Angler's Guide to[TM] the

WEST COAST
SALMON AND TUNA
Washington • Oregon • California

Robert H. Mottram

Fishing Titles Available from Wilderness Adventures Press, Inc.™

Flyfishers Guide to™

Flyfisher's Guide to Alaska

Flyfisher's Guide to Arizona

Flyfisher's Guide to the Big Apple

Flyfisher's Guide to Chesapeake Bay

Flyfisher's Guide to Colorado

Flyfisher's Guide to the Florida Keys

Flyfisher's Guide to Freshwater Florida

Flyfisher's Guide to Idaho

Flyfisher's Guide to Montana

Flyfisher's Guide to Michigan

Flyfisher's Guide to Minnesota

Flyfisher's Guide to Missouri & Arkansas

Flyfisher's Guide to Nevada

Flyfisher's Guide to the New England Coast

Flyfisher's Guide to New Mexico

Flyfisher's Guide to New York

Flyfisher's Guide to the Northeast Coast

Flyfisher's Guide to Northern California

Flyfisher's Guide to Northern New England

Flyfisher's Guide to Oregon

Flyfisher's Guide to Pennsylvania

Flyfisher's Guide to Saltwater Florida

Flyfisher's Guide to Texas

Flyfisher's Guide to the Texas Gulf Coast

Flyfisher's Guide to Utah

Flyfisher's Guide to Virginia

Flyfisher's Guide to Washington

Flyfisher's Guide to Wisconsin & Iowa

Flyfisher's Guide to Wyoming

Flyfisher's Guide to Yellowstone National Park

On the Fly Guide to™

On the Fly Guide to the Northwest

On the Fly Guide to the Northern Rockies

Anglers Guide to™

Complete Anglers Guide to Oregon

Angler's Guide to the West Coast

Saltwater Angler's Guide to the Southeast

Saltwater Angler's Guide to Southern California

Best Fishing Waters™

California's Best Fishing Waters

Colorado's Best Fishing Waters

Idaho's Best Fishing Waters

Montana's Best Fishing Waters

Oregon's Best Fishing Waters

Washington's Best Fishing Waters

Field Guide to™

Field Guide to Fishing Knots

Fly Tying

Go-To Flies™

Flyfishing Adventures™

Montana

Angler's Guide to™ the
WEST COAST
SALMON AND TUNA
Washington • Oregon • California

Robert H. Mottram

Wilderness
Adventures
Press, Inc.™

Belgrade, Montana

Angler's Guide to™ Series

>   Published by Wilderness Adventures Press, Inc.™
>   45 Buckskin Road
>   Belgrade, MT 59714
>   866-400-2012
>   Website: www.wildadvpress.com
>   email: books@wildadvpress.com

>   First Edition 2011

Printed in South Korea.

ISBN: 978-1-932098-85-3 (8-09206-98853-8)

Table of Contents

Dedication vii

Preface. 1

Trolling 7

Mooching 24

Jigging 42

Boats and Motors 55

Electronics 65

Background on Fish Management Issues 79

Salmon Identification and Reproductive Behavior 83

Washington Coast. 87

    Fisheries Management 87

    Neah Bay. 90

        Neah Bay 94

    Sekiu to Pillar Point 95

        Sekiu / Clallam Bay 99

    Port Angeles to Port Townsend 100

        Port Angeles. 106

        Port Townsend 107

    Hood Canal 108

    The San Juans 114

        Anacortes 120

    North Puget Sound. 122

        Everett. 129

    Seattle and Central Puget Sound 131

        Seattle 136

    Tacoma and South Puget Sound. 138

        Tacoma 143

        Olympia 144

    Crossing the Bar 146

    Lower Columbia River and Washington Coast 148

        La Push 155

        Westport. 155

        Ilwaco 156

Oregon Coast. 159

    Fisheries Management 159

    Columbia River. 161

Tillamook Bay 163
   Portland 165
   Astoria - Warrenton 166
   Tillamook 167
Newport and Depoe Bay. 169
   Depoe Bay 172
   Newport 172
Florence and Reedsport 174
   Reedsport. 175
Coos Bay. 177
   Coos Bay. 178
Gold Beach and Brookings. 179
   Gold Beach. 182
   Brookings 183
California Coast 185
  Fisheries Management 185
  Crescent City and Eureka 188
   Crescent City. 191
   Eureka 192
  Fort Bragg to Tomales Bay 193
   Fort Bragg. 194
  San Francisco 195
   San Francisco 199
   Sausalito. 200
   Berkeley 201
   Emeryville 202
  Monterey Bay to Morro Bay 203
   Santa Cruz 205
   Monterey 206
  Albacore Tuna. 209
   San Diego 220
  Salmon Run Charts 223
Illustrated Knots 225
  Fishing. 225
  Boating 230
How to Rig Herring. 233
Salmon Filleting 240
Coastal Tackle Shops 248
Charter Services 261
Glossary 272
Index 274

Dedication

This book is dedicated to my parents, John and Fay Mottram, who encouraged my efforts to become a writer; to my wife, Karen, who for years has patiently tolerated my absences to fish in one part of the world or another; and to Erling Bergerson, a wise and able fisherman and a good friend who years ago became my salmon-angling mentor.

Preface

The eggs had been in the gravel at the bottom of the river for about four months before the tiny fish poked its head out of the rocks for the first time, drawn by dappled sunlight on the water above him.

His mother, a magnificent chinook salmon, had deposited them the previous fall – about the middle of October – after scooping a redd in the gravel with her tail. His father had finned slowly in the clear water beside her, and released a white cloud of milt as she released her precious eggs. The milt had fertilized the eggs on contact.

It was a reproductive miracle – a miracle because both parent fish had to survive four long years in the hostile north Pacific Ocean, and then find their way back over hundreds of dangerous ocean miles to this Northwest stream. After they spawned they finally died; here in the place where they, too, had been born.

And it was a miracle that this tiny fish, still drawing nourishment from the yolk sac on his belly, had held a winning ticket in nature's lottery of life, the lottery that determines which eggs are fertilized and which find a safe place among the rocks where they will be protected from predators and where the oxygen-rich water of the river can flow freely around them.

This little fish had been especially fortunate. His parents had been among the last to spawn the fall before. That meant that other, later-spawning fish had not destroyed his mother's nest in an attempt to make their own.

Flooding was minimal that winter, so the eggs were not scoured from their protected place as so many thousands often are. And the mud slide that occurred in January – the one where half a clearcut hillside fell away in winter's rains – occurred a quarter-mile downstream. It killed tens of thousands of fertilized eggs beneath its oxygen-blocking muck, but it missed the part of the river where this fish was developing.

This little fish, its yolk sac finally consumed, began to feed instinctively on microscopic organisms in the stream. But he didn't wander far from where he had emerged. He fed and grew, dodging predators, for about three months.

Then, about the first of June, he was drawn by a new urge. His body was changing. He was starting to smolt, and he knew – without knowing why – that it was time to move downstream.

As he approached the river's mouth, the environment began to change. The water, just a little briny at first, became saltier and saltier. It would mean death for a regular freshwater fish, but this one pushed on. His genetically specialized body was ready for it, and he was able to resist the powerful, dehydrating effects of the salt.

The fish stayed just outside the river's mouth for a long time, in the estuary where freshwater and saltwater mix. Nature was bountiful here, and the tiny organisms on which he fed were everywhere.

Finally, his instincts called him on. He swam out of the estuary and turned north, responding perhaps to a signal from the earth's magnetic field. He knew innately that danger lurked in the darkness of the deeper water, and so he kept to the shallows near the beach, avoiding the lingcod and the rockfish that waited hungrily in the depths. On and on he swam, ever northward, feeding and growing as he went, eventually passing into Canada near the west coast of Vancouver Island. Day by day, the urge to travel grew weaker, and finally it was gone. Here, hundreds of miles from home, he would feed and grow some more, a mid-range predator in an eat-or-be-eaten world.

His diet by now had changed. He was feeding on herring and on candlefish, and was becoming adept at slashing through a school of them, disabling some, then turning and feeding on the injured as the rest fled. He knew that others were hunting him – sea lions and seals and roving pods of killer whales. Sometimes after he had seen or heard the killer whales, days would pass before he would be calm enough to eat again.

All summer long he fed in the rich Canadian waters, gaining skill as a predator, and gaining size and weight. Fall came and then winter approached. He drifted south and passed the darker months along the lower reaches of Vancouver Island.

As winter's gloom gave way to longer, brighter days, he drifted north once more, following his food supply. Somehow he avoided the commercial troll fishery that operates off the Vancouver Island coast, and which impacts so many runs of chinook from U.S. streams.

Life rolled on like this, precariously, for two summers more. Then, the summer after that – his fourth in the sea – a yearning began to take hold of him. It was different from anything he had known before. Some of the fish in his year-class already had left these northern waters, a few in that second summer, a few more in the third. This fish hadn't felt that urge. But now his time approached. He started to swim south. He was coming home.

Exactly when the impulse strikes, nobody knows. But by July he had reached the Strait of Juan de Fuca, which separates Canada from the United States. He was taking his time, feeding and resting as he came, putting on fat, storing up energy. By late July, the trickle of chinook at the strait had become a flood, and he was a part of it. He was as lucky as his parents. He managed to avoid the Indian troll boats, the sportfishing fleets, and the predators that remained a constant part of a salmon's life.

The urge to get home called him more and more strongly now. He was eating less and traveling faster, sensing he was near his journey's end. Soon he would be thrashing upstream through the waters of his birth, reveling in their unique delicious scent which had been implanted in his memory so long ago. Then would come an orgy of reproductive delight, draining his body of the last of its energy.

He was swimming more earnestly now, past underwater landmarks he had seen before. Finally he turned into his estuary and moved toward his river, just ahead.

But now something had caught his eye: a flash, and then another. His eye was drawn to the light like a pin to a magnet, and he moved in its direction.

Ahead, near the surface, he could see a trail of bubbles from the prop of a small boat. Behind the boat and deep – about where he was – came the flash. It appeared to follow the boat. He was closer now, and he could see the source of the light; a silver oblong rolling in lazy circles as it moved across his path. It caught the sun's rays even at this depth, and reflected them as it turned. Behind it swam what appeared to be a candlefish or a squid, moving when the oblong moved, pausing when it paused, its body swaying hypnotically. Something inside the fish stirred. He couldn't take his eyes off the object. He moved closer.

He was almost home. Just a couple of miles to go. The river called. But he couldn't leave the swimming creature. It wasn't hunger that he felt. Perhaps it was anger – the sight of this thing, moving and pausing, moving and pausing, methodically swaying, insolent, following the light.

The fish moved into position to attack.....

Downrigger trolling increases one's chances for days such as this. Photo courtesy of Wooldridge Boats.

You Can Do It

It's a heart-in-your-throat experience; the excitement you feel when you first see your salmon rod dancing in its holder on the gunwale of your boat.

All your senses snap to attention. You slide the rod from its holder, take a few quick turns on the reel, then you lean back on the rod and tie into the fish. As your rod arcs sharply toward the water, you realize he's a big one.

The fish erupts, and a shot of adrenaline goes through you as he starts to strip line from your whining reel. The fight is on.

It happens thousands of times a year, all up and down the Pacific Coast. And it can happen to you.

There's nothing magical about catching salmon – big, brawny chinook or acrobatic coho that like to dance on their tails. They're creatures of instinct and habit. And when you appeal to them in the right way, at the right time and in the right place, their impulses take over.

The rest is pure, heart-thumping thrill.

Some of the finest fishing on the Pacific Coast comes with summer. Those soft, sunny days of July and August – dog days for anglers in so much of the rest of the country – are the time when big, bright chinook surge in from the ocean in waves. They move by the thousands along the Strait of Juan de Fuca and into Puget Sound and the San Juans, up the Columbia River, and into countless bays and river systems up and down the coast from Washington to California, feeding voraciously as they close in on their home rivers. Behind them come large schools of ocean coho, scouring the currents for food as they make their way back to the gravel beds and hatcheries that spawned them, and often schools of sockeyes, pinks, and chums, depending on the year and the place.

This is the time – July into autumn – when it pays to be flexible, to follow the progress of the runs and to intercept them where you can. A good, trailerable boat and a dependable tow vehicle are all you need to turn your summer into the kind of angling experience that fishermen elsewhere dream about. And with a canopied pickup or a comfortable tent, you can do it on a financial shoestring.

Where to Fish

As a rule, mature chinook and their immature counterparts, known as blackmouth or feeder chinook, lurk in relation to bottom structure, just like the bass in a Florida lake. Migrating chinook tend to travel along the beach, often in water no deeper than 70 to 120 feet, and sometimes just a few yards from the water's edge. Blackmouth tend to spend their time around reefs or rock piles or points of land, sometimes at drop-offs or underwater holes.

They're attracted by the currents, which dip and eddy and swirl around these structures. The currents concentrate the tiny organisms upon which baitfish feed, thereby attracting the baitfish themselves. And where baitfish gather, so do salmon.

Chinook, particularly immature ones, take the course of least resistance. That means you'll find them resting close to the current but not right in it if they can help it – someplace where they can watch the action and dart out to pick up a morsel without expending too much energy. So pay attention to the tide, particularly if it's strong. If the current is swirling past a point of land, look for blackmouth on the lee side, in the back eddy where floating organisms are going around and around and the baitfish are feeding on them.

If your fathometer (fishfinder) tells you there's a ridge or a hump extending across the current, look for blackmouth on the sheltered side of it, not on the side being scoured by the water.

Coho, both mature and immature, are found less often in relation to structure. Mature fish often travel several miles from the beach, and it's common for anglers to have to run offshore to find them.

Look for coho in the rips – those places where different tidal currents come together, creating visible breaks or lines in the water. Baitfish often concentrate there, and that's where coho will be feeding.

To find the coho, first find the bait. And to find the bait, follow the birds. Gulls and terns can spot it easily from on high; and where gulls are swooping or terns are sitting on the water, dabbling, it's very likely that salmon are present also.

Approach the birds carefully, at low speed, and toss your bait or lure into the water well toward the edge of the feeding flock, so you don't disturb it, or the fish below.

Mature coho travel fast, and you have to scout for them. But when the first fish hits, you can expect others to follow. Often, a morning's fishing can mean a boat-full of anglers prospecting for two or three hours, then 20 minutes of frenzied action as they limit from the same school.

Basic Principles

Although they feed on the same things, coho and chinook respond to different presentations of bait. Chinook like a bait with a lazier roll. When plug-cutting herring for chinook, you should strive for one that revolves about 60 times a minute. If you're trolling for chinook, and nothing seems to be working, the rule of thumb is to troll slower.

Coho like a bait which spins at least twice as fast and travels more quickly through the water. The rule of thumb with coho is, when all else fails, troll a little faster.

There is more on this in the following chapters.

Despite a coho's affinity for speed, all salmon are basically lazy, and you have to keep that in mind to catch them. They're probably not going to go out of their way to take your bait or lure, and that means you have to put it where they are – in the right area, at the right depth – and present it with the kind of action that will trigger their feeding response.

Salmon are not terribly bright, the way a monkey or a dolphin is bright, and the things they get involved in tend to happen automatically. If you present an appropriate bait or lure at an appropriate time and place, with the proper action, you almost certainly will trigger a strike. There's an old saw that's been around about as long as hooks and lines: If you want to catch a big fish, use big bait.

A lot of anglers swear by that theory, and biologists say it may be supported by the principle of conservation of energy. A big fish can't afford to burn a lot of calories chasing small bait. The energy to be derived from the food must equal or surpass the energy required to catch it. So remember, to entice a large fish, the bait must pass at a speed and at a distance that make it worth pursuing. The larger the bait, the more effort a salmon may be willing to expend to get it.

Many old-timers who fished nearly year round for chinook on Puget Sound did nothing but pull plugs. And many of them pulled only large ones – 5 or 6 inches long. They said they may have gotten fewer strikes that way, but the fish they caught were bigger.

If necessary, you can stack two lines on the same downrigger. Photo courtesy of Scotty.

Trolling

I'm looking out over the bow of my boat, steering toward a distant landmark, when I hear a soft "thwunk" from the stern.

Glancing over my shoulder I notice that my rod, in its holder on the gunwale, has lost the deep arc in which it had been pinned. The rod has sprung nearly straight in its holder, and its line now enters the water at an acute angle far behind the boat.

Fish on!

I reach the rod in a couple of steps, slip it out of its holder, and crank the reel as fast as possible until I feel resistance. I strike hard, just once, and now the fish is really on.

A few minutes later a chunky, 12-pound blackmouth lies thrashing in the bottom of the boat.

He would not have been there had my ears not told me what my eyes had failed to perceive. But this is not unusual when you're trolling with a downrigger.

Why troll?

For many saltwater salmon anglers, possibly most, trolling is their principal method of fishing. A couple of things account for this. Most important is that trolling enhances an angler's exposure to fish more than any other fishing method.

"You cover more water by trolling", one professional salmon guide pointed out. "You place your lure in the strike zone and present it to the fish in a consistent manner day in and day out, hour after hour."

The more water covered, the more salmon are probably exposed to bait or lure. The more salmon exposed, the more in the boat.

The other major reason to troll is that it allows use of artificial lures when dogfish sharks and other unwanted species make fishing with bait impractical.

Trolling With Mooching Gear

Sometimes it's effective to troll with standard mooching gear, especially for young resident coho in the late spring if seasons allow it, and for returning mature coho, or silvers, in the fall. For this you simply pull a whole or plug-cut herring several feet behind the boat on regular mooching hooks that are tied below a crescent sinker of 1 to 5 ounces or more. The size of the weight and the speed of the boat, as well as the amount of line out, determine the depth at which the herring is fished. Coho often come right to the top to grab it.

You may troll with the rod in your hand or in a holder at the rail, and you strike as soon as you see or feel a hit. Often, a striking fish will hook itself, and your job simply is to give it no slack as you slide the rod from its holder.

Some anglers prefer lures over bait for young resident coho, eliminating the crescent sinker and pulling the lure behind a small barrel sinker of the type used in freshwater fishing – or, in some cases, behind a couple of split shot. The No. 50 Hot Shot is a very effective lure for this, especially in green.

One professional guide who fishes Washington's San Juan Islands often uses a crescent-sinker setup for returning adult silvers, or rigs a slider on his main line with a cannonball weight of several ounces. For this late-season fishing, he prefers fluorescent-red weights.

"I use a lot of 8-ounce weights, and right in the prop wash of the motor is a very good place" for the bait, he said.

"Strip out 12 to 15 pulls of line", he said. If you're fishing with an 8.5-foot rod and you lift your rod tip you should be able to see the herring in the bubbles.

"Oftentimes, that's the hottest rod on the boat," he said.

Planers

If you plan to buy special equipment, one of the least expensive ways to troll is with a planer. This is a round or triangular plastic about the size of a man's hand that attaches to your gear between the main line and the terminal tackle. The planer contains a device for changing its center of balance and inducing it to lower its nose in the water and dive like a deep-running lure, pulling the terminal tackle down with it.

When a fish hits the terminal tackle, the center of balance changes again and the planer loses its deep-running tendency, providing little impediment to the angler or to the fish as they battle for supremacy.

Used with whole or plug-cut herring, planers are particularly effective on mature silver salmon, and have helped put many a lunker in the boat up and down the Pacific Coast. They also can be used to pull spoons and light-weight lures.

My preference is for the Luhr Jensen Deep Six in size No. 2. I prefer it to Luhr Jensen's Pink Lady, another popular planer, because the Deep Six's release mechanism that changes the center of balance is adjustable. You can set its tension so the force of water rushing over the planer will not trip it, but the strike of a fish will.

Its disadvantage is that if the mechanism trips without a hookup, you must reel the Deep Six all the way to the boat to reset it. The Pink Lady can reset itself if you strip a little line and give it some slack.

Another popular planer is Luhr Jensen's Dipsy Diver, whose center of balance you can change not only from front to back, to induce it to dive, but also from side to side to induce it to swing out from the boat to the left or the right. People who run a lot of lines are fond of the Dipsy Diver because it can walk a line away from the boat on either side, leaving room closer to the craft to run others on downriggers or on more conventional divers.

Always attach about a foot of 40- or 50-pound monofilament to the barrel swivel at the rear of your planer, then finish off with a top-quality ball-bearing swivel at the end of that. When you fish, attach your leader and baited mooching hooks or your leader and spoon to the ball-bearing swivel so your terminal tackle may spin without twisting.

To use a planer, place its center-of-balance mechanism in the diving position, then free spool or strip enough line to get to the depth at which you want to fish. For mature silvers, this normally is between 18 and 60 feet (between 12 and 40 pulls), and usually is closer to 18 than 60.

A silver usually hits with such energy that there's no mistaking it. If it hits and misses, and you don't happen to see the strike, you'll know it has occurred because the arc of your rod will become less pronounced after the mechanism trips.

Downriggers

Downriggers are far more efficient than planers, and far more expensive. They're better than planers for controlling depth precisely; for fishing heavier terminal tackle, such as a flasher, that would trip the diving mechanism of a planer; and for fishing at depths greater than a planer can reach. The great majority of trolling for chinook salmon, a deep-running species, is done with downriggers.

A downrigger is simple in principle. It consists of a wire line, usually braided, on a large reel that an angler cranks manually or electrically. The reel includes a counter for keeping track of how much line is out. At the end of the wire is a weight, usually a "cannonball" of 10 or 12 pounds (I prefer 12 pounds). An angler attaches his fishing line to the wire line or to the weight – usually to the weight – by means of a quick-release mechanism which pinches the fishing line, then he lowers wire line and fishing line together into the water. The weight on the wire line takes both lines to the depth required. When a fish hits, it pulls the fishing line free of the release mechanism on the wire or ball, and the angler plays the fish with no weight between him and it.

Some line-release mechanisms attach to the downrigger wire above the weight, and they are useful for stacking lines when running two or more off one downrigger.

To do this, attach one line about 20 feet higher on the wire line than another, and run the lures or baits out varying distances behind the boat. When stacking, attach the bottom line first. Loosen the downrigger brake and lower the weight 20 feet, then attach the next line, and so forth.

If your partner is running the boat and you are handling both rods, you can keep one in your hand while lowering gear. Put the reel in free-spool with the clicker on, and keep your thumb on the spool as the line pays out to keep from getting a crow's nest in your reel. Place the other rod in its holder, the gears of the reel engaged, and its drag set very lightly.

The resistance offered by the drag will prevent the line from tangling as it pays out. In some cases, resistance of the clicker alone will prevent tangles. As soon as the gear has reached the proper depth, tighten the drag.

Anglers mount downriggers on a boat's gunwale, sometimes on its transom, or on both. A downrigger's pulley-equipped shaft must be long enough to clear any obstructions the boat provides, to keep the wire line clear of outboard props during tight turns, for example. But a longer shaft transmits greater torque to the gunwale in the event gear hangs up on the bottom.

Here's how to rig for fishing: With your boat moving at trolling speed and your downrigger weight barely making contact with the water, toss your bait or lure over the side and let out enough fishing line to put your lure as far behind the weight as you want it – 30 feet is about average. Now attach your fishing line a few feet from the tip of your rod to the downrigger's quick-release mechanism. Set your fishing reel to free-spool with the clicker on. With your rod in one hand, loosen the downrigger brake with the other and lower the weight in a controlled manner, letting out fishing line as the downrigger line submerges.

When you reach the depth at which you want to fish, tighten the brake on the downrigger, pop your fishing reel out of free spool, and adjust its drag. Then crank up enough turns on your fishing reel to put a sharp bend in the rod, and slip the rod into a holder. Loading the rod with tension in this manner helps to prevent a fish from gaining too much slack when it pops your fishing line from its release mechanism.

Not all downriggers have to be electric. This Fathom-Master 625 still is cranked by hand. Photo courtesy of Pure Fishing.

When the line pops loose you sometimes hear it. But since you can't count on it, glance frequently. When your gear is properly attached to the wire line or weight, your rod will arc sharply, its tip pointing toward the water, and your fishing line will enter the water beside the boat. When the line has popped loose the rod will spring straighter, and the line will enter the water farther behind the boat.

Sometimes your fishing line will remain connected to the downrigger, but the tip of your rod will vibrate. This could mean you are dragging a fish too small to trip the release, or are dragging kelp or other trash. If you see this, remove the rod from its holder, pop the release by pulling against it, then reel your gear in and check it.

Meatlines

Meatlining is a method of trolling with a short, stout fiberglass rod built with pulleys rather than guides, and equipped with a weight of 8 or 10 pounds and a large, direct-drive reel. The reel is filled with wire line, usually braided but sometimes solid. Some anglers say they prefer the solid line because it doesn't fray. But if it kinks it will break. Braided line will not.

The difference between meatlining and downrigging is that in meatlining you attach your lure permanently to the wire. When a fish strikes, both it and you must fight the weight as well as each other. The gear operates similarly to a downrigger, but is far less expensive. Why is it called meatlining? Because it's efficient. It puts a lot of meat on the table.

The practice is especially popular on South Puget Sound, and one experienced meatliner there likes to pull a 5- or 6-inch Ace Hi or Tomic plug behind 30 or 40 feet of heavy monofilament line.

"It's a real easy way to fish," he said. "And you can also do that with just herring, instead of the plug."

Most meatliners pull a plug or a flasher and hoochie. They rig by running their wire line to the top loop of a heavy-duty, three-way swivel. To the middle loop of the swivel they attach 3 or 4 feet of heavy Dacron line, and to the far end of that they tie their weight – often a lead window sash.

To the bottom loop of the swivel they attach a heavy-duty rubber snubber such as surgical tubing – everything is heavy-duty in meatlining – and to the far end of the snubber they tie their flasher or lure by means of about 30 feet of heavy-test monofilament. When a big fish hits, the snubber absorbs shock.

You fish a meatline the same as a downrigger, except you usually have no counter on your reel, so you must estimate how much line is out. Many anglers like to fish it right on the bottom, literally bumping it along. You have to pay attention to the bottom configuration, though, or you'll lose some weights.

It's surprising how well a stubby little meat pole will telegraph a hit. A fair-sized fish will have it bouncing in its holder, which must be as heavy-duty as everything else in meatlining. Many meatliners use holders of brass or steel, because the popular plastic ones won't stand the strain.

A lot of anglers also attach a bell to the tip of the pole to signal immediately the strike of a fish.

Fighting a fish on a meatline is not a pretty thing. It's just a matter of horsing it in. But things get tricky when that three-way swivel reaches the rod tip. You still have 30 feet of monofilament between you and the fish, which you have to bring in by setting your rod down and retrieving monofilament hand-over-hand. A last-minute run can be a problem now, and if you're going to lose the fish, this probably is when it will happen.

Rods

Anglers seem to be split over whether to use graphite or fiberglass rods for trolling. A majority tend to acknowledge the superiority of glass for this application. But many – if not most – continue to use graphite anyway, either because that's what they own or because graphite has some qualities that they like.

When graphite first appeared in the market place in the late 20th Century, anglers discovered it was lighter than glass and also more sensitive. But it proved to be more prone to breakage. When downrigging began to become more popular in the 1980s, graphite rods already were well established in the marketplace, so a lot of anglers purchased softer-action graphite more suited to downrigging than the customary fast-action ones they had used for mooching and casting.

"Then guys started to gravitate back toward fiberglass," said a representative of one major rod manufacturer. "They saw they could load that rod in the downrigger and, because they didn't have to hold the rod all day, its weight didn't matter. Fiberglass gave them a little extra bend. We started to sell a lot more fiberglass, and we've added to our fiberglass line."

This attention has resulted in improvements to fiberglass rods unknown in the days when that material dominated the market.

"Graphite has gone about as far as it's going to go, in terms of engineering development" the spokesman said. "There's not much more you can do. Our highest-end rods are very sensitive; you can feel a pinprick at the end of them. But they're more prone to breakage.

"But fiberglass has improved to the point where we've been able to make them lighter and still maintain their strength and durability," he said.

Graphite continues to outsell fiberglass, even for trolling, but the trend among trollers is toward glass. Rod makers also combine graphite and glass now in order to try to capture some of the best qualities of both.

"We've seen graphite become higher quality every year, and less weight," one Washington retailer said. "But for downrigger use, the old glass rods are probably still best. Shimano has turned out a series called Talora, and they're not too expensive. And they're a lot less prone to breakage than graphite."

Lamiglas also manufactures a popular glass trolling rod designed to replace a model once popular on the West Coast that Fenwick discontinued.

Still, some anglers refuse to return to glass.

"I like the graphite rods because they're light and easy to handle," observed one professional salmon-fishing guide. "The graphite composites are probably more durable, because graphite rods do blow up. If you get somebody who's really aggressive in snapping the line out of the release clip, they go in a lot of pieces."

Another salmon-fishing guide, on the other hand, doesn't use graphite.

"Graphite breaks too easily trying to yard it out of the downrigger," he said. "We use mostly straight-glass rods."

Reels

Professional fishermen say choice of a reel is more important than which rod they employ. Their gear has to withstand rough handling. They want level-wind baitcasting reels with enhanced gear ratios, and they want the best-engineered and best-constructed reel they can get for what they can afford to pay.

"You want a good-quality level-wind reel in top condition," one said. "Penn and Shimano are the two most popular ones I see."

He likes a gear ratio of 3 or 3.5 to 1, and wants a reel "that will fit in your hand. I use Shimano Charter Specials, but the Penn 209 is very popular."

Another professional uses Quantum reels with ceramic drags, "basically a level-wind with a fairly fast retrieve. These Quantums ... have been very good to me."

He has used Penns and Shimanos in the past, he said, and liked them as well.

In northern West Coast U.S. waters, direct-drive "knucklebuster" reels such as the Shimano Moocher 2000 and Moocher 4000 have become increasingly popular for many salmon-angling applications, apparently as a result of Canadian influence. That style of reel is widely used in Canada, and the practice appears to have worked its way south. However, some U.S. anglers don't like knucklebusters for trolling, complaining that their one-to-one cranking ratio is too slow.

"If somebody is fishing one of those types of reels, when they get a bite I instantly kick the kicker motor wide open to help them overcome the slack faster," one guide said.

Kings usually take the bait while coming up, and that habit means the fish may be high in the water column before it exerts enough pressure on the downrigger line-release to trip it. As soon as the mechanism trips, under these circumstances, it creates slack in the line for the fish, which by now is relatively close to the surface.

Terminal Gear

For downrigger trolling, an angler wants a sturdy line of at least 20-pound test that can resist the abrasion imparted by a downrigger release mechanism. One professional angler says he prefers a 30-pound main line, and he avoids a limp line, preferring a "hard-surface line with very little stretch. That forces your swivels to work."

Limper line tends to twist more easily, he said.

"And I prefer a variety of colors of line," he said. "That way, should a fish get you wrapped up, if you have to sacrifice something you instantly know which one to cut."

He uses 20-pound test leaders with his 30-pound main line for mature kings. In winter, he'll retain the main line and drop the leader strength to 15 pounds for immature chinook.

To the end of your main line, tie a good-quality ball-bearing swivel, and tie your clear, monofilament leader to the other end.

One professional guide who trolls a lot of plug-cut herring prefers to rig his leader in two pieces. Rather than utilize hooks with a standard 6-foot leader, he ties them with a leader of only 2 feet. Then he ties a separate, 4-foot monofilament leader to the ball-bearing swivel at the end of his main line. This leader terminates in a small barrel swivel. The hooks, on their 2-foot leader, are tied to the terminal end of the barrel swivel. This results in 6 feet of leader with a barrel swivel inserted in it 4 feet from the main line.

"The reason for that is if you get into a dogfish bite, you can have your leaders all tied up in the 2-foot length," he said. "You can quickly unwrap one, tie it on, and you're back in business. But if you've got a 6-foot chunk of leader, you've got a mess because by the time you get that unwrapped the bite's over."

Many a big chinook has been fooled by a flasher and hoochie. Photo by John Yeager for Hotspot Flashers.

Should you pull bait? Pull plugs? Pull hoochies? With attractors? Without attractors?

The possibilities are myriad, and each has advocates.

"One of the biggest trends I've seen in the last 10 years has been the resurgence in spoons for salmon," one tackle-shop operator observed. "The spoon that really did it was the Luhr Jensen Coyote. That really brought back spoon fishing to the whole Pacific Northwest.

"Then we had a couple of years when Silver Horde's little Coho Killer spoon was one of the hottest things going," he said. "And since the Coyote became so popular, there's been a big resurgence in other spoons, like the Canadian Wonder."

Spoons have proven effective both inshore and offshore. Those 3.5 inches and shorter often are fished behind a flasher or dodger. Spoons 4 inches and larger are effective fished alone.

"A second thing that's become popular has been redevelopment of in-line flashers that rotate on their own axis," the tackle-shop operator said. "They're built out of plastic, and won't impart any action to your bait, but act as an attractor. They come in a variety of sizes and finishes, and they don't have the resistance of a conventional dodger or flasher."

Examples are the Big Al's Fish Flash, a triangular attractor rather than the traditional oblong, and the Oregon-produced KoneZone, which sports a pear shape. They come in a variety of colors, reflect a lot of light and produce little drag.

"But you have to fish an action-type bait behind it, like a plug-cut herring or a whole herring or a spoon," the merchant said. "A non-action lure, like a squid or a coho fly, is useless behind it."

Some trollers prefer to fish without an attractor. Plugs usually are fished that way, and they can be very effective on chinook, both immature and returning adults. Ace Hi and Tomic produce plugs in a variety of sizes that have caught thousands of chinook.

Some trollers pull fresh or frozen herring on a downrigger all by themselves for chinook, although many run them behind a dodger for chum or coho salmon in the fall. If you plug-cut your herring you need to troll it slowly or it will rip. If you want to troll faster, you should consider using them whole, perhaps with a cap to help achieve the proper spin.

"My preference is a plug-cut (brined) herring and a really slow troll, almost a mooch," one guide said. "I like a tight, bullety-looking spin on the bait, rather than tail-wallowing. If you can fish that way, normally you will catch more and bigger fish. But sometimes dogfish and other things won't allow you to fish bait."

In that case he'll switch to plastic squid behind a flasher.

Some anglers like to tip their squid with a strip of herring fillet on the lead hook, but not this man.

"Normally, when I'm fishing artificial stuff I don't (use herring), for the reason that I'm fishing the lure in the first place. You put a piece of herring on it and you're still attracting dogfish."

Other anglers prefer to use lures most of the time.

"We're using less and less bait, because there always seems to be some lure that can come real close to the action," another professional guide said. "A good baitfisherman who really knows how to do it is going to do great. But the guy who's a novice will do better with lures. Because if you don't have the bait prepared right you're wasting your time. It's a whole lot easier to accomplish by using a lure."

Plastic squid, called "hoochies", and coho flies are fished behind a flasher or dodger. Some anglers use a piece of surgical tubing behind or ahead of the flasher or dodger to cushion a hit. They claim fewer missed fish.

Follow the attractor manufacturer's directions to attain optimum distance between attractor and lure for maximum lure action. With spoons or with bait, you can run them 6 feet or more behind the attractor, because they create their own action. Flies and hoochies take their action from the movement of the attractor, and must be closer.

However, many anglers believe that large adult chinook won't take a lure or bait that is too close to a flasher.

"Silvers will take it at 22 inches," one former commercial salmon troller observed. "Blackmouth will take it at 36. For kings, I fished 40 inches with a hoochie or a herring.

"But at Neah Bay, a lot of fish wouldn't grab the herring unless they were 5 feet or more behind the flasher," he said. "You get it 5 or 6 feet behind, then you catch those big kings."

Both squid and flies actually imitate baitfish, not invertebrates, and both come in a wide array of color combinations. A lot of Puget Sound anglers prefer shades of green or glow-in-the-dark white. Many ocean anglers tend toward blues, and brown-and-red combinations are popular on the inside waters of Canada. The Canadian colors don't seem to work as effectively farther south.

In Puget Sound, "if it's green it's going to work," one guide observed. "Or white. Green and white are the primary colors, and any combination of those in a hoochie. The same with a spoon. It might be green, two-tone green, light green and dark green, green and white, and so forth.

"Sometimes I've had some success with blue, but it has fallen by the wayside."

This man also likes glow-in-the-dark lures, such as squid.

"If it's a bright day in the middle of summer and you're fishing less than 90 feet deep, non-glow lures will work as well and sometimes better than glow-in-the-dark," he said. "But if you're fishing deeper or if there's overcast, glow-in-the-dark will out-produce non-glow day in and day out."

You should carry a variety of lures, including hoochies. The plastic squids are least expensive if you buy them without hooks and add your own snelled mooching hooks. Metallic skirts, made of aluminum foil tied to a plastic head and known as twinkle skirts, can be inserted when you install the hooks, to make the hoochie more appealing.

Abe & Al produces a popular metal flasher. Gold Star makes another, which is stronger and less prone to stretching out of shape. One of the most popular among

commercial fishermen in the Northwest is the Canadian-origin Hot Spot, a colored, plastic flasher with a metal reflector strip on each surface. I use Hot Spots almost exclusively, either green or red.

One professional angler likes a flasher that features glow-in-the-dark tape on one of its surfaces, and favors those colored green for the water he fishes.

"I think they out produce the reds and silvers and all the others," he said.

Another professional salmon guide agrees, but said he shifts to red flashers late in the season, particularly when mature coho begin to run. He also switches to red downrigger weights at that time, believing they help attract coho.

"One of the interesting things about flashers and plugs," one guide said, "but not so much about spoons and other equipment, is that some work really well, some (that appear to be identical) work part of the time and some don't work at all.

"I can't tell the difference looking at them or watching them in the water. But I know there are certain flashers on my boat that will out-produce other flashers no matter where I put them. And it's the flasher, not the terminal tackle. It will hold true with all terminal tackle."

If you run a bait or a lure that produces its own action, such as a spoon, you may run your flasher off the downrigger ball and 10 or 20 feet behind it with no lure attached. Then fasten your main line to the downrigger wire with a line-release mechanism that's designed for that purpose, running your lure or bait several feet above the flasher and several feet behind it. You must space the main line far enough from the ball to avoid entangling the flasher on the descent.

The flasher still functions as an attractor, but when you hook a salmon you can play it without the drag of the flasher between you and the fish.

Many Northwest anglers have gone to 5-inch plastic squid, instead of the formerly standard 4-inch size, matching the size of the hoochie to the size of baitfish in the area where they operate and presenting a larger silhouette to the salmon. Mini-squid, especially in bright pinks and reds, continue their popularity. Anglers fish them slowly behind a dodger, often a white dodger, for pink salmon.

One Washington tackle dealer has designed and manufactured what he calls a mini FAT Squid, which also is a 5-inch plastic squid. It is "mini" only in relation to his standard FAT Squid, which measures 9 inches long and is designed to catch halibut, marlin, sailfish, and other species. He says his mini FAT Squid is effective for salmon. It works like a standard hoochie, but has an extra hole for insertion of a chemical light or scent.

The manufacturer recommends that you tie two hooks on a leader in the standard salmon configuration, using 3/0 hooks or a 3/0 and a 4/0, and spacing the hooks 1.5 inches apart on the leader. Place two or three beads on the leader ahead of the hooks, then slide a mini FAT Squid over the leader to the hooks. Insert the small chemical light that he provides into the second hole on the hoochie. The light stick causes the hoochie to glow from within, and makes it attractive, he says, to salmon in deep water.

Fish the hoochie off a downrigger, approximately 26 to 28 inches behind a Hot Spot or Coyote flasher, with the length of the leader depending on trolling speed and

the distance of the flasher behind the downrigger ball.

"For best results," he said, "tune your mini FAT Squid leader at the boat. Start with a 28-inch leader behind the flasher, and distance the flasher 12 to 20 feet behind the downrigger ball. Lower the downrigger about 6 feet, so you can watch the action of the flasher and squid. The squid should dart from side to side. If the squid moves too slowly, shorten the leader. If it moves too quickly, lengthen it.

"After tuning your squid, maintain the same distance behind the downrigger ball," he said. "Remember, closer to the ball gives the flasher a tighter roll and more action on the lure. Farther from the ball increases the diameter of the roll and softens the action of the lure."

If you use a mini FAT Squid behind a dodger, he said, you should use a leader of approximately 18 to 22 inches.

Many anglers, including professional guides, use artificial scent on their lures.

"I believe there are certain people whose (own) scent is distracting to fish," one guide said. "I've tried many different (artificial) ones, and they all seem to work."

He considers them more a camouflage, he said, than an attractant.

Where and How to Downrigger Troll

"When I consider places to fish, I think of it in terms of river fishing," one professional guide revealed.

In this case, however, tidal currents substitute for river flow.

"Look at your charts," the guide said. "You need to do a little homework prior to fishing. Salmon like back eddies, and that's where you'll find them. The current will create a back eddy on the downstream side of points of land and underwater obstructions. In those back eddies is where the bait will accumulate, and that's where the fish will be when they're looking for lunch."

With a little practice, an angler can learn to use the bottom topography to anticipate where salmon will find conditions to their liking.

"They don't want to fight a strong current," another guide said. "If you have a point or an underwater ledge that's creating breaks in the current line, that's where these guys like to hide."

Your marine charts, issued by the National Oceanic and Atmospheric Administration in the United States and by the Canadian Hydrographic Service in Canada, will reveal the topography that determines how tidal currents will behave. Combine those with a set of current tables that reveal when and in what volume currents will run. Consider your fishing grounds a huge river. The eddies and pockets, and the holding and hiding places that salmon utilize, will be different on the flood tide from those on the ebb, and will be different to a degree from one flood to another or one ebb to another, depending on how fast the current runs at a given hour.

Like many fish, salmon hang out in slower current rather than faster, and in places where they can ambush prey that gathers or passes by. They don't like to work harder than they have to, especially bigger fish.

Besides reading your charts, watch to see where birds are working, and keep track of other anglers.

"Observe the other boats in the area," one guide said. "Look for what appears to be the local expert. It's not bad to drop in behind him. And it's not a bad idea to talk to people to find out what's happening.

"If you're fishing for kings, you want to know when the bite was yesterday and the day before," he said, "because normally a group of fish will bite on the same cycle in relation to the stage of the tide. Normally, the tide will move up about an hour every day, and many times the bite will coincide with that. So if they bit at 1 o'clock yesterday, they'll probably bite about 2 o'clock today."

You want to be in the right spot at least an hour before and an hour after the time that you anticipate the peak of the bite will occur. Often, the bite is right around the time the tide changes. But not always.

"Some fish like it right around the change," the guide said. "Some prefer it an hour after or whatever. So you get a particular race of fish, and that bunch of fish will probably follow the same pattern."

A particular race would be fish of the same species from the same river that have the same run timing. You find salmon more and more segregated by race the closer they are to their natal rivers. The farther seaward you encounter them, the more likely they are to be of mixed stocks.

Tide-change feeding is complicated by the fact that tidal currents don't necessarily go slack precisely when tide books say they should.

"When they're going to feed, with adult chinook, is generally early morning – crack of dawn – late evening right up until dark, and at or around tide changes; usually within two hours before or after the change," one professional guide explained. "But the key here is current change, rather than just the tide book. The tide controls the current, and the current – the actual movement of the water – controls the fish."

"Sometimes you have a current overlap," another guide said, "which will be after the actual tide change; especially on the bigger changes when you're moving a lot of water at higher velocity. The current will continue to run out on the surface while maybe the tide has turned and is starting to come back in underneath. So you can have water going in two directions. You'll notice it in some areas more than others. Normally, the fish will like it (for feeding) when that current stabilizes, rather than on the (technical) tide change."

Usually, tide changes are more important feeding stimulators for salmon than are sunrises or sunsets. However, chinook almost always produce a crack-of-dawn bite.

"You have a small window in the morning," one guide said. "As soon as the sun hits the water, the bite is over."

This tends to be true year round, but is most pronounced when mature fish are traveling.

"And you're fishing shallower during those periods," the guide said. "The 35- to 45-foot zone is a good place to be in that period, particularly if any bait is flipping on the surface."

As the day grows older, consider fishing deeper, especially for resident chinook. When the sun climbs, you may fish contours as deep as 200 feet, still paying attention to bottom structure and looking for the kinds of places where salmon like to hang out.

With mature returning chinook, you'll sometimes find them right off the bottom if they're feeding, and 40 or 50 feet from the surface if they're traveling. But you'll find very few immature chinook, or blackmouth, in the mid to upper water levels. Blackmouth usually live within about 20 feet of the bottom.

Anglers have tended to find returning adult salmon – even coho – deeper in recent years than they once did. Biologists debate whether this is because so many higher-running fish of all salmon species, the most accessible ones, have been picked off by sports gear and commercial nets over the years. They speculate whether this harvest has selected genetically for the deeper-running fish that may have survived to spawn in greater numbers. Nobody knows if this is so. But if you don't locate returning adults at depths where you expect to find them, consider fishing deeper.

Although salmon often like to bite at sunrise and at slack water, between dawn and the tide change you may encounter fish of a race that likes to bite part way through a tide. And often, other fish will bite sporadically if they see something that strikes their fancy. So as long as your gear is in the water, you're not wasting time.

A Fishing Scenario

You arrive in an area that's new to you and that has promising bottom structure at a variety of depths. Your fish-finder shows no bait initially, and no predator fish, but the area has a reputation of producing lots of salmon. Where and how should you begin to fish?

"If you want king salmon, a good place to start is 120 feet," said one guide. "I would drop my gear into that zone and probably bracket it, because you don't want all your gear sitting in one area.

"I would probably run the deep downrigger right to 120 feet," he said, "because you're going to be giving away about 10 feet on the line angle on your cables. So you'll probably be fishing about 10 feet off the bottom at normal trolling speed."

Sometimes before settling in to fish, he will drop his downrigger weight all the way down and bump bottom with the ball to see how much line he's actually giving away. Then he can raise it to the right depth.

"If it's winter blackmouth time and you've got a lot of spawning candlefish that hold the bottom real tight, you want to be dredging," he said. "You want to be just off bottom – 5 feet, sometimes 2. It can be hazardous to your terminal gear, but it often pays, particularly if the first fish in the boat has got his cheeks scratched from rooting around down there. Then you know they're living tight to the bottom."

This man would bracket his other downriggers in about 10-foot increments above the lowest one, unless he saw something on his fish-finder that told him to concentrate somewhere else.

"If I were in 120 feet of water and I saw bait in the 80-foot zone, I would put one of those 'riggers right at the bottom of that bait school," he said.

This professional angler runs four downriggers, something most private anglers don't do, one on each gunwale and two on the transom.

"The side ones I run back farther and deeper than the back ones," he said. "I put them in first and out last so I'm not crisscrossing gear as it's coming up and down."

He usually runs his back downrigger baits or lures about 20 feet behind the ball, and the side ones 30 to 40 feet behind, or even more. He'll troll at four different depths usually, unless he sees everything in a specific zone on his fish-finder. Then he will fish two of his rigs in that zone and bracket the others close to it.

"If I don't find fish on the fish-finder, I'll hold 120 feet for the initial pass," he said. "If nobody else is catching fish, I may continue to hold that. If others are catching fish, see what they're doing. You want the same contour and distance off the bottom that they have. When you get close, holler at them. Most fishermen will tell you what they're doing."

Under appropriate conditions, steer a zigzag course rather than a straight one. This covers more water, and causes your bait or lure to slow down or speed up as you turn toward or away from it.

Some Suggestions

Many anglers equip their boats with two downriggers, one on each gunwale. If you prefer, you can fish with one, double-stacking lines on it when you fish with a partner. In this case, you would attach one line to the downrigger ball with a line-release clip in the usual manner, and attach the second line about 20 feet above the first, using a release clip that's designed to grip the downrigger wire rather than attach to the ball.

If you mount a single downrigger and you steer your boat by means of a wheel, you probably should mount the downrigger on the port gunwale. Since most boats operate from a pilot station on the starboard side, it's easier to monitor a downrigger that's aft on the opposite side of the boat than it is to watch one located directly behind the pilot station. The disadvantage, however, is that a downrigger on the port side encourages a skipper to turn his body to port, presenting his back to that important 12-o'clock-to-3-o'clock quarter-circle forward of the starboard beam out of which approaching traffic has the right-of-way.

Don't neglect to keep a sharp lookout, especially ahead and to the right. Keep a sharp eye on your depth finder, too. If the bottom starts to come up, you'll need to raise your downrigger ball immediately to avoid the risk of hanging up.

A striking fish sometimes fails to trip the line release, so you've got to watch the gear. If you see your rod tip twitching, don't wait for the line to release. Remove the rod from its holder, pop it free of the line release yourself, and reel as fast as you can until you make contact with the fish.

Even if your gear does not twitch, you shouldn't troll for more than about 20 minutes without cranking in your line to check your bait or lure. You may be pulling an undersized fish without realizing it, or you may be pulling kelp.

To pop loose your gear from a downrigger, remove your rod from its holder, point the rod tip at the spot where your line enters the water, and reel until the line is as tight as you can get it. Then pull straight back, your rod making a straight line with the monofilament. Don't whip the rod, as though striking a fish, because you may break it, especially if you're fishing with graphite.

When fish trip the line release, they're often well hooked.

"But reel as fast as you can and give them one poke to be sure the hooks are set good," one guide said. "Then don't give them any jerks after that. Just reel."

When a fish has hit, get the rod from its holder as quickly as possible and sink the hook home. Don't stop the boat until then. After the fish is solidly hooked, you can throw the motor into neutral. If you're fishing with a friend, he should pop his gear loose from the downrigger and reel it in and should retrieve the downrigger line, if possible, before helping you net your fish. If you're fishing alone, it's nice to have an electric downrigger. Turn the switch to retrieve, and get your wire line out of the water before your fish comes close enough wrap the monofilament around it. If the lines get wrapped, the fish almost always will saw through the mono and break off.

When you pop your gear loose to check the bait or to change fishing areas, occasionally let it work its way to the surface at its own speed, rather than reeling it up. This way you're fishing through the entire water column, and sometimes you'll get a hit on the way up.

Should you troll with the current or against it? How fast?

Many anglers believe it's by far more effective to troll with the current, for a couple of reasons. For one, when trolling with the current you cover ground faster, thus potentially presenting your lure or bait to more fish. For another, fish usually lie facing into the current. So by traveling with it, you present your lure to the fish's face.

Some anglers troll against the current if they can make reasonable headway. But in many circumstances, tidal current is strong enough to hold you in one place, and your odds of encountering fish are poor. It's better to troll with the current, then pick up gear, shut off the kicker, and run up-current with the large motor to begin another downstream pass.

"In some areas, I like to troll across the current," one guide said, "so I can troll either way."

When you troll, ignore the speed-over-ground data that your electronics may be measuring. It's irrelevant. You're more interested in your speed through the water, because that is what affects the action of your bait or lure.

"I judge trolling speed by the angle in the downrigger line," one guide said. "I'm looking for 30 to 45 degrees for both coho and chinook, although occasionally I'll go a little faster when I'm fishing for coho."

"The angle depends on the species of fish," another guide said. "For adult kings, I like about a 15- to 25-degree angle. If you're going on a slack current, that will have you about 1.6 to 1.8 miles an hour.

"For blackmouth, a little faster," he said. "They're a younger fish and more aggressive. Get an angle of 20 to 30 degrees, about 1.8 to 2 miles an hour. For coho, the angle of the cable should be 30 to 40 degrees. Your speed is picking up considerably.

"For pinks, you're dead, dog slow. The downrigger is down to 10 degrees, or maybe even straight down."

Should you play out a fish before attempting to net it?

"Pretty much the fish dictates that," one guide said. "I usually get them in fairly rapidly, but still enjoying the fish – that's what you're there for. But if the bite is on, speed should come after you get him in. Sometimes the bite cycle will last only 15 minutes, so you want to take advantage of it.

"Get the gear back in the water and then celebrate. Take pictures after you get the gear trolling again."

Among those who contributed information used in this chapter, the author would like to thank:

John Posey, national sales manager for Lamiglas, Inc., Woodland, Washington; Jim Aggergaard, Catchmore Charters, Anacortes, Washington; Gary Krein, All Star Fishing Charters, Seattle and Everett, Washington; Bob Salatino, former commercial fisherman and chief fish-catcher for the Point Defiance Zoo & Aquarium, Tacoma, Washington; Mike Chamberlain, owner and operator of Ted's Sports Center, Lynnwood, Washington; John Beath, manufacturer of mini FAT Squids.

Mooching

He says it was the heavy woolen gloves that did it; gloves with the fingertips missing to permit the tying of knots and the sensitive thumbing of a reel.

He had one big chinook in the box already, and was bringing another to the side of the boat. The one on the hook weighed 18 or 20 pounds, he estimated. It came to the surface and the angler turned, his rod in his left hand, and reached for the net with his right. For a second – only a second – he took his eyes from the fish.

And that's when it happened. The chinook made a lunge and just flipped that slippery, wooden-handled rod right out of the man's grasp. Fish, rod, and reel streaked for the bottom, and the angler was left counting the rings where he'd buried his tackle at sea.

It's not an unusual case. More than one fisherman has come home without his rod and reel because of a careless moment. But it doesn't have to happen to you.

Some fish are bigger than others, and stronger than others, and do what they do better than other fish. But they all do the same things. You have a better chance of avoiding trouble, putting more fish in the box – and returning to shore with more tackle – if you know what's likely to happen next.

There are several ways to catch salmon, and all of them have their adherents. One of the most popular and least expensive methods to gear up for is mooching. Why it's called that nobody knows, but it consists basically of dangling a bait – usually a herring or an anchovy – until a fish comes along and picks it up.

Mooching Rods

Start with a medium-action rod of 8.5 or 9 feet, and a level-wind baitcasting reel of medium capacity. Neither has to be expensive, although more and more anglers are tending in that direction.

In buying a rod, you must choose between graphite and fiberglass. Over the last several decades, many moochers have switched away from glass.

Until the 1970s, almost everyone mooched with a fiberglass rod. That changed after graphite became widely available, because the more graphite and the less glass in a rod, the lighter the rod and the greater its sensitivity. This allows an angler to work a bait longer without fatigue and to detect subtler pickups. But a graphite rod doesn't have the resilience of glass, and heavy work can overstress and possibly break it.

Because of this, some fishermen have drifted back toward glass for certain angling applications, especially downrigger trolling, although graphite remains securely in first place even for that. Some fishermen also have gone back to fiberglass for mooching.

"A nice thing about fiberglass is you get a little extra action," one rod maker explained. "Wave action will bounce it up and down and 'dance' the herring a little bit.

"We've added to our fiberglass line, and guys are starting to use fiberglass a lot more," he said. "Some like the old action; it reminds them of when they started fishing."

With the ascendancy of graphite, people had gravitated toward faster-action models of rod, which bend only in the top one-third or one-quarter of the blank. Most fiberglass rods provide moderate or medium action, and bend all the way through the blank, and that's what provides the extra movement to the bait.

Graphite is strong when it's used properly, but fiberglass can take more abuse.

"The way guys break (graphite) rods – and it doesn't matter the manufacturer – is mostly by overstressing them," the rod maker said. "By high-sticking them; getting the line up over their heads. And sometimes they get hung up and are stressing them trying to get free."

Despite this problem, graphite is not going out of favor, the manufacturer said. Nevertheless, rod makers are covering all their bases.

"We've worked to develop our fiberglass rods so they don't feel like your dad's fiberglass rods," he said. "They're lighter, a lot more responsive. When a guy picks one up he's not sure it's fiberglass."

At least one manufacturer, Lamiglas, has developed a line of rods it calls Triflex that combines graphite and glass. It has done so primarily to respond to an increasing switch to braided lines, which are smaller in diameter than monofilament of the same strength.

"As guys switched from monofilament they weren't paying attention to rod ratings," a spokesman said.

If a rod is rated for line of 12 to 25 pounds, for example, it means that a 25-pound line would break before your rod would.

"So we went to Triflex, which is a combination that has some glass in there to toughen them up," the spokesman said. "Otherwise, if a guy is putting 80-pound braided line on his reel and he gets hung up, he turns around and his rod tip is busted."

No matter the material it's made from, the length of the rod you buy is likely to depend on where you live. The closer you fish to Canada, the more you see long mooching rods – often exceeding 10 feet – equipped with "knucklebuster" reels. That's probably because so many Northwesterners fish in Canada and have adopted Canadian styles of fishing. In California, anglers favor shorter rods.

Lines

Regardless of the rod you choose, fill your reel with top-quality line of 12- to 20-pound test monofilament. In winter, a lot of anglers lean toward the lower-test line, or at least a lower-test leader, when they're fishing for resident blackmouth (immature chinook). They switch to the heavier line and leader in summer, when they target mature migrating fish.

Don't compromise on quality at any time of year. Some anglers prefer brown or green line, believing it's less visible to the fish. Others believe colored line can put fish off the bite, and swear by a line that's clear. Personally, I like a monofilament of light green when fishing green water, or one that's clear, in either case teamed with clear leader. Some tackle stores stock line in bulk, and you can take your reel in and have it filled for a fraction of what it costs to buy the line on an individual spool.

Remember, the heavier the test, the greater the diameter of the line and the harder it is to handle at greater depths and in stronger currents. You need more weight to get it down, making your tackle less responsive. With a lighter-weight line you may occasionally have to fire up the engine and chase a big chinook, but you're more likely to have hooked him in the first place.

Some anglers have abandoned their old monofilament and have gone to new styles of line.

"I think the number one thing that's revolutionized gear is the emergence of 'superline'," a manufacturers' representative said. "In older days, nobody would fish with anything other than monofilament. Now half the fishermen I know are fishing with superlines like FireLine and Spiderwire."

"One trend I've seen is the utilization of fluorescent lines," a tackle-shop operator observed, "in greens and chartreuses and hot pinks, so people can see where their lines are and be able to follow the fish better."

Nobody ties such colored line directly to a lure or bait. Instead, anglers employ a clear leader, and a trend in that area has been toward fluorocarbon, which is nearly invisible in water.

"A lot of companies are coming out with it," the shop operator said. "It's expensive, but if conditions are touchy and visibility is high, sometimes it pays to have fluorocarbon leaders.

Reels

The smaller the reel, the less weight it adds to the rod. So the smaller the reel the better, to a point, but be sure that it has the capacity for 200 yards or more of whatever line you plan to use.

Smaller reels are "lighter and easier to handle," a manufacturers' representative said. "A great big reel has so much cross section that when you're cranking on a fish you tend to rotate the rod in your hand."

The challenge a small reel presents to its manufacturer is providing an adequate drag, he said. He represents Abu Garcia, and he recommends that company's Big Game 7000.

"I consider it to be the premier salmon reel in the world," he said. "What I love about it is it's got plenty of line capacity, but on a narrow spool that's deep. And it's got a highly adjustable lever drag.

"Also, it's got a level-wind, which is absolutely critical," he said. "Because when you're fighting a fish, it's easy to bunch the line up at one end of the spool. Having a level-wind is crucial to getting a nice even spread across the reel, and even more crucial with superlines, because they're thinner and it's easier for them to dig into the other line on the spool and hang up."

The Penn 209 has been one of the stand-bys of Northwest moochers for years. Photo courtesy of Pure Fishing.

With a lever-drag reel, as opposed to star-drag models, an angler adjusts the amount of tension by pulling or pushing the lever rather than by turning a wheel. When you bring the lever all the way back, the reel goes into free-spool. You can pre-set the maximum amount of drag for the lever's farthest-forward position, called the strike point, and if you have loosened the drag, you can come back to your pre-set maximum almost instantly and know you will not exceed it. With a star drag, you must strip line from your reel to test its resistance as you reset it.

Some experienced moochers like a direct-drive reel that provides one turn of the spool for each crank of the handle, such as the old Penn 109. They believe this gives them a better feel for the fish and a more enjoyable fishing experience. But reels like those have become harder to find. Others prefer the high-speed retrieve they can attain with higher gear ratios.

Some moochers also prefer a reel they can crank in free-spool while retrieving line, such as the 109, controlling a fish by thumbing the reel rather than by using the drag.

However, the facts of economic life dictate that fishing gear manufacturers look to big angling states such as Florida and Texas to determine trends in anglers' tastes, and the fact that certain gear finds a niche among some West Coast fishermen doesn't guarantee its continued availability. The result is that direct-drive baitcasting reels have become tough to find outside of garage sales. Penn, for example, quit production of the 109 about 2001, although it continued to manufacture the 209, also a popular Northwest salmon-fishing model but with a greater line capacity and a higher gear

Abu Garcia's Ambassadeur Big Game 7000. Photo courtesy of Pure Fishing.

ratio than the 109. Penn shifted manufacture of the 209 to China in 2005, by the way, and at the same time upgraded from brass construction to stainless steel.

It also has introduced the 310 GTi, virtually the same size as the old 109, and the 320 GT2, equivalent to the old 209, a Penn sales rep said, but both with a graphite composition body and higher-speed retrieve. That's okay with a lot of anglers, apparently. The 320 has become Penn's best selling model among Northwest salmon fishermen.

In California, the Penn 500L won wide popularity. It's a conventional level-wind reel with a bit more line capacity than the 320.

"It started out in southern California as being a hot reel and – as far as California goes – just moved its way up through the rest of the state," the sales rep said.

Despite some lingering desire for low gear ratios, a majority of anglers all along the West Coast have gravitated to retrieves of 5.3-to-1 and even 6.2-to-1 to be able to stay on fast-moving fish.

"When you get on a coho and he's ripping across the surface and giving you slack, you want a big rod and a high-speed retrieve to recover that line," a manufacturers' representative said. "In the old days, people didn't want high speed. They wanted more power. But these days you've got better gearing and better rods, so you've got plenty of power in any of these reels to handle a fish."

Overall, the quality of reels has increased over time, and many manufacturers have gone to unitized, one-piece frames and away from those constructed of component parts that could come apart or loosen.

Throughout the West Coast, however, anglers have shown increasing interest in line-counting reels and those manufactured with tight tolerances.

People "want good engineering so you don't get line stuck between the spool and the frame the way we used to," one manufacturers' rep said. "And people want higher and higher quality drag material and more focus on corrosion resistance. They're spending more money on reels now, and they want them to last."

Two of the beneficiaries of this trend have been the lever-drag Shimano TR1000 and TR2000, known as "Charter Specials", which have become popular among upgrading salmon anglers.

Shimano also produces a reel called the Tekota in a 500, 600, and 700 size suitable for salmon angling. They have a die-cast aluminum frame and conventional star drag, but with far better drag systems than older reels, and many anglers buy those.

Shimano also builds line-counter reels that tell an angler how much line he has in the water. And Daiwa builds several models of line-counter reels that it calls "Accudepth".

"I was anti-line-counter, because they're a little bulkier," a shop owner said. "But I've seen the light. I tell people fish are 80 feet down, they put out 80 feet of line, and they're right on them."

Terminal Gear

You'll need some crescent sinkers of 2 to 6 ounces, preferably the kind with a barrel swivel at one end and a chain swivel at the other. Some anglers use sinkers painted fluorescent red, so they can double as an attractor. Others like the natural metal color. I prefer red.

Tie your main line to the barrel swivel, and your leader to the chain. The 3- and 4-ounce sinkers are most popular for mooching, but anglers should carry a variety of sizes for different conditions. Some anglers tend toward the larger sinker sizes even when conditions don't demand them.

"Most guys use a 2-, 3-, or 4-ounce sinker," one productive salmon moocher said. "I use a 5- and 6-ounce sinker. It takes the herring down a lot faster, and the herring works better because there's more drag against it. It has more action."

A few anglers use a crescent-shaped sinker with a small-diameter tube through the length of it, sliding their line through the sinker and tying it off to a swivel on the far side. This allows the sinker to slide up and down the line.

That's all right for trolling, but it doesn't work as well for mooching, because a chinook often will pick up your bait as you let line out. If you're using a hollow sinker, the sinker will slide back along your line as you continue to unspool it, keeping tension on the line and making it harder to detect that a fish is holding the bait.

If you're using a sinker that's tied solidly to the end of your line, you'll feel the premature slack when the fish picks up the bait. Reel as fast as you can, taking up that slack, until you make contact with the fish. As soon as you feel resistance, set the hooks.

You'll need a 6-foot leader, tipped by a single hook or a pair of hooks, one above the other about 2 to 4 inches apart, depending on the size of your bait. Most salmon anglers use the two-hook setup, and many of them use an upper hook that's one size larger than the trailing one.

Hooks of 3/0 and 2/0 are good for blackmouth most of the year, and for coho when they're running in from the ocean. For mature chinook, you might want to go to a 4/0 and 3/0 combination or to 5/0 and 4/0. When fishing for blackmouth in winter, anglers sometimes downsize to 1/0 to better fit the smaller herring that are prevalent then.

If you're fishing in marine areas of Washington, Oregon, or California, regulations may require you to use hooks that are barbless. Some anglers prefer to start with a barbed hook and pinch the barb flat with pliers. They believe that the tiny, smooth bump below the point of the hook that results helps to prevent a fish from throwing the hook. Others prefer to purchase hooks manufactured without a barb on the theory that their streamlined shape allows the hook to penetrate more easily.

Some anglers look for leading-edge technology when shopping for hooks, preferring brands such as Gamakatsu with its chemically sharpened points. Others remain content with old-standby manufacturers such as Mustad and Wright-McGill.

Sharpen your hooks before using them, especially if they're not manufactured sticky-sharp, and always sharpen after catching a fish or snagging bottom. A small,

flat file works well for this. Even better is a tube-shaped file with a groove that runs the length of the tube. You insert the point of a hook in the groove, with the point facing away from you, and strip the hook toward you to sharpen.

Bait

Anglers on large inside waters, such as Puget Sound, almost always bait with herring. On the ocean, herring, anchovies, and sardines work well, and anchovies are the most popular choice in many areas.

Bait may be alive or dead, frozen or fresh. Usually it's dead, but live bait works wonderfully well. Even if you don't fish it alive, buy your bait fresh if you can. Frozen bait often is mushy, less appealing to salmon, and doesn't stay on the hook as well. If your boat is not equipped with a live well, dip a bucket of sea water and put your live bait in that, keeping it out of the sun if you can. The cold marine water will keep it in relatively good condition for hours, even though it will die in the bucket.

If you want, you can keep it alive longer in a minnow bucket, the kind that lake fishermen use in some states. The bucket floats overboard, and you tie it off to a cleat. Many Northwest tackle shops carry these. Use a plastic one for saltwater, and don't forget to bring it into the boat before you run to a new fishing area.

Buy frozen bait if you can't buy it or catch it fresh. If you buy it on the day that you fish, remove it from its package and put it in a bucket of sea water, just like fresh bait. The water will thaw it, and then will maintain it in relatively good condition. Don't let it sit in the sun in its plastic package, which will transfer heat to it. Salmon will not accept tainted bait.

Even better, if you know that you'll be fishing with frozen bait, or even if you'll fish with fresh but need to keep it for several days while fishing in a remote location, buy it in advance and brine it at home to toughen and preserve it.

Obtain the best quality bait that you can, because salmon know the difference. Bait with missing scales or mushy texture will not fish effectively. Some anglers carry their baitfish on ice in an insulated cooler. Put them in a sturdy lock-top plastic bag before placing them in the cooler, however, because freshwater produced by melting ice will spoil them.

If you plan to be on the water for an extended period, you can plug-cut your herring a day in advance.

"I fill the body cavities with Borax, then roll the bait in the Borax," one long-time moocher said. "Then I put them in a (lock-top plastic) bag and lay them flat and put them in the refrigerator. When I go to fish, I'll put ice in the bottom of a cooler, put the bags of bait on top of the ice, then put more ice on top. I can fish bait like that for a minimum of three days."

Some anglers brine their bait to toughen them and increase their brightness and color. A simple way to brine bait on the water during an extended trip is to fill a five-gallon bucket about one-third full of rock salt, then add seawater, stir, and add bait. Herring will last as long as a week this way if you keep the water cool.

Many anglers use more elaborate brining methods, utilizing ingredients such as powdered milk and bluing agents to increase toughness and brightness. A popular brining recipe follows at the end of this chapter.

Anglers usually use anchovies and sardines whole, and often with a plastic "cap", because they tear if you try to fish them plug cut. You insert the baitfish's head into the cap and fasten it there with a plastic or wooden pin, such as a toothpick. The cap imparts action to the bait.

Sometimes even a carelessly cut or rigged bait will catch salmon if the fish are on a strong bite. But that's unusual. Most of the time, the bait and the way that it's rigged must be just right, and all of the time, well-handled bait will outfish one that's poorly cut or rigged.

You may use herring either whole or plug cut, and you have a choice among several ways to rig it while using each of those options. All of the alternatives have their adherents, and some alternatives work better than others under particular conditions.

A whole herring works better if the bait is small and you don't want to lessen its length even further by removing its head. It also works better if the bait is soft rather than firm and fresh, or if you plan to cast it or work it against a strong current, because it's less likely to tear. Some anglers also believe that it produces less scent than plug-cut, making it less attractive to pesky dogfish.

A disadvantage to whole herring is that they're a bit trickier than plug-cut to rig in a way that produces life-like action in the water. Success comes with practice. One way to rig them is with a plastic cap, like those used for anchovies. Some anglers like the caps, and some don't, believing they can attain better action without them.

Rigging Whole Herring

Salmon possess notoriously sensitive olfactory senses. Let that work for you, not against you. Always start with clean hands when touching bait or, for that matter, when handling any salmon-catching gear. If you shave on days you fish, forget about the after-shave. If you use sunscreen, apply it before you leave home, and then wash your hands with warm water and soap. If you must re-apply sunscreen in the boat, wash hands again before touching any gear or bait. A lot of anglers carry a bottle of dishwashing soap and use it for personal cleanup. Many swear by Lemon Joy.

Many anglers avoid bananas on days they fish, or any product with bananas in it, such as banana bread. Some think it's the potassium in bananas that salmon don't like. Whatever it is, some West Coast charter skippers say they won't allow a banana aboard their boat.

Working with clean hands, a good way to rig whole herring without a cap is to pinch the herring's mouth shut, then run your leading hook sideways through the lips, pinning the mouth closed. This is important, because a herring will not spin properly in the water with its mouth gaping. After pushing the point of the hook through the lips, from one side of the head to the other, turn the hook and pass its point back through the head just behind the top edge of the eye, to the side where

you started. The hook's point and its eye now both protrude from the same side of the head. You can let the trailing hook dangle, or you can pin it in the side of the herring along the midline by piercing the herring's side and running the point of the hook in a head-to-tail direction. The point should emerge closer to the tail than where it went in. The eye of the hook remains outside the herring, pointing toward the head. The trailing hook should be pinned about three-quarters of the way to the tail on the side of the herring opposite the one on which the point of the leading hood protrudes.

It's not necessary to pin a bend into the herring's body. The lead hook alone, rigged through the head in the manner described, should give your bait a nice spin.

"I like my herring straight," one expert moocher said of this rigging technique. "Because, the straighter the herring, the tighter the spin."

This angler always pins his trailing hook to the bait, however.

"I always put mine in because if it's dangling, the salmon can grab the herring and miss the hook. If I put it in, when they grab the herring I know they've got the hook."

If the action is not right, remove the point of the lead hook from behind the eye and insert it again, but this time behind the middle of the eye. If the bait still doesn't work properly, re-hook it near the bottom of the eye. Often, these small corrections will improve the bait's action significantly.

Another method of rigging whole herring is to start with the trailing hook and run the entire hook through the eye sockets from one side of the herring's head to the other. Go through at the edge of the socket, in order to avoid damage to the eyeballs. Follow the trailing hook with the leading hook, so both have passed entirely through the sockets. Now, holding the herring parallel to the ground, reach over the top of the bait from the entry side, grasp the leading hook and bring it back over the top of the herring. This creates a noose that comes over the nose of the fish. Pass the point of the hook through the herring's body from one side to the other just behind the gill plate. You can let the trailing hook dangle, or you can pin it into the herring's side along the fish's midline near the tail. When you tighten the line, the noose that you created will pin the herring's mouth shut. You also can use this method with only a single hook for an excellent way to rig small whole herring.

Plug Cutting Herring

A plug-cut herring is one with its head lopped off at an angle, and the angle of the cut adds enticing movement to the bait. In cutting the plug, you actually impart two angles, one on the horizontal plane, the other on the vertical. With the bait lying flat on its side, its belly toward you, start your cut where the fish's head meets the top of its back, placing your knife so its handle is closer to the bait's tail than is the tip of the blade. The angle of the knife should be about 30 degrees from vertical. At the same time, tip the cutting edge of the blade toward the tail a few degrees so that when the cut is complete the side of the bait away from you will be about one-quarter inch shorter than the side that faces you. If you have started with a whole bait lying on its left side, for example, head to the right, you should end up with a headless herring

whose front-end silhouette goes from upper right to lower left, and with the side on which it reposes about 0.25 inch shorter, measured from the tail, than the side that is visible to you.

After removing a herring's head, discard the entrails, sliding them out of the body cavity with the point of your knife, because they will interfere with the bait's action.

If you lack experience plug-cutting herring, you can buy a plastic or metal cutting guide at nearly any marine tackle shop. You place the herring in the guide and your knife blade in the guide's slot. After you've cut a few dozen baits successfully, you can throw the guide away.

Rigging Plug-cut Herring

Anglers have developed a variety of ways to rig a plug-cut herring. One of the easiest and most effective ways is to run the trailing hook through the herring's side at the midline, from the inside of the body cavity out, pulling the entire hook, including the eye out through the side. Then place the point of the leading hook through the top of the back directly beside the backbone, also from the inside of the body cavity to the outside. The point of the hook should penetrate the back no more than about 0.125 inch into the cavity. If you bury the hook too far back inside the cavity, it will dampen the bait's action.

You can leave the trailing hook to dangle near the tail, which is what a lot of anglers do, or you can pin the hook along the herring's midline near the tail. To do so, run the point of the hook into the herring's side and then out again, parallel to the herring's back, with the point emerging closer to the tail of the herring than where it went in. You can leave it pinned in that position with both the point and the eye exposed, or you can slide the eye on a shallow angle into the hole located closest to it, burying the eye and leaving only the point of the hook exposed.

An alternate method of rigging a plug-cut herring, effective with larger baits, is to push the point of your trailing hook through the herring, emerging near the backbone high on the short side of the fish. However, instead of starting this hook up inside the body cavity, start by pushing the point into the fleshy part of the herring above the body cavity at the front of the fish. Pull the entire trailing hook all the way through the hole, and let it dangle. Now insert the leading hook into the same hole, starting in the fleshy portion at the front of the herring. Pull the leading hook all the way through the hole, and then pin it high on the herring's side near the spine, parallel to the backbone. Now pull on the leader above the lead hook, drawing the hook's eye back into the hole through which both hooks originally emerged. The herring is ready to fish.

If your herring are small or if the salmon are finicky and it seems more practical to fish with a single hook, you can run the hook entirely through the bait, starting on the outside of the short side near the herring's lateral line and emerging on the outside at the lateral line on the long side of the bait, starting about 0.125 inch from the front on the short side and emerging about 0.25 inch from the front on the long side. Pull the entire hook through both holes, and then pin it on the long side of the herring.

"Especially in winter, that's a real good bait," one mooching expert said. "You don't have to work it as fast. If you want to drift-fish, just a little current will make it turn pretty easily."

Another version of this is to bring the entire hook all the way through the herring's body as in the previous method, from short side to long side, then go back about 0.25 inch toward the tail and penetrate through the body again in the opposite direction. The entire hook now emerges on the side on which you started. You can let the hook dangle, or you can pin it into that side.

"This works well with bigger herring," one experienced moocher said. "I've caught fish this way when nobody else was catching them, using just one hook. I wonder if sometimes salmon see that leading hook and won't bite it."

After rigging a baitfish, whether whole or plug-cut, drag it through the water at the side of the boat to check its action. If it doesn't spin easily and tightly, re-rig it. If necessary, throw it away and cut and rig another.

Trolling can cover a lot of water and a lot of fish. Photo by Bob Mottram.

Mooching Techniques

When do you mooch, and where? On inside waters, it depends on the currents. Tide changes often stimulate salmon to feed, but the size of the tide can affect the length of those feeding periods or "bites". Generally, the larger the tidal exchange, the smaller the window around the change in which you can expect salmon to go on the bite. On a big tide, the feeding window may be no more than an hour. On a smaller tide, you can expect a wider window spanning slack water. The other side of that coin is that sometimes a big tide will produce a good bite within the smaller window, because the salmon have less time during which they may capture food relatively easily.

Figure out where to fish by finding the bait. Look for feeding birds, and for signs of baitfish on your electronic fish-finder. Salmon will be where their prey is. Often, in the case of chinook on inside waters, this will be in eddies created by points of land or by underwater structure such as ridges. It also may be in places where different tidal currents come together. You'll be able to see the confluence of currents by a seam in the water. Places such as eddies and seams are gathering spots for the microorganisms on which baitfish feed, and the baitfish are what attract salmon. Determine the direction of tidal flow, then look "downstream" from points of land to find the eddies. Get out of the main current there and right into the backwater to locate the fish.

In the ocean, look for feeding birds. Also tap local knowledge, because fish often gather in particular offshore areas, near banks or reefs, for example.

Chinook are caught most of the time – although not always – near the bottom. Coho tend to hang higher in the water column. In winter, it's common to mooch near the bottom in water of 100 to 180 feet, or even deeper. Anglers in some Washington waters, for example, go to depths of 200 to 250 feet. When mature fish are migrating toward their natal rivers, they tend to travel at shallower depths; however, chinook are often intercepted as shallow as 40 or 45 feet in deep waters of the ocean and Puget Sound and in water as shallow as 6 feet in Washington's Willapa Bay and on parts of the Columbia River.

Moochers divide into two schools over how best to get their bait to the bottom – the stripping school and the free-spooling. Both methods work.

Strippers drop a bait over the side and, holding their rod in one hand, pull line off their reel with the other. If lowering a bait from directly beside the boat, it's better to strip than it is to free-spool, for a couple of reasons. For one, the gear will descend more slowly, making it less likely the leader will come back and tangle around the main line.

For the other, if you count pulls as you strip, you'll know where your bait is at all times. Each pull extends from the reel to the first guide on your pole. Figure 1.5 feet per pull. If bottom is 110 feet down, and your line goes slack after 60 pulls, you'll know that something has taken your bait at 90 feet. Because you've counted the pulls, you'll know not only that a fish has picked up the bait, but also at what depth it is feeding, and you'll be able to return to that depth after the first fish is in the boat.

If you get all the way to the bottom without a hit, reel up immediately 10 or 12 turns to keep from getting hung up. Wait for a few moments or a few minutes, and

then begin to reel the bait back to the boat. Pause every 10 or 12 turns. When the bait reaches top, repeat the process.

To free-spool, begin by casting your bait away from the boat 10 to 30 feet. Try to cast in the direction in which your line would naturally extend if you had lowered it instead of casting, and cast so that your baitfish lands beyond your sinker. Then free-spool to the bottom, controlling the descent with your thumb to prevent your reel from backlashing. The bait will follow the sinker down, and the angle of the line from the boat will prevent the leader from wrapping around the main line.

Sometimes you'll feel a bump on the way down. That's a strike. Crank your reel as fast as you can, and when you make contact with the fish, get a hook into it.

If your bait goes down unmolested, as soon as the sinker touches bottom reel up 10 or 12 turns.

"The bait still is up 5 or 6 feet off bottom when your weight hits," one long-time moocher explained. "When you begin to reel, the bait will continue down and then turn and follow the sinker up."

After the first dozen turns, pause for a second or two.

"Now the bait is 5 or 6 feet off the bottom again, and you've got about a 40-degree angle on your line, which is perfect," the angler said, "because as you reel up, your bait will be coming in at an angle."

Reel 10 or 12 turns more, pause, then 10 or 12 more, and so on until you've reeled several groups of 12. Your line should continue to enter the water at an angle in the direction toward which you cast. When you estimate that your bait has traveled 50 or 60 feet from the bottom, free-spool again to the bottom and repeat the process. Under moderate current conditions, each series of three to five groups of 12 turns should bring your line closer to vertical as the bait gradually makes its way back toward your boat. After several series, when your line has approached the vertical, reel all the way to the surface and repeat the process by casting again.

If you feel no immediate hits, vary the speed of retrieve and the number of turns in a group to change your bait's action and provoke a strike. If nothing else works, reel slowly all the way to the surface, allowing the bait to work all the way up. Chinook have been known to grab a bait within view of the boat.

"A lot of times I reel in three or four cranks and stop, three or four cranks and stop, and I'm stopping for just a fraction of a second, just to change the action a little," one moocher said. "A lot of times I can look down and see a fish, and when I stop they grab it."

If your line seems to be returning to the vertical too quickly, you can pop your kicker motor into forward gear for a minute to get some angle back in the line. Conversely, if a strong current makes it difficult to get to the bottom, you can put the kicker into reverse and back into the current in order to get the bait to drop.

Usually a salmon will grab your bait on the stop or during its descent. Often, the hit comes right after you have touched bottom and started to crank. Other times salmon will follow the bait up through a series of stops, then slack-line you as you start to free-spool again toward bottom.

A lot of anglers who free-spool with level-wind reels count the number of times the line leveler traverses the reel on the descent. As a rule of thumb, figure you're unwinding 6 feet of line for each traverse. If the line stops prematurely, it means a fish has grabbed your bait. Don't expect the fish to take line. Reel as quickly as possible until you make contact with the fish, then – unless regulations have required you to rig with circle hooks – sink the hooks in the fish's mouth. If you are equipped with circle hooks (which California, for example, has required in the past) you need to use a little more finesse to achieve a hookup. Reel until you feel resistance from the fish, and then simply continue to reel. With luck, the hook will turn and penetrate the fish's jaw as it was designed to do. Jerking a circle hook probably will result in a missed fish.

If you do miss the fish, free-spool your bait toward the bottom. Often a salmon will grab it again on the way down.

Another good way to mooch is to free-spool all the way down, immediately turn 10 or 12 cranks of the reel, then let the bait dangle there, a few feet off the bottom. After three or four minutes, drop it back to the bottom and repeat the process. If the current is moving your boat, you can leave the herring just off the bottom for the entire drift. If the current is weak, you can kick your motor into and out of gear from time to time to cause the bait to rise and fall. A weak-current situation is also a good time to cast and free-spool down, then reel all the way back to the boat, covering all depths. Many times both chinook and coho will grab the bait just before it gets to the boat.

Coho often sock a bait and run with it right away. Chinook rarely do. A chinook, large or small, typically will tap a mooched bait. Watch the tip of your rod, and when you see the tap, tap, tap evolve into a long, gentle pull, that's the time to react.

Playing the Fish

If he's a fair-to-middling-sized fish, he's going to take some line on you, and you've got to be ready for it. Have your reel's drag pre-adjusted, so the fish can't put too much strain on your knots – the weakest links between you and him. You want him to be able to take line, but you want him to have to work for it.

If he's really a large one, he's going to take lots of line, and there's nothing to compare with the feeling that comes when you see that rotating spool getting smaller and smaller. If moderate pressure won't turn him, you're headed for trouble, because when he hits the end of that line it's going to pop like a thread.

All you can do is start up the engine and go after him. This is a time you'll be especially glad to have someone with you, because it's tough to run a boat and play a big fish simultaneously.

Have your companion take the tiller or the wheel and start out after the fish around trolling speed. You'll see which way the line is pointed; there'll be no doubt about it. You play the fish just as you would if he didn't need chasing – holding your rod tip up and letting it absorb the shock, reeling when you can. But don't high-stick the fish by raising your rod to a 90-degree angle – or more – from the water. This can put as many as 180 degrees between your rod tip and the fish, and can place great

stress on a graphite rod, which bends only in the top section of the blank. Point the tip away from the fish, to relieve direct pressure on your line and knots, but keep the angle to the fish well under 180 degrees.

Eventually the fish will stop or turn, and you stop your boat and fight him in the standard way. If you need to turn him to keep him off an obstruction or out of traffic, point your bow away at an angle from the course you're on, and get a little lateral distance between you and the fish. This gives you more leverage in inducing him to turn.

If you're fishing in marine waters anywhere from Washington to California you may be using barbless hooks, so be especially careful not to give the fish any slack. You don't have to lean back on the rod all the time, but you do have to maintain solid contact, enough to put a bow in your rod tip.

Let the fish fight the rod, not the line. Pump the rod, bringing the fish gently closer on the upstroke, and reel to gain line on the down stroke. If your line goes slack, reel as fast as you can, because he may be running toward the boat. It's not uncommon, and often you catch up with him and re-establish contact. It's a risky period, though, during which he may throw the hook.

Netting the Fish

When you get a large fish to the side of the boat, the fight is usually not over yet. The sight of the net seems to put new life in a tired fish, and he'll usually make at least one more line-stripping run. This is a critical time. Once they've gotten a fish to the boat, many novice anglers don't want it to run again. They clamp down on the spool, the panicked fish puts a strain on the knots, and it's goodbye salmon.

Resist the urge to do that. Your drag already is working all right or you wouldn't have gotten him this far. Let him run. Some will make two or three line-stripping runs from the side of the boat, each shorter than the last. Just keep the tension on, bring him back each time by pumping and reeling, and let him tell you when he's ready for the net.

When you can lead him with your rod, slip your net into the water and lead him into it. Don't try to scoop him up, or you may lose him. And don't ever chase him with the net, or you'll surely lose him. Always net him head-first.

If he tries to fight the net, lift him into the boat with the net's handle perpendicular to the water. That closes off the mouth, and he can't escape.

When you bring the fish aboard, be very careful while he's thrashing that he doesn't sink a hook into your hand. If your hooks are as sharp as they should be they'll go right to the bone. Whack the fish sharply between the eyes with a club, and immediately cut a gill to bleed him. This improves the quality of the meat. Of course, hold him over the side of the boat or over a bucket when you cut so you don't get blood all over your boat.

Identifying Species

In many waters, size limits apply to various salmon, depending on time, place, and species. To comply with these, you need to be able to tell one kind of salmon from another, and to avoid the rough handling that can kill a fish you need to be able to distinguish them while they're still in the water. If your fish is a sub-legal chinook, for example, carefully release it without netting it and without bringing it into the boat. That will increase its chances of survival significantly.

How do you tell the species apart?

Most often, anglers need to distinguish between chinook and coho salmon. As you bring your salmon toward the net, look at its sides. If you see a purple iridescence, it is a chinook. As the fish comes closer alongside, you can glance inside its mouth. If it's a chinook, the gum line will be black where the teeth protrude. If it's a coho, the entire inside of the mouth will be gray. Also look at the tip of its lower jaw. A chinook's will come to a point. A coho's will be round.

You also can look at the tail. A coho's tail will be lightly spotted, and only on the upper lobe. A chinook's tail will be heavily spotted on both the upper and lower lobes.

Suppose, however, that your fish is a pink salmon. Like a chinook, it will be heavily spotted on the back and on both lobes of the tail, but the spots of a pink will be larger than those of a chinook, and those on the tail will be oval. A pink also can be identified by its tiny scales.

Chum and sockeye salmon look very much alike in their ocean phase, with a noticeable lack of spotting on backs and tails, although chum are able to grow to about 30 pounds, about twice the size of the largest sockeye. Some differences are detectable, however. A sockeye's teeth are soft, and the sockeye has prominent eyes with a glassy appearance. Mature chum often display dark vertical bars on their sides, although the bars may be faint. Chum also have an unusually narrow caudal peduncle, the waist-shaped area just ahead of the tail.

Brining Herring

Tom Pollack, an employee of many years at Auburn Sports & Marine in Auburn, Washington, recommends this method of brining herring.

Ingredients:
Powdered Borax
2.5 gallons water, chlorine-free
4 cups non-iodized salt
3 T Mrs. Stuart's Concentrated Liquid Bluing
1 cup powdered milk
Scent (optional)

Let 2.5 gallons of tap water sit in a bucket overnight, allowing the chlorine to dissipate. Then add salt (canning salt, rock salt, kosher salt or road salt), liquid bluing, powdered milk and garlic scent, anise scent or any other fish-attracting scent (optional). You may use a prepared fishing scent for this, or oil from a jar of minced garlic.

The bluing will brighten scales and skin, and make the bait more visible. The powdered milk will make the bait firm, and the salt will preserve it.

Plug-cut four dozen to six dozen herring, and dip the cut end in Borax to harden the end. Then place the baitfish in brine mixture, and brine them overnight at room temperature. After initial brining, store herring in the brine in the refrigerator. They should remain in good condition that way for several weeks.

Among those who contributed information used in this chapter, the author would like to thank:

John Posey, national sales manager, Lamiglas, Inc., Woodland, Washington; Jim Martin, Pure Fishing, Portland, Oregon; Jeff Collier, Penn Reels, Portland, Oregon; Mike Chamberlain, Ted's Sports Center, Lynnwood, Washington; Bob Salatino, formerly with the Point Defiance Zoo & Aquarium, Tacoma, Washington; Tom Cromie, Point Defiance Boathouse & Marina, Tacoma, Washington; Tom Pollack, Auburn Sports & Marine, Auburn, Washington.

Jigging

The angler dangled a 4-ounce chunk of lead over the gunwale of his boat and free-spooled it toward the bottom, about 100 feet below the keel. He wondered if this would be a waste of time. The oblong scrap of metal was painted solid white and, except for its silhouette, it didn't look like any fish he'd ever seen.

The angler lightly thumbed the spool of his baitcasting reel to prevent a backlash, and counted the number of times the level-wind traversed the face of the reel. Each trip from left to right, or back again, indicated about six feet more line in the water.

Beneath the boat, the piece of lead had lain over on its side, and fluttered its way toward deeper water. All of a sudden – bam! – the angler felt a bump. He reeled up what little slack his line contained, and raised his rod tip. Yes! He felt the satisfying resistance of a large fish, in this case a chinook, which began to shake its head.

And now he faced the challenge of getting it safely to the boat – sometimes easier said than done when fishing this kind of gear.

Some lures are designed to catch fish, they say, and some to catch fishermen. Lead jigs, the kind that work best in salmon country, are designed for the fish. Because to look at them, it's hard for a fisherman to believe they'd do the job.

Experience shows, however, that they do.

People jig for salmon for a couple of reasons; many because they simply enjoy this style of fishing more than any other kind, and many because they catch a lot of fish this way.

"I prefer it," said one long-time successful jigger, "because you can feel the bait, you can feel the hit and you're pretty much in control once the salmon hits."

This contrasts with trolling, for example, where the rod usually isn't even in an angler's hand at the critical moment of the strike.

Jigging can be so addictive, in fact, that often the issue is not whether a person should jig on a particular day. It's where he should jig and with what equipment.

Where and When to Jig

Ninety percent of successful salmon fishing is being in the right place at the right time, regardless of your style of fishing. But many times, jigs will work when you have located fish and can't induce them to bite any other way.

On the contrary, jigging may not be the best way to find fish whose location is unknown.

"If I get a report there are fish in an area, I go out there," one expert said. "If I don't see a bunch of bait or bird activity or something I want to explore, then I go into a search pattern. And that's usually easier with bait or downrigger.

"But if I discover there's a bunch of birds working bait at the right depth in an area where I think there should be fish, then I'll go to jigs, and try to match the hatch."

It's best to fish where bait is schooling or where salmon have been taken historically, and birds working the water broadcast the location of bait schools over long distances. If birds are not feeding, keep an eye on your fish-finder. When you spot a school of bait on the screen, its configuration will tell you what's happening where the school is. If the bait is spread out, it's probably feeding peacefully. If the school is compact, predators probably are working it. This is the best possible place to fish.

How important is tide?

"In most cases, tide dictates where I fish," one angler said. "But there isn't a time when you shouldn't go out. It's just a matter of looking for them in different spots. They're going to feed somewhere sometime during the course of the day."

Other anglers prefer to fish at specific times in relation to the tide.

Jigging can produce a lot of fish. Photo by Bob Mottram.

"I'm going to go almost always the hour before or the hour after the change," one jigger said. "I want some movement. If I've got less than a foot-and-a-half of interchange, I don't play with it. I like it when I've got several feet, 4 or 5. If you don't have enough water moving through, you don't get the bait clumped up. And if you don't get the bait clumped up, your chances of success go down.

"But I don't like a 9- to 10-foot exchange," he said, "because it's not going to be very long when I have optimal conditions."

Like moochers, jiggers look for structure, especially if they seek chinook. Points of land are good places to explore, and so are underwater humps, because they're likely places to find bait. They're usually much more productive than places where the bottom is uniform.

When fishing an eddy in the lee of a point, one experienced jigger likes to get in close to the beach in 35 to 40 feet of water, then fish his way out, keeping his jig working no more than a yard above bottom.

Another likes to fish contour lines. He believes that salmon follow well-defined routes, the way crabs do.

"The fish follow current patterns," he said. "I can't see the current, so the only thing I have to follow is the contour lines.

"You first have to figure out what contour they're over. They may be in 90 feet of water, but may be only 45 feet down. So first you've got to be in that 90 feet of water, then you've got to figure out what depth they're at."

As you're setting up to fish, observe specifically where others are catching. That may tell you what contour the fish are traveling. And if others around you are catching, don't procrastinate.

"Generally you have a limited time to intercept the fish," this angler said. "An hour later they'll be down the bay or up the bay or whatever."

Sometimes, if you're part of a sportfishing fleet, you can see a bite start at one point then move along a beach or a wall to another point before stopping.

"The fish haven't quit feeding," this angler contends. "They've just moved off to someplace that people haven't figured out."

People tend to fish deeper now than they did a few years ago, in the belief that chinook travel patterns are changing.

"The fish that once moved along the shorelines where they did traditionally have been cropped by nets," one angler said. "Now the ones that are surviving are moving out through deeper water. People who are catching them may be out there pounding the bottom in 180 feet."

That opinion is not unanimous, however. One experienced Washington jigger likes to fish for chinook right next to the kelp along the edges of the Strait of Juan de Fuca, when seasons allow.

"The kings come right along the kelp" he said. "I get in there and have, like, 20 feet of line out."

Typically, chinook hang near the bottom, one experienced angler said.

"I set my windows up to 30 feet off the bottom, because that's where the bait

usually is," he said. "Whether I'm in 60 feet of water, 100 feet, or 180 feet, that's where I'm fishing."

People fish deeper contours now than they did historically, and modern gear enables them to do so.

"The non-stretch lines, for example, allow us to fish at depths that formerly you could not," this angler said.

Occasionally, though, salmon will hang higher in the water and, especially on the ocean, you can use your boat as an attractor by fishing in its shadow. Baitfish often find shelter in a boat's shadow, or in the shadow of any flotsam or jetsam they encounter at sea, and this attracts salmon to the same location.

A good fish-finder and Global Positioning System receiver (GPS) are nearly mandatory for consistent success. You need to be able to locate salmon, schools of bait, or bottom structure and, in the case of structure, to return to it. Many jiggers enter permanent waypoints in their GPS to mark the locations of salmon encounters, pinnacles or depressions on the bottom, and places where other anglers have caught fish, so they can come back to these places again and again.

Choosing a Jig

If you see birds diving on bait, let the birds tell you how to rig up. Are they catching herring or candlefish? How large? Try to match what you see in their beaks. If the bait has that distinctive herring shape, tie on a jig with a herring silhouette. Conversely, tie on a candlefish jig if candlefish are what the birds are catching. Salmon appear to prefer candlefish over herring, given a choice. But if they're feeding on herring at the moment, you'll have little success if you dunk the wrong jig.

The bait in the school will be uniform in size, and you should strive to match its length. You'll catch fewer fish if your lure is more than about 0.25 inch too long or too short.

"You'll be catching enough that you'll probably continue to do what you're doing," one experienced jigger explained. "But if you're able to match the hatch, you'll get fish after fish after fish. If you have the right lure and there are predators around, every drop you'll get a hit."

While size and shape are important, color is less so.

"I've caught fish on every color there is," one long-time jigger said. "But the best color is white. It's the one you can count on."

"If I could have only one," another angler said, "I'd pick a white, 2-ounce jig. It will work about anywhere."

Many others agree. If they had to choose one, it would be solid white.

But you should carry a variety in your tackle box.

"Normally, what you want on a lure to be effective is a clear lateral-line area," one expert said. "Most lures are two-tone, because most fish have a color pattern where they look silver from below and dark from above."

Tackle shops are full of good choices.

"As far as herring imitators, there are none I would say are excellent," one long-time jigger said. "There are many that are satisfactory. For candlefish imitators, you're looking at the Point Wilson Dart and the Dungeness Stinger. If you can't catch fish on them, you're doing something wrong."

"The jig that seems to work extremely well for me is the Point Wilson Dart," another angler said. "I've got a box of jigs that has lots of different colors, lots of different sizes, ranging from 1 ounce to 5 or 6 ounces. Over the years, the one that's worked best for me is dark green on top, silver on the belly, and kind of a light green on the sides."

Size sometimes is a compromise, however, especially if birds aren't bringing up bait to show you.

"The bigger the jig, the easier it is for the fish to throw it," one angler said. "I can get more bites on a big jig, but my fish-in-the-boat ratio goes down. So if I want to get fish in the boat, I go to a smaller jig."

One jigger usually starts with the smallest lure he can get down and keep down, because a lot of the bait where he fishes is small.

"I'll go as small as I can at first, and then I'll go bigger. I'm changing fairly frequently," he said. "But every once in a while I'll put a monster on. Sometimes you've got to change to change your luck."

Some people bend their jigs, and some don't.

"Sometimes I bend them a little bit right at the front, just behind the eye," one jigger said. "But not always. Sometimes you buy jigs that work just perfect."

Others think it's a mistake to bend.

"On my homemade jigs, I bend them," one long-time jig fisherman said. "But for the average person I would say no, I would not bend the jigs. Leave them straight. Most of the commercial jigs are not made to be bent. It will destroy the coating, and that's the major reason that you don't do it."

If you can, check in the area where you propose to fish to learn local angler preferences. Sometimes they seem unusual. On the Nisqually Flats of south Puget Sound in Washington, for example, lime-green jigs were killers for many years. But they weren't terribly effective most other places. Many anglers who fished the Columbia River at its confluence with the Little White Salmon River preferred white jigs with a green back. Near Campbell River, B.C., a luminous jig with a dark back was popular and effective.

"As you get closer to terminal areas, in the case of chinook, the chartreuse colors tend to work well, particularly in cloudy waters," one jigger noted. "But predetermine, if possible, the local favorites. That can save you a lot of time in a new area."

In general, the closer to the ocean one fishes, the less discriminating the salmon tend to be. This is where white lures work best. As salmon arrive in their terminal areas they tend to acclimate to the indigenous bait.

"White catches what I call 'virgin' fish," one jigger said, "ones that haven't yet acclimated to a specific bait. If I wanted to catch larger fish and 'fresh' fish into the area I would use a 6-ounce white Dart or Stinger. That won't catch the most fish, but

it will catch the larger and the most aggressive. Fish in the ocean tend to grab a larger white lure, because these are fresh fish and they tend to be less discriminating."

The closer to their terminal areas salmon travel, the more discriminating they become. By the time they've been in terminal areas a week, this angler said, they've acclimated to the local bait.

Choosing a Hook

A lot of anglers prefer treble hooks over single siwash hooks if regulations permit their use. They do so for a couple of reasons. For one, a treble is more likely than a siwash to hook a fish. For another, many anglers say, it's less likely than a siwash to kill that fish.

"I think you kill more small fish with siwash hooks because they take a deeper bite," one angler said, "and it ends up going through the eye or the brain.

"I also prefer treble hooks because I get three times as many bites that I recognize with treble hooks," he said. "When you hook them with a siwash hook they're generally well hooked. But I hook markedly more fish with a treble hook."

"I always use a treble hook with a jig," another angler said. "With a siwash hook, you can't believe how many fish grab the jig and miss the hook."

Unfortunately, however, management agencies of the Pacific Coast states aren't always in accord with such anglers on the safety benefits of treble hooks for fish. At various times the agencies in each of the states have banned use of trebles on grounds that they tend to kill fish that ought to be released. Check your regulations pamphlet carefully before deciding which style of hook to use.

Siwash hooks that are made barbless by crimping the barb are not particularly effective at either hooking or holding fish. Canadian anglers change them to increase their effectiveness by putting a twist in the shank so the tip is off center, then bending the tip into a modified circle shape.

Even when rules allow the use of trebles, many experienced jiggers switch the treble hooks on most new jigs before putting the lures in the water. Most of the hooks that come with the jigs are too heavy to penetrate salmon well, they contend, and are so heavy in fact that they cause you to break off the jig when you snag bottom.

"I think the manufacturers use them because you lose the jig, then you've got to buy another jig," one angler said.

Some brands of jigs are okay right out of the package. But with others, anglers remove the factory hooks and replace them with hooks made from lighter wire.

"If you've got 40-pound-test line and get hung up you can straighten the hook out and get your jig back," one angler said. "But it will hold 99 percent of the time on fish."

Some anglers not only go lighter with hooks, they also go larger.

"I always put on a bigger one," an experienced jigger said. "If I've got a 1-ounce jig and it's got a small treble, I'll put the hook for a 5-ouncer on my 1-ouncer. It seems to give me a lot better chance of hooking a fish."

The larger hooks are more inclined than smaller ones to hang up on the bottom, but the light wire usually allows this angler to retrieve his jig at the expense only of

replacing the hook. He says the larger hook is worth the small additional risk of losing the jig in return for the increased likelihood of hooking a salmon.

"If I go for the smaller hook because I'm afraid of losing the bait, then I'm focusing on the wrong objective," he said.

He has lost a few large fish, however, because they straightened the lighter wire.

Choosing Rod, Reel, and Line

An angler can use virtually any rod to jig, but some are better than others.

Graphite is the rod material of choice for three reasons: sensitivity, backbone, and light weight. Jigging is work. The rod stays in the angler's hand virtually the entire time he is fishing, rather than in a holder, and the relative weight of that rod becomes important by the end of the day. This is especially true when fishing at greater depths with heavier jigs.

In jigging, fish take the lure most of the time on the downward flutter when line is slack. It's easy to overlook a bite, so the greater sensitivity of graphite compared to fiberglass means more fish in the boat.

Jiggers prefer a fairly beefy and fast or moderately fast rod, meaning one that bends only in about the top one-quarter of the blank. This transfers more of the jigging action from the angler's arm to the lure, and less of the action is lost in the bending of a more pliable rod. Jiggers also prefer a relatively short rod – 7 or 7.5 feet – because it's less strain on an angler to jig with a short rod than it is with a long one.

Baitcasting reels are the favorite model by far among jiggers, although large saltwater models of spinning reel are popular among Canadians who jig at great depths in waters around Campbell River, B.C. They apparently like the high gear ratio and quick retrieve that the spinning reels provide, as well as their free-spool capabilities.

In the United States, however, nearly all jiggers use bait casters because of the control it gives them over their lure. By thumbing the reel they can regulate the rate of drop. They also can free-spool the lure for a while, stop it with thumb pressure on the spool and jig it a few times, then drop it and jig it, drop it and jig it, all the way to the bottom. This is harder to do with a spinning reel. Many baitcast anglers prefer level-wind models because they not only distribute retrieved line on the reel's spool, but their travel back and forth across the spool, providing a way to measure line let out or retrieved.

"You can count crossings as you're dropping," one angler said. "Or you can figure out where fish are relative to the bottom; how many crossings up."

Some jiggers prefer a baitcasting reel that lacks the level-wind feature. They usually track the whereabouts of a lure on the drop by counting seconds. But that is harder and usually less accurate than counting crossings.

The major exception to the preference for bait casters in the United States occurs when people fish with Buzz Bombs, a type of jig that stimulates bites primarily through sound rather than sight. Unlike most jigs, they are cast rather than free-spooled, and then retrieved in a rise-and-fall manner. Many anglers use spinning reels to cast and retrieve them.

In recent years, more and more anglers have turned away from monofilament and adopted braided lines for jigging for several reasons. One, modern braided lines are more sensitive than monofilament, and transmit the touch of a fish more clearly. Two, braided lines don't stretch, while monofilament does. It's easier to work a jig with braided line, especially at greater depths, because energy transmitted from the angler to the jig is not lost in expansion and contraction of the line. And monofilament, because of its stretch, has a tendency to dampen the action of a lure. Three, braided line is significantly smaller in diameter than monofilament of equivalent strength, allowing an angler to go deeper with smaller jigs than is possible with mono.

Some anglers use monofilament when jigging in shallow water, because it has greater hang time. And many anglers who jig with braided line tip that line with 3 to 10 feet or more of clear monofilament, usually of less breaking strength than the main line, primarily in the belief that fish can't see it. The monofilament leader also fulfills a shock-absorbing function.

They'll also tie a good swivel into their system somewhere to keep their line from twisting.

One experienced jigger uses braided line of 20- to 40-pound test, depending on how deep he's fishing and how heavy the jigs are. He uses the lighter test to fish a small lure, going to heavier line only when using a heavier lure.

Another jigger says he almost always uses braided line of 65 pounds.

The switch to braided line has lessened the need for vigorous working of the jig.

"There are times you don't have to do a thing," one jigger said. "You can put your pole in the holder, and the boat's action, moving up and down, will impart all the action you need. There's a tendency to give it too much action and make it harder for fish to successfully intercept the bait."

Another potential problem, especially with braided line, is that too much action may cause the hook to flip around and snag the line.

"You have to be sensitive to it not feeling right," the angler said. "That's an indicator that you're clearly doing something wrong."

How to Jig

Fishing with a standard jig for salmon primarily is fishing for chinook.

Find your spot, preferably on a school of bait, and free-spool your jig toward the bottom. Stay alert while the lure is on its way down, because that's when it's most likely to attract a bite.

"You've got to have slack line going down," one jigger said. "As it goes down it should lie flat in the water and flutter."

The flutter not only attracts fish, it slows the descent and makes the jig easier to catch.

"Watch your line going down," one long-time jigger advised. "When it stops, that's when you've got to set the hook, real fast."

This man often fishes at depths as great as 200 feet, and says he usually sees the take before he feels it. Others say they usually feel it first.

Sometimes it can be surprisingly hard to detect.

"I've fished where I can see the jig, and you'd be surprised how many fish grab it and you can't even feel it," one jigger said. "You can't feel it unless he grabs the hook."

On a few occasions, being able to see his jig made all the difference for this man.

"It was kind of thrilling," he said. "It would come up and go down, and then it would disappear. When it disappeared I'd set the hook, and there would be a big old king."

Do salmon always take it on the descent?

"No, they'll follow it up and swallow it," one jigger said. "But probably in excess of 75 percent of the time I catch my fish on the drop."

It's important to maintain your line in a near-vertical position, and experienced jiggers use their motors to help do this.

"You may have to motor forward or back," one said.

"Use of a boat is almost mandatory in jigging," he said. "Almost any size boat is useable. But you've got to maintain line angle by backing into the current, which can be quite a challenge for boats over 25 feet. And because backing into swells is often routine, hardcore jiggers sometimes modify their transoms to block or slow incoming water."

Some experienced anglers always fasten a jig to their line with a snap swivel. Others always tie the line directly to the jig.

Failing to use a snap "changes the action; impedes it in most cases," one expert said. "The jig will be slightly more erratic if it's got a snap on it. Also, the metal takes most of the abuse from the bottom, rather than the nylon knot.

"It's critical that you frequently check your knot and the line immediately around it," he said. "It's pounding on the bottom and maybe rubbing on barnacles. So as frequently as you sharpen your hooks, you want to check that knot.

"And if you use a snap swivel, make sure the snap closes tightly. A lot of times they should be crimped to make sure they don't come unsnapped."

Another jigger likes the action he gets by tying direct, but acknowledges that his line takes a beating where it goes through the eye of the jig.

"Sometimes the fish break off," he said. "So after a half hour I almost always pull up and retie. Oftentimes if the fish break off it's because I waited too long to retie."

Many jiggers drop their lure all the way to the bottom to start, then immediately reel up several turns to keep from hanging up. Ideally, they'll drop where there's bait.

"I'm going to drop through the bait ball," one man said, "and I'll always go all the way to the bottom. Then I'll reel up a couple of turns, and then just bring it up slowly with the rod tip and let it back down. They hit it when it's fluttering on the way down. Occasionally while coming up it will get a whack, but that's the exception.

"Then I'll come up and try to get right below the ball. Then I'll get into it, and sometimes even come above it."

If you're too far below the bait, the salmon may never see your jig. But as long as you're not too low, virtually any place around the ball should be productive. And as you fish, you tend to focus more on your line and lure and less on your electronic fish-finder, thus losing track of the ball.

"What happens is, I'm drifting," this long-time jigger said, "so I'm going to drift through the ball. I get in it, get around it, get alongside it. I don't know that it's made a great deal of difference where I am – whether I'm in it or alongside it – regarding whether I get a hit."

Some anglers use scent on their jigs, and some don't.

"I always use scent, and every time I bring it up and check it I always put a little more scent on it," one man said. "I'm doing anything I can to enhance my chances of getting bit."

He uses a variety of standard aromas, he said, and isn't aware of any outperforming the others.

"This is a sight fishery," another jigger observed. "The addition of scent doesn't seem to make a lot of difference. But what does make a difference is I use clear nylon for a tippet. I don't use any of the colors. I use a clear line that has a lower visibility to the fish."

On that the scent fisherman agrees.

"I've gone to fluorocarbon line," he said, "and if I have braided line I'll use 20 to 30 feet of monofilament fluorocarbon as a leader, because the fish can't see it."

How should you move your rod to impart the best action to your jig? The experts are unanimous: Vary what you do.

One experienced jig fisherman likes to raise his rod to about 15 or 20 degrees short of vertical.

"Sometimes I let it down really quickly, so the jig flutters," he said. "Other times I let it down real slowly. About every fourth or fifth time, if I'm near the bottom, I like to touch the bottom.

"But if you hit bottom every time, you're hitting it too much," he said.

"When you get around river mouths, a lot of times fish will take it when you jig it just a little bit," another jigger said. "But you've got to keep it moving."

In deeper water he jigs with larger strokes or jerks.

"But you can get them that way, too, in shallow water," he said. "If they're not biting the little jerk, then I go to the big swing. You've got to change when you're jigging."

Another knowledgeable jigger says an average stroke would be 2 or 3 feet, but he also varies it. Sometimes he raises his rod 6 or 7 feet; other times just inches, depending on how deep he's fishing and what kind of baitfish he's imitating. It's possible to "over-actionize" your bait, he said, and the fish themselves have taught him this.

"There have been times ... when we've tried everything to get fish to take," he said. "We could see bait, we could see fish, and we couldn't get a hit. So I've said, 'The heck with it. I'm going to have lunch,' and I've put my pole in the holder and it's just going up and down with the boat, and fish take it."

Should you use a fluid motion or a jerky one when moving your jig?

"Don't get locked into any one thing," this angler said. "Sometimes one thing will work, sometimes another. Try a variety of actions until you find the right one.

"Above all else, keep an open mind," he said. "Don't get locked into one lure, one jig stroke, one depth, one color."

There are subtleties in jigging that a lot of people miss.

"The average fisherman is not aware of a high percentage of the fish takes that he has," one jigger observed. "You'll get a tick or something where it behaves funny on the drop – a momentary hesitation. Or the jig goes slack, and you're 30 feet down in 60 feet of water.

"A lot of time, with sensitive lines, you can tell that a fish is interested. You're dropping it erratically, and a fish is swimming around, ticking it, trying to grab it and missing. So you can change your tactics. Slow it down and the fish will grab it."

Feeling fish hit the jig is part of the fun of jigging.

"Strike as quickly as you can," one veteran advised. "But you don't want to pull it out of the fish's mouth. If you keep your arm straight and then raise it, that's a better way than bending at the elbow. You don't get the speed, but you get a nice, solid set."

When jigging, unlike when mooching, it's best to fish with your line nearly vertical.

"In most cases if it's not vertical you're not close to the bottom," one jigger said. "And it's harder to feel the ticks, because you don't have the sensitivity."

If the current is too strong to allow him to lower his jig vertically, this angler will use his motor to back into the current to get the jig down. Or, he'll toss the jig out down-current, then jig as he drifts over it, and reel it up after he has passed it.

"That's far more effective," he said, "than just letting it drift out and continuing to jig."

Fishing at a large angle works with a Buzz Bomb, which operates differently than other jigs, but that's an exception to the rule.

Coho on Jigs

It's possible to catch coho salmon on jigs, too, but coho occupy a different ecological niche than do chinook. While chinook usually hang from midwater to bottom in the water column, coho – and pink salmon – more commonly travel and feed midwater and above. And so the technique for jigging coho is different than it is for jigging chinook.

One expert uses a light, level-wind reel for coho, although a spinning reel also would be appropriate, and he snaps on a herring jig or a Dart of 2 or 3 ounces. But he fishes the lure as though it were a Buzz Bomb or a spinner.

"I'll cast it out 60 or 70 feet, and let it sink 10 feet or so, then I'll pull back so it rises up in the water column," he said. "Then I'll let it sink again about 10 feet."

He'll repeat the procedure, reeling a few feet, letting it sink, then reeling a few feet, until the jig is back at the boat.

"Sometimes I work it along the shoreline, and sometimes out in the rips," he said.

Fighting the Fish

Fish that you catch on jigs fight differently than those you catch on flasher gear or mooched bait.

"Normally, when you get a fish on a flasher the fish takes off, the flasher is hitting him in the tail, and he's going 90 miles an hour," one jigger said. "He fights until he's exhausted. When you catch a fish on bait, he reacts not quite as violently. He does take off, and the sinker is chasing him, so he tends to run away from the sinker.

"With a jig, the weight is right there outside his mouth. Some will sit there and shake their heads. Others will take off in a slow, steady run. But their behavior will be different than it is with flashers or bait.

"Often you can pull them up and net them even before they realize they're hooked."

Others say that a salmon jigged in deep water may behave with restraint, but one hooked by a jig in shallow water will take off like a shot.

The problem is, whether water is shallow or deep, the weight of the jig hanging right outside the fish's mouth gives the fish something to work against in ridding itself of the hook.

"You've got to keep a real tight line," one jigger said. "When you're mooching, you've got the sinker away from your hooks, so the fish has got nothing to jerk against. When you're jigging, the sinker is right up against the hooks, so they've got something to jerk against every time they shake their head. They can throw that jig right out of their mouth.

"When I first started fishing with jigs, I used to just thumb the reel when a fish was taking line," he said. "I lost a lot of fish that way. Now I use a star drag, and I set the drag pretty tight, because the fish is jerking the rod tip up and down, and that's creating some slack. I use heavy leader, and as soon as the fish stops going out, I start cranking."

You're going to lose more fish on jigs than you will with other gear, another angler said.

"This is the cost of doing business," he said. "But I find that I get more bites on jigs than I do on other things. I have a tendency with jigs to try to net the fish faster because I know the jigs are going to come out."

Not all jiggers behave likewise, however.

"I like to play them out, rather than bring them in too green," another jig fisherman said. "If you bring them in too hot they're going to come right to the surface, and once they come to the surface they're going to jump and splash and twist."

He'll do whatever he can, he said, to keep a fish from surfacing prematurely, including plunging his rod tip into the water to try to hold the fish at bay.

"If they do come up and jump," he said, "I take a chapter from my days as a fly fisherman. If they jump, I bow."

His bending at the waist, he said, serves to lower his rod tip.

"I honor the fish by bowing, and it takes the extra tension off," he said. "It still allows tension, but not that severe tension that breaks them off or pulls it out of their

mouths. A lot of time when a fish jumps, people do exactly the wrong thing; they pull back. It adds too much tension, and they lose the fish."

Creating a Starter Kit

Here is a collection of lures that one successful jigger of many decades recommends for starting out in the sport. This mix will work in a variety of situations while keeping cash outlay to a minimum.

"If I were going to buy 10 jigs," he said, "60 percent would be candlefish. I would pick 2 ounce, 4 ounce, and 6 ounce, one of each of those sizes in white. Then I would pick one of each of those sizes in chrome with a green back. That would give me six of those.

"Then, of the herring imitators, I would pick the 3-ounce size and the 5-ounce size. One of each would be white. And then, instead of chrome and green, I would pick one each of chrome and blue if I were planning to fish in the ocean. But if I were planning to fish inside, I would pick chrome and green again."

Among those who contributed information used in this chapter, the author would like to thank:

Mark Carr, retired fisheries biologist for the Washington Department of Fish and Wildlife; Chuck Wahtola, former president, Fidalgo Island Chapter of Puget Sound Anglers; Bob Salatino, former commercial fisherman and chief fish-catcher for the Point Defiance Zoo & Aquarium, Tacoma, Washington; John Posey, national sales manager for Lamiglas, Inc., Woodland, Washington.

Boats and Motors

Frankly, I was worried. It was early May, and I had pointed my fiberglass runabout down the west side of Blakely Island in the Washington San Juans, heading for Thatcher Pass and then the final sprint to Anacortes.

I'd been fishing with friends for a couple of days, and now family obligations called me home. To get there, I had to Cross Rosario Strait to the public ramp at Washington Park, where I'd left my trailer and truck. But a strong southwest wind was raising whitecaps even there on the protected waters between Blakely and Lopez Islands, and it made me uneasy. When I turned the corner into Thatcher Pass my heart sank.

Rosario Strait, open to the wind all way from the Olympic Peninsula, was a cauldron of seething white. It was more than I wanted to risk in my small boat.

I found a place to go ashore just outside the mouth of the pass on state-owned James Island which offered a tiny bay that was somewhat protected, in which was located a float to tie up to. The island itself was a good place from which to watch the strait.

At first it looked as though I could be stuck there for days. The wind howled without let-up, driving rain nearly horizontally up the strait. Fortunately, I had a weatherproof backpacker's tent in my boat, and enough food and drink in the ice chest to see me through. But I fretted about what my family might think.

The worry turned out to be for nothing, however. A couple of hours later the wind abated briefly, and I cast off quickly and made the 20-minute run to the other side during a window of relative calm. Even then, though, the water was lumpy. Hurrying across the strait in my little boat was a bone-jarring ride, and a wet one.

I've fished the San Juans for many years since then, and have crossed Rosario Strait numerous times. But there was a lesson to be learned from the experience that May: Gear up for the kinds of waters you plan to fish, and for goodness sake get a boat with a hull that will cut through a chop. Mine had been relatively flat-bottomed, and flat-bottomed boats ride like a buckboard when the water kicks up.

My current boat is longer than that other, a lot beamier, has more freeboard, and provides a covered pilot station that's a godsend when heavy seas splash over the bow. It also has a modified deep-V hull that cuts through chop like a chainsaw through balsa, flattening out the ride and making windy days mild.

Why this talk about boats? Because saltwater salmon fishing is boat fishing. There are places that salmon can be caught at times from the beach, but success in marine waters throughout a season requires flexibility, and flexibility requires that you be able to fish from a boat.

Depending on where you live and what waters you fish, your boat might not have to be a big one. For years on central and southern Puget Sound, for example, a popular boat was the 12-foot fiberglass Hi-Laker. It worked well for a single occupant in the protected waters around Commencement Bay and Vashon Island, and produced many fine salmon. It didn't require much to push it, either, and a lot of fishermen used motors of 9.9 to 15 horsepower.

Fourteen-foot aluminum Lunds are widespread in western Washington. A 9.9 motor will move them nicely with just one person aboard, but they're more commonly powered by 20 or 25 horses.

As one travels north and west out of Puget Sound and then down the coasts of Washington, Oregon, and California, however, the nature of fishing changes. The water gets bigger, and the protected places where one can fish become fewer. The nature of boats changes also.

In the last few years, the pace of change has increased. One of the major modifications has been a swing toward outboard power and away from inboard-powered boats. Another has been a trend toward bigger boats.

Boats

Growth in the popularity of larger boats – but larger only to a point – reflects the changing nature of salmon fisheries up and down the coast. As conservation requirements dictate the constraint of seasons by time and area, people who fish must often run farther to do it. For this they want boats that are safer and that can cover water quickly. This often means boats that are longer, sometimes beamier, and that sometimes incorporate a flared bow that turns water down and out instead of letting it encroach on the deck and windshield in heavy seas.

However, those same season constraints also often dictate that people trailer long distances to waters that are open to fishing, and many anglers don't want their boats to exceed a size convenient for towing.

One of the first things you need to consider in buying a boat is whether you want a deep-V or modified deep-V hull or whether you prefer a flatter bottom. A deeper-V hull provides a smoother ride in rough water, but a trade-off is a fishing platform with less stability than one with a flatter hull. At least one manufacturer attempts to address this by installing a wide, flat chine along the hull near each side of the boat so when the boat is at rest in the water it's sitting on that chine.

"Fifteen years ago, you would find avid anglers buying a 14-foot skiff and a 15-horsepower motor," one Seattle boat retailer observed. "Now they have bigger boats, because they end up in bigger water and more distant destinations."

For this dealer, the change has meant a shift by anglers to manufacturers who make larger boats and then a trend toward buying the larger boats in those manufacturers' lines.

His own line of premium offshore fiberglass fishing boats, the merchant said, which run from 18 to 36 feet, "allows fishermen to pick up and run to far-off places to fish."

Besides considering hull configuration, you must decide whether you want a self-bailing deck that allows any water taken on board – either rain water or sea water – to run out through scuppers into the sea. A self-bailer has an obvious advantage if you intend to moor your boat in a marina or at a private moorage for long periods, especially if you're not able to check it often. With a non-self-bailing deck, any water that collects on the deck runs into the bilge and must be pumped overboard.

However, to build a self-bailer, the manufacturer must place the deck several inches above the water line so sea water won't enter the boat through the scuppers.

One Northwest manufacturer of fiberglass fishing boats builds most of his models as non-bailers with the deck located at the waterline because, he says, it provides greater stability to the boat and gunwales that are higher and more secure relative to a person standing on the deck. It also allows a person to reach over a gunwale and reach the water more easily.

"Two of the most important things we've found: People want the ability to have two or three full-size adults standing on one side of the boat," a factory representative said. "And they want to be able to touch the water with their hands to release a fish.

"With a self-bailing deck, you've got to put it up six or eight inches. Most of us can't touch our toes, so how are we going to touch the water? Also, when you raise the deck you raise the center of gravity, and the boat gets a little listier." With a deck at waterline, a boat is "extremely stable and untippy."

Placing motor outside the transom, instead of on it, provides a quieter ride and, in many cases, better handling. Photo courtesy of Honda Marine.

This manufacturer makes boats of 15 to 22 feet, and those near the upper end of the range, from 19 to 21 feet, have become the most popular in his line with salmon anglers.

The spike in fuel prices that occurred early in the 21st century resulted in a noticeable surge in the sale of somewhat smaller fiberglass boats. But not, apparently, because anglers didn't want to buy gas for larger boats. In fact, the phenomenon appeared to be related to pickup trucks.

"Guys are downsizing their towing vehicles," the factory spokesman said, "and this bounces back. When everybody owns a big-size pickup or diesel truck, towing is not a problem. But when gas doubled, guys were downsizing tow rigs and we saw a jump in demand for 17-footers. There was a new interest in little boats, although there hadn't been a drop-off yet in big boats."

Tastes in boats among anglers run about the same in Washington and Oregon, but change somewhat off the California coast.

"In California they don't have nice bays with good fishing," the factory spokesman said. "They've got to commit to the big ocean. In California, everybody wants a bigger boat."

Still, the boats that anglers use in northern California are much like those you find through Oregon and Washington. They usually provide some sort of protection from the weather, such as a cabin, a hard-top or a fabric top. And metal boats have become more popular in California in recent years, as they have elsewhere, although the sport fleet still consists primarily of fiberglass.

That brings up another decision a salmon angler must make. A person who plans to trailer often to remote locations to take advantage of those windows of fishing opportunity should weigh the merits of an aluminum boat.

Aluminum provides several advantages. For one, you can run it up on the beach if you should decide to go ashore somewhere, without worrying about chipping or scraping a delicate fiberglass bottom. For another, a manufacturer can incorporate custom features during manufacturing more easily with aluminum than with fiberglass.

"A glass boat comes out of a mold, and nobody's going to build a new mold for you," observed one manufacturer of aluminum boats. "But if you want a cabin a foot longer or you want the fish box this way or that way, I can do a lot of that."

Some anglers prefer fiberglass over aluminum because of the weight and stability that glass provides. But weight can be both a plus and a minus. And some anglers prefer aluminum precisely because it provides more boat with less weight. One Northwest manufacturer produces a line of metal boats with exactly that in mind. He builds two models, with lengths of 17 to 21 feet in one model and 18 to 24 feet in the other, and he'll customize them to be longer.

"We aim for a boat that will do a good job in open water that a private party can afford and also can tow," he said. And it's the towable part of the equation that he thinks is of prime importance. He points to one of his popular 23-foot boats, for example, which comes with a bracket outside the transom for the main outboard.

"It will be powered typically by a four-stroke motor which is quiet, efficient, and takes a lot less room than an inboard, and weighs less than an inboard" he said. "So you can pull it with your half-ton pickup, which with a glass boat would be a chore."

He builds his boats with a deep-V hull for rough water, and with an aluminum cabin that contains the pilot's station, a portable toilet and opportunity to choose among an array of options that include a dinette, benches for passengers, or a counter with a one-burner stove.

"We're seeing more deeper-V boats of 23 to 25 feet, with cabins, than we ever used to," the manufacturer said. "People are looking for a boat in that size that's fuel efficient and that's what an aluminum boat is."

If you're looking for a boat in the 20-foot-or-larger category, keep this in mind:

Federal regulations require boats less than 20 feet long, whether fiberglass or metal, to be equipped with floatation that will float them level if completely swamped. No floatation is required for boats 20 feet or longer, although some manufacturers install it anyway. Some such boats, depending on the manufacturer, float level when swamped. Others float bow up, stern submerged.

Here are some other points to keep in mind, when shopping for a boat. Length overall means little if a lot of the length is in front of the windshield under a covered bow. The space that counts is what's usable for fishing. In a wide-open utility boat, like a Lund, the entire boat is usable. In a runabout with a windshield, you're often confined to the cockpit unless you have a walk-around deck or a walk-through windshield with an open bow. Some boaters don't like an open bow, however, in heavy seas.

You want fishing room for at least two people. Room for three or more is better. You'll need space for a fish box, if none is built in, for tackle boxes and for stowing a long-handled landing net. You'll want gunwale-mounted rod holders, one per angler, because sooner or later you'll have to set a rod down to pour a cup of coffee.

Holders for storing and transporting rods horizontally along the sides of the boat or rocket-launcher holders for carrying rods vertically on a cabin roof are very handy. They keep the rods where you can get at them, and save many a tip from being broken. You need enough holder capacity for all the rods you expect to carry on any trip. That's usually at least two per angler.

If you plan to fish through the winter, consider a boat with some shelter, at least a canvas top. You can feel 15 degrees warmer on a blustery day just by stepping out of the wind. If your cover is fabric, consider the kind that's higher than the top of the windshield. This extra head room makes for a pilot house that's easier to get out of when a rod is dancing in its holder on the stern.

It's nice to have a cabin or canopy you can see over when standing in the cockpit of the boat. You'll probably fish at least some of the time in crowded waterways, and you've got to have a 360-degree view to avoid collisions. If your cabin top is too high to see over, then make sure it's high enough so you can look through the windshield from the cockpit without bending too far. If you can't, one member of the party will have to serve as fulltime skipper.

If your main source of power is inboard/outboard, or an outboard of 50 horsepower or more, you may want a bracket-mounted outboard auxiliary, 6 to 10 horsepower motor with which to troll. It will double as insurance on bigger waters to get you home in the unlikely event that the big motor fails.

Consider an auxiliary that will run off the same fuel supply as the main engine. That means that if the big one's an inboard or a four-stroke or oil-injected outboard, you should consider a four-stroke auxiliary for which gas and oil aren't mixed.

Motors

A marine salmon angler must choose among three types of propulsion: inboard motors, inboard/outboards, and outboard motors.

An inboard consists of an engine mounted below the deck, usually amidships, with a fixed propeller below the hull and a separate rudder for steering. An inboard/outboard, also called a stern drive, contains an engine below the deck near the stern of the boat. The engine connects to a lower unit, also called an outdrive, which looks much like the lower part of an outboard motor. A skipper steers the boat by turning the entire lower unit, which contains the propeller, similar to steering an outboard.

An outboard motor mounts entirely outside of the boat, either on the transom or on an extension or bracket extending aft from the transom.

With a wide beam and a deck that's built at water level, this Arima gives an angler a stable fishing platform and puts him close to the action. Photo courtesy of Arima Marine International.

A major change has taken place in recent years in marine propulsion, and salmon anglers have been right in the middle of it. The change has involved a dramatic shift to outboard power from inboard or inboard/outboard on larger boats.

"The outboard is probably safer," one boat dealer explained. "And it's simpler, and therefore more reliable than the stern drive."

Anglers gain a lot of advantages by placing a gasoline motor outside a boat's transom. For one, it reduces the risk of explosion and fire, because they're no longer igniting an unstable fuel in a confined space inside the hull. For another, outboard motors weigh less than equivalent inboard ones, and operate more dependably. Outboards are easier to access for maintenance and repairs and easier to switch if the need arises. Outboards also leave more room in a boat's cockpit by eliminating the need for the engine box that occupies valuable space in a boat with an inboard motor. If the outboard is mounted on a bracket, it's also quieter than any other motor.

"And it's easier to build an unsinkable boat with an outboard," one dealer said, "because the inboard has a big hole in the cockpit sole where the engine sits. Obviously, if you flood the cockpit it floods the bilge."

A major part of the propulsion evolution has been the switch from two-stroke outboards to four-stroke. California started it.

In the mid-1990s, the California Air Resources Board established internal combustion emission standards for motors sold in that state that surpassed what the federal Environmental Protection Agency required. With populous California comprising such a large part of the U.S. market, its standards became the impetus for the blossoming – nationwide – of the four-stroke outboard motor. And the four-stroke has helped fuel the switch to outboards because of its efficiency, dependability, and longevity; its anticipated useful life being twice as long as that of a two-stroke operated under the same conditions.

Carbureted two-stroke engines expel significantly more smoke, fumes, and unburned fuel from their cylinders than do four-strokes. For that reason, they are more polluting and less efficient than four-strokes at converting fuel to energy.

A four-stroke outboard lubricates itself the way an automobile engine does. It utilizes oil that's carried in a reservoir inside the motor to bathe its moving parts, rather than mixing its lubricating oil with gasoline and burning both oil and gasoline inside the cylinder the way two-stroke engines do. It's called a four-stroke because its pistons make four thrusts, or strokes, during every cycle of drawing fuel into the cylinder and expelling exhaust from it.

The pistons of a two-stroke outboard make just two thrusts, or strokes, during every cycle.

"Four strokes are the predominant thing we sell, because that's what the customer wants," the aluminum-boat manufacturer said.

Why?

Because of their fuel efficiency, their quietness, their dependability, and the ability of four-strokes large and small to run for hours at trolling speed without fouling spark plugs and piston rings with carbon.

Manufacturers promise 25 percent better fuel efficiency with four-stroke motors, the retailer said. "But I have customers who tell me they've doubled the range of the boat with the four-stroke."

Development of four-stroke engines resulted in another phenomenon as well – a trend toward elimination of the second large outboard from the transoms of many boats.

"It's mostly single motors on the back now," a spokesman for one major outboard manufacturer said. "Four-strokes are very reliable, compared to two-strokes. In the old days, it was common sense to use two motors, because one was likely to break down. Now, most people go with one big four-stroke and one kicker."

In recent years, virtually the only people installing more than one large outboard on their boats are those with boats whose weight surpasses the ability of a single four-stroke to push it. But the size and power of four-strokes has increased rapidly. Until 2001, for example, the largest four-stroke outboard available was the Honda 130 horsepower. It had followed Honda's 75 and 90 into production. Just four years later, Honda was producing a 225, and Mercury and Yamaha had introduced a 250. Honda was following suit, and designs for larger four-strokes were on manufacturers' planning tables.

The increasing popularity of four-stroke outboards has pushed many boat builders to begin to modify their products for outboards. Redesigns sometimes are necessary because large four-stroke outboards are heavy. A Yamaha 250, for example, weighs 592 pounds. That much heft on or behind a transom can change a boat's planing characteristics, and some boat builders have worked to develop hulls that will accommodate this.

Four-stroke outboards initially gained popularity among salmon anglers in the 1970s as trolling kickers aboard boats with inboard or inboard/outboard engines. Only smaller four-strokes were available then, and anglers could plug them into the fuel supply for their primary motors and avoid having to mix oil and gas. Also, they could troll with a four-stroke at the slow speeds required for salmon angling and not foul the engine. Carbureted two-stroke kickers, because of their gas and oil mixture, would carbon-up quickly at trolling speeds.

"A lot of anglers have found they can troll now with the main motor," a spokesman for one major outboard manufacturer said. "That used to be something you didn't want to do, because you didn't want to idle a two-stroke for any length of time. The plugs would foul, and carbon buildup in the rings could lead to catastrophic failure. But a four-stroke is like a car engine. You can idle it for hours on end."

The main disadvantage to four-strokes is their weight.

"Generally speaking, a two-stroke is going to be smaller, lighter, a little faster," a manufacturer's rep said. "A four-stroke will be bigger, heavier, more expensive but more fuel-efficient."

Some manufacturers have responded to increasingly stringent clean-air regulations by developing fuel-injected two-stroke outboards to replace the old carbureted models. They inject the fuel directly into the cylinders at pressures of as

much as 1,000 pounds per square inch. The high pressure better atomizes the fuel, and it burns cleaner.

"That allows them to burn their fuel and oil fully, and makes them much cleaner than they were before, and more efficient," the manufacturer's rep said. "Many of those motors are comparable to a four-stroke in efficiency. But when you do that, you add a lot of weight and complexity, and some of them weigh and cost nearly as much as four-strokes. So you're taking away a lot of the advantages the old two-strokes had."

Some of the 200 horsepower two-strokes with direct injection and 200 horsepower four-strokes have almost identical fuel economy, another manufacturer's spokesman said.

"The difference is, two-strokes are going to be a lot stronger, with more torque, at lower rpm," he said. "Every internal combustion engine has a torque curve, and with a two-stroke you get more torque in a lower range. Because outboards don't change gears, you're always in the same gear. Two-strokes, with sparkplugs firing every two strokes instead of four, you've just got a little more oomph right off the line when you're trying to get going.

"So if you have a big boat and you're trying to get up on plane, a two-stroke application might make more sense than a four-stroke."

But, while that may be important to water skiers, salmon anglers don't care whether they get up on plane in two boat lengths.

"And at wide-open throttle, a 250 is the same whether it's two-stroke or four-stroke," the manufacturer's rep said.

Meanwhile, even though the fuel efficiency of direct-injection two-strokes approaches that of a four-stroke, a four-stroke operator does not mix oil with his gasoline. That is a significant savings.

"If you look at the new-technology two-stroke, they're more fuel-efficient, but you're still burning oil, so you still have that cost," the rep said.

Among those who contributed information used in this chapter, the author would like to thank:

Terry McCartney, Jacobsen's Marine, Seattle; Don Gross, Arima Marine, Auburn, Washington; Glen Wooldridge, Wooldridge Boats, Inc., Seattle; Mike Connor, Honda Marine, Olympia, Washington; Richard Burton, Honda Marine, Clovis, CA; Dennis Phillips, Mike Walker Agency and Yamaha Motor Corp., Scottsdale, AZ.

Electronics

It happened several years ago off the corner of an island in northwest Washington. A friend and I had come there to fish. We were staying in a rented cabin on the island for several days, fishing each day from first light until evening, having a good time on the water.

This was in an era when the electronics on most boats, including mine, were much less sophisticated than they are today. My little fiberglass runabout boasted a Citizens' Band (CB) radio and a flasher-type depth sounder, both state-of-the-art for that period. I had mounted the CB under the dash of my open-cockpit boat, and then permanently enclosed all of it but the microphone and its cord in a transparent plastic bag to keep rain water and sea water away from its internal parts. Corrosion was evident on the radio's metal body in spite of the bag, but the instrument continued to work.

I had mounted my flasher out in the weather, on the dash, but it was advertised as waterproof.

While monitoring the flasher, my partner and I had discovered a pinnacle about 100 yards off the northwest corner of our island, and every time we drifted over the pinnacle one or both of us got a strike. We thought we had found fishing's mother lode.

With our limits in the boat we headed for our cabin, determined to return to the same spot the next day and pick up where we'd left off. But sometime between turning my flasher off in the afternoon and turning it on again the next morning, the unit failed. The screen stood blank.

If you've been in that position, you know what I felt. My partner and I had several days more to fish, no way to fix the unit – which ultimately had to be shipped back to the manufacturer for repair – and no way to replace it.

Not until that moment did I realize how much I had come to depend on this electronic aid. I reminded myself that I'd fished for a lifetime without one before buying the unit several years before. Certainly I could do so again.

My partner and I set out in the morning as planned, but never relocated the pinnacle for sure, and never found fish again on this trip in such a big way as we had at that spot. I tried to dredge up all the former fishing skills I'd used in years past – taking more careful note of sea birds and currents, examining shoreside topography for clues to how the bottom lay offshore and for evidence of our position in relation to charted bottom features – but it was like hunting for elusive game with one eye shut and the other blurred.

It was a lesson in how much we come to rely on technology once we start to use it. And it's something to take to heart. Because advancement in technology continues, and the degree to which anglers have adapted to it has been remarkable. Some younger anglers have never fished without electronic aids.

Technology not only grows better, but grows different. Fish flashers, for example, have become virtually obsolete in recent years. By 2005, Boater's World Marine Centers, a national retailer, sold fewer than a dozen flashers a year throughout its entire system, and sold most of those to people who replaced an existing one. Nearly everyone had switched by then to liquid crystal display screens that drew pictures of bottom topography and marked fish and other targets in relation to their place in the water column.

By the early 2000s, fewer anglers relied on CB radios. Many had switched to sophisticated very high frequency (VHF) marine radios or, in some cases, to cell phones. Global Positioning System (GPS) marine navigation units had gone into widespread use, and many anglers took that another step to GPS/chartplotter units. Radar became more common on smaller boats, with many anglers using it not only for navigation and safety, but also as a fishing aid. And still other electronic aids, though not yet widely used, were gaining popularity among cutting-edge anglers.

GPS chartplotters have changed the face of marine electronics. This model has a touchscreen interface and no buttons. Photo courtesy of Garmin.

"It used to be a guy was happy with a fish finder and a VHF radio," one Seattle boat retailer observed. "Now they all want a GPS with plotter and radar, with color monitors and brighter screens and bigger screens."

He sells a lot of autopilots, too, he said, which connect to a boat's main engine and the kicker engine. They work on a compass heading, and also can be tied to the GPS so they'll run a programmed course.

"A lot of guys will use it just with the compass heading," he said, "so they can go back and tend to their downriggers and their gear."

Choices are plentiful. Almost bewildering. If you're outfitting a new boat or upgrading an old one, you have many things to consider. Here is what's available, what's popular and why, and what you should think about in making buying decisions.

Multifunction Units

Generally, boat buyers mount a multifunction monitor for their marine electronics, then hook up as many individual units to their monitor as they want or can afford. These include fish finder/depth sounder units, GPS, chartplotter, and radar. Units may be installed all at once, or over a period of time as need for them develops.

"If you've got the space to mount separately it's nice to do it, because you've got (separate) large displays and they're easier to look at," the manager of one marine equipment store said. "There's also a school of thought that if you've got two separate units, you've got an extra as backup. So if you're entering a shallow-water area, for example, and you lose your GPS, you'd still have a depth sounder to make sure you're not going to run aground."

With a single unit, if you lose its connection to your power source, you lose all its functions.

The advantage to a multifunction unit, however, is it requires less space, and many boats don't provide much space in which to mount electronics. It's also usually less expensive than units purchased separately. You can view each function by itself on a multifunction monitor full-screen size, switching for example from fish finder to radar to chart plotter. Or you can view two or more functions simultaneously by splitting the screen.

Over the past few years, anglers as well as other boaters increasingly have voted with their pocketbooks for multifunction displays.

"Five years ago you couldn't give one away, because there were a lot more failures in electronics than there are now," said an electronics buyer for a major national boating-equipment retailer. "People were afraid that if something went wrong they would lose everything. Now, people are switching. Our best-selling model is not just a GPS/chartplotter, but a GPS/chartplotter/sounder. And now a lot of them are capable of adding radar on top of that.

"It's very unlikely now that a unit might go out," the buyer said. "Something might stop working, such as a radar antenna or a GPS antenna. But it's very unlikely that a unit just goes dead."

The operator of a marine-electronics specialty shop in the Northwest agrees that equipment has become more dependable.

"I've rarely seen a multifunction unit fail in such a way you just can't use it anymore," he said. "If something quits, it's usually just one function or another."

However, he thinks a buyer should consider separate units in some circumstances. If a buyer is a serious angler, this shop owner would rather see him put radar and a chartplotter on one screen and reserve an independent screen for the fish finder.

"It seems to me if your main purpose is to fish, put a good chunk of money into a really good fish finder, then get a radar and chartplotter that will get you by, because you want to step your fish finder up to the next level. And when you have an all-in-one, you pretty much have an all-in-one."

With at least one manufacturer, however, "you can mix and match really good equipment in a multifunction device," he said, and that might be worth considering.

Fish Finders

"With sport fishermen, a fish finder with a large, readable screen is the first thing they look at" when they come into the store, said the manager of a major nautical-supply outlet in Seattle. "A lot of people will opt for a smaller or hand-held portable GPS. But a lot of anglers, especially smaller-boat owners, are looking at combination units that are GPS and fish finder in one unit."

At least two major national marine equipment retailers say several of their most popular fish finders are, in fact, combination products that package the fish-finding function and GPS/chartplotting in the same unit.

Whether or not the fish finder you purchase is part of a multifunction unit, you want a liquid crystal display screen that's large enough to read from the place in the boat where you do most of your fishing, and which might be near the stern. You also want one you can read in full sunlight. A monochrome screen draws less power, but color screens are the overwhelming favorite among purchasers.

Fish finders work by transmitting sonar signals into the water from a transducer mounted on or in the hull of the boat. The transducer receives return echoes and transmits them to the display unit, which shows them as a graphic portraying bottom characteristics and topography, and everything that's in the water between the bottom and the boat. This may be fish, debris, or other material such as vegetation. It's important to choose a unit with a transducer appropriate to the kind of water you fish.

"Don't scrimp on a transducer," the marine electronics shop operator warned. "If you're going to put a high-quality fish finder on a boat, don't limit yourself to a plastic stern-mount transducer. You should be looking at a through-the-hull bronze transducer, if it's a fiberglass boat."

If you operate an aluminum boat, you're essentially limited to a non-metal transducer, he said, because of electrolysis problems generated by metal-on-metal contact in saltwater.

"I would definitely recommend a dual-frequency transducer as opposed to a single-frequency unit," the nautical-supply store manager said. "Typically they provide 50 kHz and 200."

The 200 kHz option provides greater resolution for better detail, but has trouble penetrating greater depths.

"The 50 is better for deeper water," the manager said, "and generally transmits in a narrower cone. The lower frequency allows you to punch through deep water, especially saltwater, to give you a better bottom return."

As a rule of thumb, use the 200 kHz setting for depths to 200 feet, and the 50 for deeper water. Some units switch automatically between settings for optimal results, and also allow manual override.

To get the cone angle, or beam width, that you prefer, you have to look at products offered by different manufacturers. A wider beam covers more bottom area, and the deeper the bottom, the more area it covers. A narrow beam focuses on the area more directly beneath the boat. Cone angles vary from about 9 degrees to 45, depending on the manufacturer. And, because transducers are manufacturer- and model-specific, you should know what type of angle you prefer before you pick your brand.

Chartplotters

A chartplotter function combines GPS with an on-screen nautical chart, and places an icon on the chart to represent your boat. Very few mountable GPS units are available anymore that don't have chartplotting abilities.

"It's like looking at a map with you on it," the electronics buyer explained.

Sales of such units have been huge, and the sales have followed the trend set with fish finders; from monochrome purchases a few years ago to virtually 100 percent color today.

The advantage of using a chartplotter?

"Peace of mind," the buyer said. "It shows you where you are in relation to buoys and to the land base."

GPS receivers pull their data from a network of satellites in orbit around the earth and operated by the U.S. Air Force. The receiver reads timed signals broadcast by the satellites and, by reading multiple satellites simultaneously, can calculate its own position anywhere on the planet to within a few feet. Combined with a chartplotter function, it then illustrates that position on your electronic chart.

What you see is where you are in relation to land, to navigation aids, to navigational hazards, and to charted underwater topographical features such as pinnacles, reefs, and banks.

A GPS/chartplotter feature not only shows you where you are, however. It also shows you how to get from there to any other place on your chart. You can navigate to any preselected destination that you've input into your GPS or to any spot on your electronic chart where you place your cursor. The unit tells you the distance and compass bearing to your target, the speed at which you are approaching it, your

estimated time of arrival, and any deviation you may be taking from the most direct route. It also draws a picture of that route on your chart, which you can follow by manipulating your boat icon as though playing a video game.

You may zoom in on the chart to see smaller areas in greater detail, or zoom out to see larger areas in less detail.

If you have radar as part of your integrated system, you may overlay a radar image on your chart to help differentiate between radar returns that indicate charted objects such as buoys and those that indicate other objects such as vessels.

You can create GPS "waypoints" to mark places at which you have encountered fish, for example, and return to a waypoint in the future by following a route created for you by your GPS. With an integrated multifunction system, you even can create waypoints by clicking on underwater objects displayed on your fish finder screen, such as rock piles or pinnacles.

"To be able to look at your fish finder and see a ledge or something that you passed several minutes ago, and to be able to put a cursor on it and mark it, that's a powerful thing," one marine electronics retailer said.

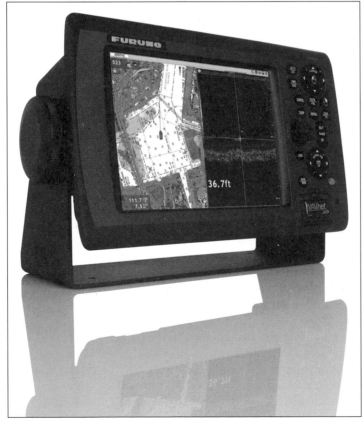

Split-screen electronics can give you both chart-plotter and fishfinder simultaneously, a great advantage when fishing underwater structure. Sometimes, also radar as well. Photo courtesy of Furuno USA Inc.

Radar

Not long ago, only larger private boats – those longer than about 30 feet – usually were equipped with radar. In recent years, as units of increasing quality have grown less and less expensive, radar has become common on smaller boats. In many cases, you will see a radar dome on vessels less than 20 feet, depending on the kind of water on which they're used and the prevailing weather conditions there.

So, is radar a necessity? Or a luxury?

One marine equipment retailer describes it as "kind of a luxury", but one that many more-intense marine anglers opt for.

"A lot of guys start fishing and then realize they'd be a lot safer with radar," the retailer said, "and would have a lot more fishing opportunities with radar."

Radar is the third leg in the multi-function unit stool, and one that an angler doesn't necessarily have to buy when he installs a fish finder and GPS/chartplotter. If he prefers, he can install a radar unit later. Or never. But its availability gives him certain advantages, the major one of which is an added layer of safety. If he fishes where he has to cross commercial shipping lanes or if he is overtaken on the water by darkness or fog, he'll be glad he has it. The instrument provides a way to detect other vessels, fixed objects on the water such as buoys, and rock piles or points of land before they can be seen under conditions of poor visibility. The technology has become so sophisticated that a boater can use his cursor to click on a radar target, such as another vessel, and his radar will compute its speed and direction and advise whether it is on a collision course. If it is not, it will tell the operator how close to his own vessel the target will pass, absent any course changes, and when it will reach that point. Once locked on, it will continue to track the target, and is capable of tracking multiple targets simultaneously.

Radar has other uses as well.

"Radar can be used for navigation, in the fog or at any other time," one marine electronics retailer said. "And it can be used when coupled with a proper GPS for finding out what fishing spot a boat two miles away from you is sitting on. You can use it to steal their latitude and longitude.

"You can also use it to find flocks of birds on top of feeding fish," he said.

Radar also is useful for spotting and monitoring approaching weather fronts, and can be used to measure distances.

"A chartplotter/GPS system is only as accurate as the survey that made the charts," the marine electronics retailer said. "Sometimes, it's not all that accurate. But if a radar tells you a target is 1.2 miles away, you can bet it's 1.2 miles away. It's a completely self-reliant unit."

Radar can be either a luxury or a necessity depending on what a boater does on the water and where he does it, a marine electronics buyer said.

"A lot of people are running out and using radar to find where other boats are and where the fish are," he said. "It's called 'finding the fleet.'"

Radar comes in a variety of sizes, or powers, providing coverage that ranges from a maximum of 16 miles on the smallest sets to 120 miles or more on larger. Typically

recreational boaters, including anglers, choose a unit that transmits at 2 kilowatts or 4 kilowatts, depending on the size of their boat, with boats less than 30 feet generally carrying 2-kilowatt units. The more kilowatts the greater the range. The smaller units provide ranges of 16 to 24 miles, depending on manufacturer, and the larger units 24 to 48 miles. A 24-mile unit actually scans 12 miles ahead of the boat and 12 miles behind it.

"The farther you can see the more expensive it gets," the buyer said. "Usually the guys who are buying the longer-range radar are operating fly-bridge boats."

A reason for this is that radar is a line-of-sight instrument, and the curvature of the earth renders it ineffective beyond more than a few miles unless it's mounted high above the surface to obtain a better "view".

"The smaller boats that have just T-tops and radar arches, the biggest they're getting is 24 miles, because if they get any bigger they're not going to see any farther anyway," the buyer said. "If you've got a small boat and you put a 34-mile radar on it you can't see farther, but you can see a little more accurately. You might be able to pick up birds, for example, to see if they're fishing. And you might pick up buoys better than with a 16-mile radar."

You need to consider how much detail you want to be able to see, known as target resolution, the marine electronics shop operator said, balanced by how much you can spend and how big a product fits your boat.

"It's important to realize that at a 1-mile range, a 48-mile radar is going to show much greater target resolution, and have a lot better chance of seeing a small target, than a 24-mile radar," he said. "A guy in a kayak paddling along in the fog and wearing a wristwatch, the only thing metal, is going to have a much greater chance of showing up on a 48-mile radar than a 24-mile one.

"The other thing is, two boats coming at you in the fog have a better chance of showing up as two boats – as opposed to one big blob – on a 48-mile radar."

The only downsides to a large unit on a small boat, besides cost, are cosmetics and potential stresses in mounting. A 2-kilowatt radome unit weighs about 15 pounds and a 4-kilowatt unit about 25 pounds. That difference can be significant if the radome is mounted on a rail.

Other technologies under development may someday reduce the usefulness of radar to a degree. For example, if an angler fishes in areas of heavy commercial traffic – and that includes much of the West Coast – he can consider installing an Automatic Identification System (AIS) receiver aboard his boat. For about half the cost of a good radar, he can obtain a color chartplotter with an AIS receiver that will display the name, location, speed, and direction of every commercial vessel in the vicinity. All commercial vessels 65 feet and longer are required to broadcast the information.

"For knowing where commercial vessels are it's a lot more accurate and easier to use than radar," the electronics retailer observed. "But it's showing you only some of the vessels."

For anglers who run far offshore, other computer-based technologies can provide weather maps that superimpose over an electronic chart like Doppler radar

pictures on TV. You can utilize a satellite link to receive these chartplotter weather reports, including sea surface temperatures around a region, weather conditions, and wave heights at offshore buoys and so forth. These are subscriber-based services that require an up-front fee for equipment and software and a monthly fee for the service.

Radios

Anglers have choices today about how to communicate from vessel to vessel and from ship to shore. The choices include very high frequency (VHF) radios, citizens' band (CB) radios, cell phone conversations, and even text messaging via cell phone. And, while cell phones bestow on communicators some privacy, and a vast amount of fishing information changes hands by way of CB radio, only one form of communication provides a dependable safety net for boaters. That is VHF. It is the most reliable way to reach professional assistance quickly in an emergency.

Boaters who plan to rely on a cell phone in emergencies may find themselves outside the range of a cell phone tower when they need one the most. And the ability to attract assistance via CB can be hit-or-miss. Even if a boater in distress is able to establish communications with someone via CB, the person with whom he has connected may not be in a position to assist or even to relay the distress message to an appropriate agency.

All commercial marine traffic, and much recreational traffic, monitors VHF Channel 16, and so does the U.S. Coast Guard, around the clock. In addition, Coast Guard and commercial assistance vessels are equipped with radio-direction finders to home in on VHF radio transmissions in order to locate and go to a vessel producing them. It's an invaluable benefit for a boater adrift who might not be sure of his own position, and something that is not possible with a cell telephone call.

Modern VHF radios also can be programmed to transmit a distress message automatically in emergencies and to provide position data automatically to potential rescuers.

And a VHF allows you to connect with a marine telephone operator to make a call to or receive one from a land-based telephone.

Despite the benefits of VHF, at least one member of the marine communications industry sees VHF radios as a declining market, for two reasons.

One is that some boaters, including anglers, use cell phones instead of VHF despite the reasons not to.

The other is that "radios being built now are 100 times better than they used to be," the industry rep said. "Now, every radio comes pretty much with a three-year waterproof warranty. It used to be you had to replace them almost every year."

So, if you decide you want a VHF, how should you choose among the bewildering proliferation of brands and models? All of the brands and models are more similar to each other than they are dissimilar. Two of the differences among them are color and size, and those might influence your decision. You will want to match your radio to the space available for it, and will want its appearance to be compatible with other

electronics and with the boat itself. Other than that, you should use several criteria in comparing radios.

"On a smaller boat, the quality of the brand is the choice to make," said the proprietor of the marine electronics shop. "Different price points reflect different audio qualities. The audio on a $300 radio is going to be clearer and easier to hear, especially at higher volumes when you've got a lot of background noise, than the quality of a $120 VHF."

Also, although all VHF radios provide a digital selective calling feature, higher-priced radios offer more additional features and the digital selective calling on them is easier to use. Some models are able to scan multiple channels and stop on a channel where someone is talking. Some provide "select scan" that allows you to choose which channels you scan. And some radios include loud hailers that enable you to connect a loudspeaker and use it to hail nearby vessels.

Another feature on higher-end radios is second-station capability, which allows you to run a second microphone from a remote location. On a boat with a fly bridge, for example, a skipper often installs the radio below in the pilot house and installs a remote on the bridge. Or, he may install a main radio at the pilot's station and a remote in the stern near trolling motor and downriggers.

In making a final decision among makes and models, check out the visibility of their screens. Are you able to read them easily to see what channel is transmitting? Does the radio have a rotary knob that allows you to change channels quickly? After hailing another boater or being hailed on VHF Channel 16, it's easier to spin a knob to go up to a conversation channel – which might be Channel 68, 69, 71, or 72 for example – than it is to click your way up channel-by-channel if your radio comes equipped only with an "up" key and a "down" key.

In some cases, especially on smaller waters, a hand-held VHF radio may suffice. If you decide to go that route, spend a little more for one that's fully submersible. The opportunities for a hand-held to get soaked with sea water are much greater than they are for a mounted model.

Since 1999, the Federal Communications Commission has required that new, fixed-mount VHF marine radios come equipped with digital selective calling (DSC), which allows you to tap into a global system used to send and receive digital calls. Its most important function is to allow you to make automated distress calls. After installing a VHF radio, interfacing it with a GPS or Loran of any manufacturer and registering a permanent, nine-digit Marine Mobile Service Identity (MMSI) number, you or anyone on your boat, including a child, can transmit a distress call by opening a spring-loaded door on the radio's front panel and pressing a single key. The radio will digitally transmit on VHF Channel 70, which is dedicated for that purpose, your MMSI number, your position and – if your radio offers the option – a description of your distress, such as fire or flooding. And it will continue to transmit this information even if you become incapacitated. After transmitting, the radio automatically resets itself to Channel 16 to allow you to monitor and respond to replies from search-and-rescue officials or from other DSC-equipped vessels within range of your call.

Through your MMSI number, the transmission allows access to a U.S. Coast Guard national distress data base that contains information about you which might be useful to a rescuer, including a description of your boat, names and telephone numbers of emergency contacts that you have provided, and the number of any cell phone that you may routinely carry aboard your boat.

It is capability such as this that makes VHF radios indispensable to many, in spite of the growing popularity of cell phones.

"There's always that one incident," the electronics buyer said. "You're out there fishing and none of your buddies are there and your boat starts to sink. Who you gonna call? That's when you need a VHF."

In non-emergencies, you may use another person's MMSI number to funnel hailing calls directly and exclusively to his radio, much the way a telephone system directs calls to a phone. The advantage is that he doesn't have to constantly monitor heavy traffic on the public hailing channel (Channel 16) or on the auxiliary public

When everything comes together right, this can be the result. Photo courtesy of Wooldridge Boats.

hailing channel (Channel 9) with the associated risk of missing a call. The radio rings when someone who has his number is calling, and when he answers, it switches automatically to a working channel on which the caller is standing by. At that point, the privacy of the communication ends.

Your VHF also allows you to transmit a group hailing call that's received only by vessels that share a common group MMSI number, such as a club or a collection of friends who comprise a sportfishing fleet.

It also allows you to transmit an "all ships" call that goes to all vessels within range of your radio, enabling you to advise them of a hazard to navigation or to tell them that you need assistance. In the former instance, the transmission is known as a "safety" call. In the latter case it's an "urgency" call, used when an emergency is serious but not serious enough to merit a distress call.

You also may use your VHF to digitally request the geographical position of anyone whose MMSI number you know or to respond with your own position to someone who requests it. Anglers often use this to track the locations of fishing friends without giving the locations away to others. If the person whose position you have requested has interfaced his radio with a GPS, his radio can respond with a latitude-longitude message on your radio's screen. He may set his radio to respond automatically to such requests or set it to alert him and give him the option of responding or not.

If your boating is confined to U.S. waters, you may obtain an MMSI number online and register your information in the national distress data base by going to www.boatus.com.

BoatU.S. is working with the Federal Communications Commission and the Coast Guard to provide that service free.

Otherwise, you obtain the number when applying to the Federal Communications Commission for a ship station radio license, which is not required if you don't boat outside of the United States.

These capabilities won't do much for you though, if you fail to implement them.

"Do what's necessary to activate your Digital Selective Calling feature on the radio," the electronics shop operator urged, "because it's a safety issue. Make sure the radio is properly interfaced to your GPS. And obtain and properly program your MMSI number."

Laptop Computers

Several makers of electronic maps have designed marine navigation programs for laptop computers. They enable you to download the program into the laptop you use at home or at work and carry it aboard your boat to use as your nautical navigation center. The marine electronics shop operator warns against using a laptop, however, for your primary nautical system. Carry one if you wish as a backup, he said, but not to use as your main means of navigating. Such units are not dependable enough. It's not the navigation software that's a problem, he said, but the laptop itself. A working

laptop onboard a vessel will be the weakest link on the boat.

"I've had customers in with 2,000 waypoints on a computer that they've lost in a crash," he said. "I've had customers who have lost hundreds of crab pots in a computer crash.

"I had one customer almost in tears," he said, "because he couldn't recover the hard drive and couldn't recover the crab pots."

Mounted multifunction units are far more dependable, the shop owner said, and the reliability of laptops will always lag behind them.

The Future

Judging by recent trends in development and marketing of marine electronics, in what direction can you expect to move during the years ahead?

Expect more and more integration of fish finders, GPS/chartplotters, and radars, more reliance on multifunction units – some of them custom-designed for a purchaser's individual needs – and less emphasis on installation of independent units.

Look for more and more emphasis on color display screens on navigation units and fish finders, and for units that are less and less costly in relation to the value of the dollar.

Look for increasing numbers of chartplotter manufacturers to come out with units that come preloaded with sophisticated base charts, reducing or even eliminating the need to buy additional mapping chips. Depending on the size of the area over which an angler ranges, the savings can amount to hundreds of dollars.

Look for units with touch-screen technology rather than alpha-numeric keypads. One major manufacturer of GPS units led the way with such technology for automobiles, and nautical versions were expected to follow after producers determined how to reduce costs that were prohibitively expensive in larger-screen applications.

Look for continued reduction in sales of hand-held GPS receivers as mounted GPS/chartplotter units continue to increase in popularity, and look for increasing availability of mounted multifunction units with an internal GPS antenna, eliminating the need for a separate antenna.

Look for increasing use by boaters of satellite-feed real-time weather and water temperatures that overlay a GPS/chartplotter screen. Such services may marginally lessen the popularity of radar, which many boaters use to find and track storms. You receive the weather data from a dedicated antenna that mounts on your boat, and you pay an activation fee and monthly service charges.

A Final Bit of Advice

Remember that the equipment that best suits your needs on the water may not be the same as that which best suits another angler. Much depends on where you fish, how far you run, how much traffic you encounter, and other factors unique to your situation.

"What I tell people is don't worry so much about selecting the perfect electronics," the marine electronics shop operator said, "but work at selecting a knowledgeable provider who can work with you and ask the right questions. He can direct you to the products that are best for you.

"If you walk into a shop and say you want electronics, and the guy says, 'This is the best thing in electronics,' right out of his mouth, you're probably in the wrong shop."

Among those who contributed information used in this chapter, the author would like to thank:

David McLain, Boater's World Marine Center, Beltsville, MD; Paul Marander, West Marine, Seattle, Washington; Terry McCartney, Jacobsen's Marine, Seattle; Brian Hennessy, Anacortes Marine Electronics, Anacortes, Washington.

A Tomic spoon did this king in. Photo courtesy of Tomic Lures.

Background on Fish Management Issues

It's entirely counter-intuitive, but fishery managers focus less and less on how many hatchery salmon or thriving wild fish are out there for you to catch, and more and more on what the bycatch will be.

Bycatch consists of fish not specifically targeted for catching, but caught incidentally along with those that are targeted.

Salmon lay their eggs in freshwater and die soon afterward. Their newly hatched offspring spend varying amounts of time in the freshwater, depending on species and sometimes on latitude, ranging from virtually no time for pink salmon to as long as two years for some sockeye. At some point, they migrate to saltwater to finish growing and maturing before returning to the place they were born to reproduce.

From a geographical standpoint, the great majority of salmon-angling opportunity occurs – or would if it could – in what biologists refer to as "mixed-stock areas". These are places where the runs from different river systems and different hatcheries mingle while migrating or feeding, before sorting themselves out to travel to their separate spawning areas. Various groups travel more-or-less together over vast saltwater reaches, often not separating until arriving at or near the areas where they will enter freshwater.

A problem occurs when fish from weak or even endangered runs mix with fish from strong runs. Managers must determine how much fishing mortality, if any, the weak runs can tolerate, and terminate fishing before the mortality reaches that point, even if such closure leaves thousands of fish from the strong runs uncaught. The weak fish, in such cases, comprise the bycatch. In order to exploit the stronger runs as much as possible, managers try to focus fishing at places and times weak runs are not expected to be present, and also utilize what they call "selective" fisheries.

A selective fishery is possible when anglers can determine the origins of individual fish, and can retain them or release them as required. Identification usually involves fin-clipping hatchery salmon, which reproduce more efficiently than wild fish, and requiring anglers at certain times and places to refrain from retaining unclipped fish. Since a certain amount of mortality occurs even among fish that are caught and released, however, managers must calculate the presumed catch rate for unclipped fish, determine how much mortality that population will sustain as a result of it, and close the entire fishery before a critical level of bycatch mortality occurs. While not necessarily permitting full exploitation of the harvestable portion of the

strongest runs, a selective fishery usually permits greater exploitation than could occur if anglers retained fish from the weaker runs.

Why worry about weak wild runs? Why not just produce all salmon efficiently in hatcheries, where they're not subject to the vagaries of an uncontrolled environment? Many biologists, as well as many anglers, consider wild fish to be superior to hatchery ones in several ways, and they see the great genetic diversity that exists among the numerous wild stocks as insurance against potential environmental disasters. Hatchery systems often place most of their eggs in one genetic basket, which can be an important weakness in the event of serious outbreak of disease or in case of changing environmental conditions. Also, despite their more efficient reproduction in a controlled environment, hatchery fish are considered to be less adept at survival outside of the hatchery than are wild fish.

Weak wild stocks thus become "drivers" of the fisheries every year, dictating how many fish may be harvested in any area and triggering fishing season closures. The identity of drivers varies from location to location, and often changes in a particular location from year to year, but in any particular place and any particular year the weakest stocks will drive the fisheries.

Adding complexity to the management mix are:

- Federal court rulings that require equal sharing of harvestable salmon between treaty Indians and the rest of the citizenry in Washington and parts of Oregon and California
- Court decisions that have elevated Indian tribes to co-managers of the resource, and to policy-setters, along with states and the federal government
- A policy of splitting the non-Indian share of fish between recreational and commercial fishermen according to predetermined ratios
- The fact that salmon are wide-ranging fish which cross state and national boundaries, where stocks from one jurisdiction are taken by harvesters from the other

So, what are some of the recurring issues that managers must consider in establishing fishing seasons and other regulations along the coast? Unique issues that drive the fisheries along the Northwest Coast are addressed in the respective states' sections. Many of the principles managers consider in Washington are considered in Oregon and California as well.

Salmon Season-Setting

The states of Washington, Oregon, and California develop annual salmon fishery management plans in conjunction with the federal Pacific Fishery Management Council (PFMC). The PFMC is responsible for developing ocean fishing regulations for the area between 3 and 200 miles offshore. Each plan contains two major parts: conservation objectives and allocation objectives.

Conservation objectives are annual goals for the escapement of mature fish to the spawning grounds for reproduction, while allocation objectives aim to split the harvest equitably among groups such as tribal, non-tribal commercial, and recreational fishermen. Allocation is further apportioned among various ocean ports and between ocean and inland fisheries.

The process begins in February of each year when the PFMC distributes reports detailing how the previous harvest season turned out and estimating the abundance of various salmon stocks for the coming season. The estimates consider environmental factors and anticipated Alaskan and Canadian harvests of Washington, Oregon, and California fish. In March, the PFMC holds a public meeting to propose a series of alternative salmon-fishing options. It then holds public hearings on the options in March or April, and adopts a final recommendation on commercial and recreational ocean-fishing seasons and catch limits for referral to the U.S. Secretary of Commerce in April.

The Commerce Secretary and his or her National Marine Fisheries Service may adopt or reject the recommendation, but aims to implement new regulations in May.

After ocean regulations take shape, the states and tribes develop their own compatible regulations for inshore areas and freshwater areas, allocating returning salmon among tribal, non-tribal commercial, and recreational fishermen, and meeting obligations under fish-sharing treaties with Canada and under the federal Endangered Species Act.

Salmon Identification and Reproductive Behavior

Five species of native salmon are found on the Pacific Coast of North America. They are:

Chinook

Chinook *(Oncorhynchus tshawytscha)* – Also known as king, spring salmon, tyee (in Canada), blackmouth (in immature form), usually matures in three, four, or five years, although a few individuals are believed to live as long as nine. The largest of the Pacific salmon and the most sought after by anglers, mature specimens commonly exceed 20 pounds, and often will weigh in the 30s and 40s. Larger individuals are not as common, but are not unusual. An all-tackle world record of 97 pounds, 4 ounces was taken in 1985 in Alaska's Kenai River. In the 1950s, a chinook weighing 102 pounds was gaffed in Washington's Elwha River. Chinook can be persistent fighters, and large ones can strip a reel. Recognizable by a heavily spotted back, spots on both lobes of the tail, and a black gum line at the base of its teeth on its lower jaw. The tip of its lower jaw is pointed.

Chinook, like all Pacific salmon, die immediately after spawning. Most chinook spawn in the mainstem of large rivers, such as the Columbia and Sacramento and others, sometimes traveling hundreds of miles upstream to reach spawning grounds. All chinook spawn in the fall, but some enter freshwater much earlier, comprising spring and summer runs. Those that enter freshwater the latest spawn closest to the ocean, and are the strain of chinook usually found in smaller streams along the coast. Spring and summer runs often travel far enough from the sea to cross mountain ranges. Chinook are able to spawn in larger gravel than most other salmon, because of their size, and prefer a high flow of water in their spawning area.

Chinook fry live in freshwater for three months to a year after hatching, depending on their strain and their spawning location, generally remaining in freshwater longer the farther north they are produced. The young inhabit both mainstem rivers and their tributaries. Spring chinook also tend to stay in freshwater longer than most others, usually about a year.

Coho

Coho *(Oncorhynchus kisutch)* – Also known as silver salmon, a coho matures at two or three years, and may exceed 30 pounds. A coho weighing in the low to middle teens is considered large, however. A coho is more lightly spotted on its back than a chinook, and its tail has spots only on the upper lobe. The lower gum line is gray at the base of the teeth, and the lower jaw is rounded at the tip. Spectacular fighters, they love to leap out of the water when hooked.

Coho spawn in small coastal streams and in the tributaries of large rivers, and will even reproduce in small, neighborhood waterways if the water is clean and cold and present year round. They like areas with less water velocity than those favored by chinook, and with smaller gravel.

Young coho spend more time in freshwater than do most chinook. The species spawns in the fall, and the fry hatch and emerge from the gravel the following spring. The fry then spend the next 12 months in freshwater, finally migrating to sea as one-year-olds, about a year and a half after they were deposited as eggs in the gravel.

Pink

Pink *(Oncorhynchus gorbuscha)* – Also known as humpback or humpy, pink salmon mature at two years. They are the smallest of the Pacific salmon of North America, and may weigh into the middle teens, although usually smaller. They're considered hard fighters, and are particularly good for smoking. Heavily spotted on back and tail, pinks can be identified by unusually small scales and the oval shape of the tail spots. They run primarily in odd-numbered years in much of their range, including Washington, Oregon, and California.

Pinks spawn in the fall in the mainstems of large rivers and in some large tributaries, usually not far from saltwater. Sometimes, in fact, they will spawn in water that is salty or brackish. The young migrate out of the river immediately after hatching, spending several months feeding and growing in their river's estuary, then moving out to sea. They mature and return to spawn as two-year-olds. Pinks are the only salmon species that returns primarily every other year. Some observers speculate that some great bygone natural disaster might have virtually eliminated even-year runs.

Chum

Chum *(Oncorhynchus keta)* – Chum salmon are also known as dog salmon, perhaps because of the toothy lower jaw at maturity. It lives three to five years, and may weigh as much as 30 pounds. It is the second largest of the Pacific salmon after chinook. It is the most abundant of the Pacific salmon in Washington, but not found in abundance south beyond northern Oregon, and virtually absent from California. Mature specimens commonly reach the high teens and low 20s. It does not take bait or lures readily, but when it does it is a tenacious fighter, possibly tougher pound-for-pound

than any other Pacific salmon. It lacks prominent spots on back and tail. Its scales are large, and mature chum may be recognized by vertical shading on sides. Also, for their size, chum are unusually small in circumference at the spot just ahead of the lobes of the tail, known as the caudal peduncle.

Chum spawn as far south as Tillamook Bay, Oregon, in the same small coastal streams and larger rivers that coho use, but in each case the chum utilize portions of those waterways closer to saltwater than do coho. The young leave freshwater within days of hatching, moving into the estuary for several months of feeding and growing and then head out to sea.

Sockeye

Sockeye *(Oncorhynchus nerka)* – Also known as red salmon and blue back, sockeye are the third most abundant Pacific salmon after pink and chum. It typically returns to freshwater at age four. It is not abundant in Oregon and rarely seen off the coast of California. It is found landlocked in some western lakes, never traveling to sea, where it is known as kokanee salmon or silver trout. Once rarely taken on sport gear in saltwater, but more commonly taken now as effective sportfishing techniques evolve, such as slow-trolling with bare black or red hooks behind a flasher. Anglers also sometimes take them on small red hoochies or lures, trolled deep and slow. A sport fishery also takes place some years in Lake Washington, at Seattle, where anglers troll Flatfish or bare, colored hooks for returning ocean fish. Only fair fighters, they can grow to about 15 pounds, although mature specimens more commonly run 6 to 10 pounds, and are highly valued for their fine flavor. The sockeye lacks prominent spots on back and tail and is often recognized by its prominent golden eyes.

Sockeye spawn only as far south as the Columbia River system. They require a lake in the river system in which they spawn – the only Pacific salmon to do so – but are flexible in terms of river water velocity and gravel size. Spawning occurs in the river above the lake, and juvenile fish live one or two years in the lake before migrating to sea.

Washington Coast

Fisheries Management

The first things that managers look at in Washington are preseason forecasts for the various salmon species and stocks. Chinook and coho salmon comprise the major recreational species most years, although anglers sometimes also take tens of thousands of pink salmon when they return from the sea, primarily in odd-numbered years. Anglers also take lesser numbers of the other two North American species of Pacific salmon – chum and sockeye – which are harvested primarily in commercial nets.

Forecasts may be based on several things, including the number of unusually young but sexually precocious males – or "jacks" – that returned the previous year, and the age structure of chinook populations that returned the previous two years. Managers also look at various immediate environmental factors, such as current ocean conditions and river conditions, and former environmental factors, such as droughts or floods that may have impacted freshwater spawning and rearing areas when this generation of fish was being produced.

With their preseason forecasts in hand, and spawning-escapement objectives established for each stock in order to try to ensure an appropriate supply of fish into future generations, the managers subtract spawning-escapement objectives from forecasted run size to determine how many fish are harvestable, stock by stock.

This is when federal Endangered Species Act (ESA) constraints enter the picture. Managers must determine what proportions of threatened and endangered runs fishermen can be allowed to impact while harvesting healthier stocks. Only very limited impacts are permitted on some ESA-listed stocks.

In mixed-stock areas, the goal generally is to allow the most fishing possible within the constraints posed by ESA-listed stocks and other weak stocks. On the Washington coast, for example, fishery managers often require selective fishing for coho, in order to harvest hatchery fish while protecting wild ones. While anglers were able to pursue chinook without selective-fishery requirements on the coast into the early years of the 21st century, selective-fishery requirements for chinook had become common in Puget Sound.

On the Strait of Juan de Fuca, the major coho constraint in recent years has been a limitation imposed in Washington on the harvest of wild Thompson River fish – a Canadian stock from the Fraser River drainage – in order to meet Washington's

responsibility under the U.S.-Canada Pacific Salmon Treaty. The treaty requires that exploitation of those fish in Washington be capped at 10 percent of the run. That provision is the main reason that Washington has imposed a selective fishery for coho in the strait, targeting only hatchery fish.

Regarding chinook salmon in the strait, impact limits imposed by the Endangered Species Act have resulted in a constrained selective fishery there during July and August in many years in order to allow catch of some Puget Sound hatchery chinook while releasing wild Puget Sound fish. This ESA constraint has driven the summer chinook fishery in the strait for years, as well as in several other Puget Sound locations.

Look for increasing numbers of selective fisheries throughout Washington as managers try to find ways to keep more areas open longer without harm to weak and endangered stocks.

Those who manage for the state in Washington have to consider the impacts of state and tribal fisheries together, in order to share both catch and impacts with tribal fishermen. On both the ocean and the strait, managers have manipulated the fisheries not only by selective-fishing rules but also by harvest quotas and guidelines. When a predetermined number of fish of a particular species in a certain area has been taken, the fishery closes. Quotas and guidelines essentially are the same thing, but a quota is considered a "hard" number, and attaining it triggers an immediate fishing shutdown. Managers play "guidelines" a little looser.

While fishing on the U.S. side of the border is often constrained by the needs of Canadian stocks that swim there, it also can be constrained by the impacts Canadians have in Canada on stocks of U.S. origin before they return home. For example, Canadian sport and commercial fisheries on the west coast of Vancouver Island can have tremendous impact on Washington chinook, which migrate north after reaching the sea. Those fisheries play a major role in determining what kind of seasons Washington can set on its own fish in its own waters as the fish return to their natal streams.

Washington fishery managers say that, while the Canadians in general abide by provisions of the international agreement, within its constraints they have shifted some of their fisheries in the past in order to target more on Washington stocks and less on their own. Canadians often were reluctant to shift their impacts away from Washington stocks to their own because their own chinook also migrate north, into Alaskan waters, where Alaskans harvest many of them. Canadians maintained that Alaskans weren't inclined to reduce their impacts on Canadian fish, so why should Canadians reduce theirs on U.S. stocks? Late in 2008, however, U.S. and Canadian negotiators agreed on an annex to the Pacific Salmon Treaty which addressed itself to that problem, at least in part. The annex called for reducing chinook commercial and sport catch limits from 2009 through 2018 by 15 percent in Southeast Alaska and by 30 percent off the west coast of Vancouver Island from then-current limits to allow more of those fish to return to their southerly homes.

Washington Fishing Licenses

Annual saltwater, resident $22.20
Annual saltwater, nonresident $45.80

Freshwater/saltwater/shellfish combination:
One-day, resident - $10.18
One-day, nonresident - $17.82
Two-day, resident - $13.46
Two-day, nonresident - $24.36
Three-day, resident - $16.73
Three-day, nonresident - $30.91
Four-day, resident - $18.91
Four-day, nonresident - $35.27
Five-day, resident - $21.09
Five-day, nonresident - $39.64
Annual, resident - $48.20
Annual, nonresident - $91.40
Catch record card (required for salmon angling, good for recording 26 fish) First
    card free, additional cards $12 each

Columbia River salmon/steelhead endorsement:
Resident - $8.75
Nonresident - $8.75
Dealer fees extra

Washington Information Sources

National Association of Charterboat Operators / www.nacocharters.org
Charterboat Association of Puget Sound / www.capscharters.com
Westport Charterboat Association / www.charterwestport.com
Washington State Hotel & Lodging Association / www.wshla.com

Among those who contributed information used in this chapter, the author would
like to thank:
    *Tim Flint, former regional fish program manager, Washington Department of
Fish and Wildlife; and Steve Thiesfeld, Puget Sound salmon manager, Washington
Department of Fish and Wildlife.*

Neah Bay

Peel away all of the mystery that envelops salmon fishing, and you're left with one basic principle: To catch fish, you have to be where fish are.

It couldn't have been impressed upon me any more clearly that late-summer day at the Strait of Juan de Fuca's western entrance, from which the Pacific Ocean stretches a nearly 100-mile-long arm inland between Washington state and Canada's Vancouver Island.

We were fishing out of Neah Bay on the Makah Indian Reservation, the last town in Washington before you reach Cape Flattery on Washington's northwest tip. It's a good place to intercept ocean fish that funnel through the strait toward their natal rivers farther east. But it had been frustrating. We'd been dragging cut-plug herring through the rips for hours, and hadn't been able to find a fish.

It was late August – coho time – but those big, hooknose silvers were nowhere to be found. We'd worked our way as far west as the Whistler Buoy, about a mile and a quarter northwest of Tatoosh Island and just outside the mouth of the strait. The Whistler is usually a sure thing this time of year, giving up limit after easy limit, but we couldn't raise so much as a tap. We were fishing with planers, and we knew we were doing it right. It was only a matter of finding a school.

Just then Al Seda, one of my companions, looked out over the rolling swells seaward and saw what we'd been searching for – gulls, hundreds of them, circling and swooping 3 or 4 miles away. Seda knew what that meant. The birds had found bait, and where there was bait there were bound to be salmon.

We pulled in our gear and ran to the spot as quickly as we could, tossed a couple of planers over the stern, and almost instantly had two hookups. Silvers hammered our bait as fast as we could get it into the water, sometimes grabbing it right next to the boat and snapping our leaders in two. Sometimes they leaped and contorted as only coho can, throwing our barbless hooks before we could bring them to the net. We re-rigged, re-baited, and fought coho for about 15 wonderful minutes, and then our limits were in the box. We'd been fishing all morning without result. Then, once the action had started, it was over in a quarter-hour.

That's the way it can be with silvers, and the Neah Bay area is one of the prime places on the Pacific Coast to go after them.

The town of Neah Bay provides the best access to this area, and launching and moorage are available there. The bay is protected from ocean swells by a rock jetty that extends most of the way across its entrance.

Years ago, when seasons were more liberal, this area often was excellent in March and April for feeder chinook which were working their way toward the ocean. These

typically ran 8 to 12 pounds, with some into the middle and high teens. It was mainly a downrigger fishery, with anglers trolling a flasher and hoochie just off the bottom in about 180 feet of water. These were outbound salmon, so anglers fished the ebb tide – the stronger the better. One that started about daylight was ideal.

About this time, Puget Sound coho were passing through the area in huge numbers on their way to the ocean, where they would spend the summer feeding and growing, just west of the mouth of the strait. By the middle of May the outbound chinook would be gone, and the coho would be, too.

Sportfishing seasons are shorter now as a result of bycatch concerns and court-ordered sharing of harvests with treaty tribes, often not opening in the ocean here until late June or early July. But about the last week of June or the first week of July, the first runs of fall chinook begin gathering off Skagway Rocks and Makah Bay, just south of Tatoosh on the ocean side of the cape.

A lot of anglers mooch for them with 3 or 4 ounces of lead. Others troll with flasher and hoochie, or flasher and bait. The fish will be 3 or 4 pounds short of their spawning weight, and will feed voraciously, so nearly anything works. They'll continue to congregate here into August.

If fish is small, you might get away with bring it to the boat with other lines still in the water. Generally, however, it's best to get other lines out of the way. Photo courtesy of Scotty.

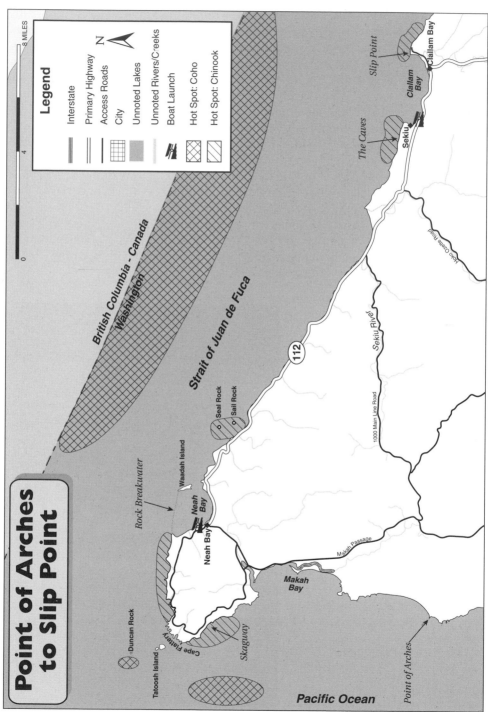

Point of Arches to Slip Point

Legend

	Interstate
	Primary Highway
	Access Roads
	City
	Unnoted Lakes
	Unnoted Rivers/Creeks
	Boat Launch
	Hot Spot: Coho
	Hot Spot: Chinook

N

8 MILES

4

0

British Columbia - Canada

Washington

Strait of Juan de Fuca

Slip Point

Clallam Bay

Clallam Bay

The Caves

Sekiu

Lyre Ozette Road

Sekiu River

112

1000 Main Line Road

Seal Rock

Sail Rock

Waadah Island

Rock Breakwater

Neah Bay

Neah Bay

Makah Passage

Makah Bay

Duncan Rock

Tatoosh Island

Cape Flattery

Skaguay

Point of Arches

Pacific Ocean

At Skagway, about a mile south of Tatoosh, rocks stick out about half a mile from the beach. Behind them is a sort of bay, and a popular gathering place for candlefish. The bottom comes up from 30 or 35 fathoms to about 10 fathoms in the bay, and big kings move right into those shallows after the bait. Anglers anchor there to mooch for the kings. Skagway tends to be best on a tide change, and generally on low slack. But it can vary.

As soon as that first group of fall chinook arrives, a few of the fish begin moving into the strait. Seasons here can close at any time if quotas are attained, but from early July into August more and more chinook will move inside. Many anglers like to fish for them there, where they don't have to contend with the ocean's heavy swells. Fish the tide changes in the strait, and stay close to the beach. High slack can be especially productive.

Meanwhile, silvers are available in the ocean as long as quotas or guidelines last. These are the fish that moved out through the strait in April and May. As a rule, you motor 3 to 4 miles off the coast, and you're into them. These fish, 15 to 22 inches long when they came through the strait, have been stuffing themselves with krill in the ocean, and they're gaining a pound every couple of weeks.

In about the middle of July, you can begin to take them on coho flies trolled on the surface with no weight. Blue is a productive color here. Locate a school, strip out 20 or 30 feet of line, and troll fast – so that the fly skips on top of the water. Then stand back. The fish will boil up and slam your fly right in the boat's wake.

About the middle of August, the silvers that have been putting on pounds in the ocean start to move into the strait, and you can go out in the rips beyond Waadah Island and catch them with flies, with cut-plug herring behind planers, or with cut-plugs and 3 or 4 ounces of lead. This action continues until about the middle of September, providing often incredible fishing, provided the allocation doesn't run out.

A lot of these silvers run up to 12 pounds, some as large as 20, and the action can be so good that anglers sort for larger fish, releasing any under the 10-pound mark. These silvers are hungry, and nearly anyone can catch them.

Another is happening at this time. Most migrating fall chinook will have moved on by the first or second week of August. But some of Washington's finest big-fish angling once occurred in this part of the strait in September. From Neah Bay all the way to Sekiu, anglers boated fish in the 40-, 50-, and even the 60-pound class. It was just a trickle of fish, but their size made the effort worthwhile.

Most of them were caught on a flasher and hoochie or flasher and bait, not far from the beach. A trolled plug was effective, provided an angler used a large one and trolled it deep and slow. Some anglers used spinner baits cut from the sides of large herring and fished behind 2 or 3 ounces of lead. Nowadays, however, chinook harvest guidelines are virtually never generous enough to extend the fishery that far toward autumn.

Among those who contributed information used in this chapter, the author would like to thank:

Al Seda, former operator of Big Salmon Resort, Neah Bay, Washington.

Hub City Information
Neah Bay
Population - 794 Area Code – 360 County – Clallam

Hotels & Motels

Cape Motel & Rv Park, 1510 Bayview Ave / 645-2250
Carol's Tyee Motel, 1230 Bayview Ave / 645-2223
Hobuck Beach Resort, 2726 Makah Passage, Po Box 115 / 645-2339 /
www.hobuckbeachresort.com
The Village Rv Park, Front Street / 645-4008

Restaurants

Warm House Restaurant / Seafood, Steaks / 645-2924
Natalie's Pizza / Espresso, Pizza / 645-2670

Charters

Jambo's Sportfishing / 425-788-5955
Big Salmon Resort, Bayview Ave. / 1-866-787-1900 / www.bigsalmonresort.net

Launching

Big Salmon Resort / Also Moorage, Fuel, Boat Rentals

Fishing Tackle

Big Salmon Resort, Bayview Ave. / 1-866-787-1900 / www.bigsalmonresort.net

Hospital

Forks Community Hospital, 530 Bogachiel Way, Forks / 374-6271

Sekiu to Pillar Point

You roll out of your sleeping bag early at Sekiu, when the summer sky is still black. By four in the morning the whole town is stirring, like an anthill that's been kicked by some giant boot. Already you can see the running lights of small boats moving slowly out of Clallam Bay, feeling their way in the dark into the Strait of Juan de Fuca, where they'll set up drifts to intercept big king salmon at first light.

If you're camping, you walk to the washroom and find a line stretching out of the building and around the corner. Doors bang, people curse and laugh, and another day is under way. The bait shops are open, spilling light from their windows, and people head for their brightness like moths. Frozen herring is what they're after, and a brisk trade is going on in packages of them.

There's a special feeling here, a special excitement. Your senses are super-sharp, despite the early hour, and you know that there's potential for great things – for the kind of day, perhaps, on which fish stories come true.

Darkness still hangs heavily when you reach the float where you've moored your boat. You give your engine a couple of minutes' warm-up, then cast off and move slowly out of the basin and toward the strait, straining your eyes for deadheads in the water. At the end of the bay is Sekiu Point, and as you turn the corner into the strait you can't believe your eyes.

To the west as far as you can see, it seems, are running lights bobbing quietly in the dark. The boats are gathered off the caves, a popular mooching spot, where anglers will try their early morning luck. If the first half hour of daylight doesn't produce a big king, many will move on, into the rips, in search of silvers.

Summer isn't the only time the fishing's good at Sekiu, however. February through March, local waters produce blackmouth, mostly 5 to 7 pounds, fish which usually take a bait or a lure readily when weather permits boats to venture out.

At this time of year, too, good fishing can be found off the caves and from there to Eagle Bay, about 3 miles to the west. It also can be good off Slip Point, at the eastern entrance to Clallam Bay, and from there to Mussolini Rock, an outcropping just east of Slip. A lot of anglers like heavy gear at this season. Meatlines are popular for pulling a flasher and a coho fly, and usually are fished deep.

If you are driving very far to get here, you want to allow several days at Sekiu if you can, however, because of Washington's unstable winter weather. In a typical week you might get four days of fishing, and the rest of the time storms might keep you on the beach.

By April, the blackmouth have grown much larger. Fishing is productive now all the way from Eagle Bay to the coal mine, about 6 miles east of Sekiu. Many anglers

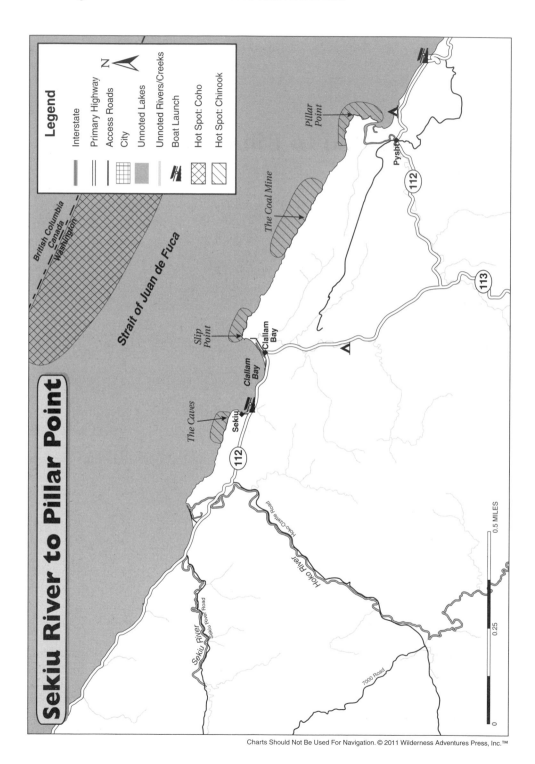

Sekiu River to Pillar Point

Legend

Interstate	
Primary Highway	
Access Roads	
City	
Unnoted Lakes	
Unnoted Rivers/Creeks	
Boat Launch	
Hot Spot: Coho	
Hot Spot: Chinook	

N

British Columbia
Canada
Washington

Strait of Juan de Fuca

Pillar Point

The Coal Mine

Pysht

112

113

Slip Point

Clallam Bay

Clallam Bay

The Caves

Sekiu

112

Sekiu River Road

Sekiu River

Hoko-Ozette Road

HOKO RIVER

7000 Road

0   0.25   0.5 MILES

use downriggers, pulling flashers and flies. Summer fishing often opens around July 1, with a chinook quota in place, and in July, many anglers switch to hoochies.

The fish are close to the rocks now, in 40 or 50 feet of water, and fishing is good around the caves, at Sekiu Point, and at Slip Point. The coal mine can be excellent, too, especially in the evenings through July.

From late June into August, kings from 30 to 50 pounds are arriving from the ocean, and are not uncommon. They're still tight along the beach, and you'll find them in the same places you were taking smaller fish in the spring.

But nothing lasts forever. By the middle of August, kings are becoming scarce around Sekiu, even if some of the quota still remains uncaught, and ocean silvers are starting to show. You've got to go offshore to find the silvers, into the shipping lanes 4 to 6 miles from the beach. From the middle of August to early September, silvers run mostly 4 to 8 pounds, but by mid-September they've undergone a change. Now they're typically 10 to 14 pounds, with a few into the 20s. And in a good year they'll continue passing this area through September, at the end of which the state often shuts it down.

Lund boats, manufactured in the Midwest, are popular on lower Puget Sound. Photo courtesy of Lund Boats.

Sometimes, chinook fishing will reopen for November.

Anglers fishing the Sekiu area may launch and moor, for a fee, at any of several resorts in the town of Sekiu. Keep in mind, however, that the facilities sometimes become jammed, particularly on holiday weekends.

Good fishing also is available near Pillar Point, 10 miles to the east, which shares seasons with Sekiu, and some anglers fish east and west of there for both coho and chinook. Like Sekiu, Pillar Point is a blackmouth show in November and again from February through March or early April, with fish running mostly 6 to 8 pounds, and occasionally into the teens.

In April, the first spring fish arrive. You can get them two ways. You can troll a herring, a hoochie, or a spoon – slow and deep – or you can mooch the holes around the point. Pillar is mainly a mooching area by tradition, and a place where you don't have to go very deep. Water of 30 to 50 feet often holds very nice fish.

One productive hole is located on the eastern side of Pillar, where the Pysht River empties into the strait. Another lies just to the west of the point, where a little reef comes out. Go around the reef, east to west, then back along its far side, and there's a hole on the western edge. Another hole lies farther west, between Pillar Point and Codfish Bay, and another lies in your path as you enter the bay. All are places where fish gather.

As you come out of Codfish Bay going west, the water drops off deeply. It's an excellent spot for chinook, right in close – no more than 100 yards from the beach. About 4 miles west of Pillar, halfway between it and Clallam Bay is the coal mine, where boats from Pillar and Sekiu often meet.

Anglers take a lot of chinook to the east of Pillar, as well, off the mouth of the West Twin River, about 6.5 miles up the strait.

Fishing often closes here about mid April. As at Sekiu, it often reopens in July, and kings continue to come through in waves in July and August.

Sometime in August, the first ocean silvers reach the point. Their runs usually continue through September. By late September these are big fish, often running into the middle and high teens.

A final run of kings – white-meated fish – shows up at Pillar around the end of September. Some of these weigh well into the 40s, but by then, chinook fishing usually has closed.

Among those who contributed information used in this chapter the author would like to thank:

Donalynn Olson, Olson's Resort, Sekiu; Paul Collins, Port Angeles, Washington, John Haller, Pysht, Washington.

Hub City Information
Sekiu / Clallam Bay

Clallam Bay – Sekiu Chamber of Commerce / www.clallambay.com
Population – Sekiu 225, Clallam Bay 900 Area Code – 360
County – Clallam

Hotels & Motels

Anglers Hideaway, Airport Road, Sekiu / 963-2750 / www.anglershideaway.com
Bay Motel and Marina, 15562 Highway 112, Sekiu / 963-2444 /
    www.northolympic.com/baymotel/
Olson's Resort, 444 Front St., PO Box 216, Sekiu / 963-2311 /
    www.olsonsresort.com
Van Riper's Resort, 280 Front St., Sekiu / 888-462-0803 / www.vanripersresort.com
Straitside Resort, 241 Front St., Sekiu / 963-2100 / www.straitsideresort.com

Restaurants

By The Bay Café, 343 Front St., Sekiu / Sandwiches, Pizza
Breakwater Inn, Clallam Bay / American

Launching

Olson's Resort
Van Riper's Resort

Fishing Tackle

Olson's Resort
Van Riper's Resort

Port Angeles to Port Townsend

Nothing about the strike indicated it was anything out of the ordinary. It was mushy, uncertain, a tentative tap on the way down by what might have been an undersized blackmouth.

I'd been stripping line out when it happened, trying to get a plug-cut herring to the bottom on the 20-fathom line just outside Ediz Hook at Port Angeles.

The pick-up had been so subtle I'd almost missed it. I started to reel as fast as possible, and when I finally made contact with the fish, I leaned back and gave the rod a hard pull. That's when the salmon took off.

My rod doubled over, and my reel started to hum in a way that's music to an angler's ears.

The fish, stung by the barbless hook, headed west along the beach, in the general direction of Sekiu and the Pacific Ocean, peeling off line and taking it smack through the middle of what looked like the largest armada assembled since the Normandy invasion. The only thing to do was keep the pressure on and wait for him to turn. But this guy didn't.

I watched in dismay as the line melted from my reel, getting closer to the bare metal, the fish on the other end of it getting farther into the fleet.

My companion started our engine, and kicked it gently into gear. We followed the salmon into the crowd, my partner steering a course among the other craft, and I standing in the stern trying to gain line. From time to time I took my hand from the reel to wave off boats that were about to cross my line. Most of them paid heed. Some of them didn't, and my language could have raised blisters on a horsehide glove.

As luck would have it, though, the fish was deep enough that the outboard props whirring back and forth across the line failed to reach it. About when I began to think the contest might go on forever, the fish finally ran out of steam and came to the side of the boat. My partner slipped the net around him and we hauled him aboard – 24.5 pounds of nickel-bright chinook salmon.

We were delighted, but not surprised. It was July, and the waters off Port Angeles often are alive with big chinook at that time of year. The size of the fleet was testimony to the fact that this was no secret.

Fishing can be good around Port Angeles any time. In winter, it's blackmouth that bring the locals out. They find them in the Winter Hole, about a mile off the Nippon Paper Industries Mill, formerly known as the Daishowa Mill and as the Crown Zellerbach Mill; and on the humps beyond the hole.

July and August mean runs of mature ocean chinook, and the fishing then can be superb. Like migrating chinook everywhere, these tend to follow the beach, and the best place to find them is right outside the hook.

You can launch at the ramp just outside the gate of the U.S. Coast Guard station that occupies the end of the hook. You also can launch at the West Boat Haven ramp next door to the Port Angeles Yacht Club near downtown. Both launching and parking are free on the hook, and parking both places is more than ample, particularly on the hook. Downtown you pay a fee to launch and park.

As always, it's easier to fish on a day when the tidal exchange is moderate. You need to fish when the fish are running, however, and if that happens to be a day with strong tides you'll need to fish around the high and low slacks.

Often if a fish has an adipose fin, it must be released without coming aboard. Photo courtesy of Tomic Lures.

More and more Port Angeles anglers have turned to downrigger trolling at all of the popular local fishing spots. For years, however, mooching was the predominant method here, and many anglers still prefer to fish that way. The key to ocean-run chinook at Port Angeles in July and August is that 20-fathom line. Find it, drop your herring to the bottom, then reel up a couple of turns and drift the line either east or west along the hook, depending on which way the tide is running. If it's early morning and still dark on the water, start at 12 to 15 fathoms, and go deeper as the sun gains strength. If the 20-fathom line is not productive, work all the way to 40, keeping your herring always just off the bottom. If you prefer, you can work the same contours with a downrigger.

At different times the fish will concentrate at different places along the hook – near the Coast Guard station, the Puget Sound Pilot station, or other landmarks. Channel 40 is the CB station anglers use here, and Channel 68 is the one they use with VHF. You can monitor them to learn where and when the bite is on. Because Canadian anglers across the strait also talk on 68, it's important that you broadcast at only 1 watt.

If the water is crowded off the hook, don't neglect the Winter Hole, even in July or August. Especially in July or August, in fact. Migratory chinook often rest there. It's worth a try at any time, especially on an ebb tide, if you can bring yourself to run past the big fish you suspect must be holding off the hook.

To find the hole, if you don't have a chartplotter, set a course between 250 and 260 degrees, magnetic, from the end of the hook, and run until you pass the K&D Mill. About half a mile beyond the mill the bottom will pop up from 35 or 40 fathoms to about 10. Turn back to the drop-off and you're over the hole.

The area known as the First Hump forms the seaward side of the Winter Hole. To find it, go northeast out of the hole until the bottom comes up. Then bear north until you drop over the far edge.

To find the Second Hump, go northwest from the First Hump toward the nearest red buoy until the bottom comes up to about 10 fathoms from 35.

The Third Hump is still farther northwest. Continue toward the red buoy until the tallest stack at the Nippon Paper Industries Mill to your southeast lines up with Mount Pleasant, the highest hill in the Olympic Range just east of Port Angeles. There, the bottom pops up to 30 fathoms from about 75, and you're over the spot.

You should be at the Winter Hole about an hour before high slack, and fish through the change. When the bite ceases there, run for the Second Hump. When the bite stops again, run for the Third. As low slack approaches, reverse the procedure. Be back at the Winter Hole by low slack.

Experienced Port Angeles anglers try to be in position at tide changes. As the change approaches, remember: If the fish aren't feeding yet, they are going to be. So be on the humps and be patient. Don't be caught screaming around on the change, and miss the bite entirely.

Waters east of the east end of Ediz Hook have been closed in recent summers for the retention of chinook, although they've been open during fall and winter seasons. If the hook and the hole and the humps aren't producing, and chinook retention is

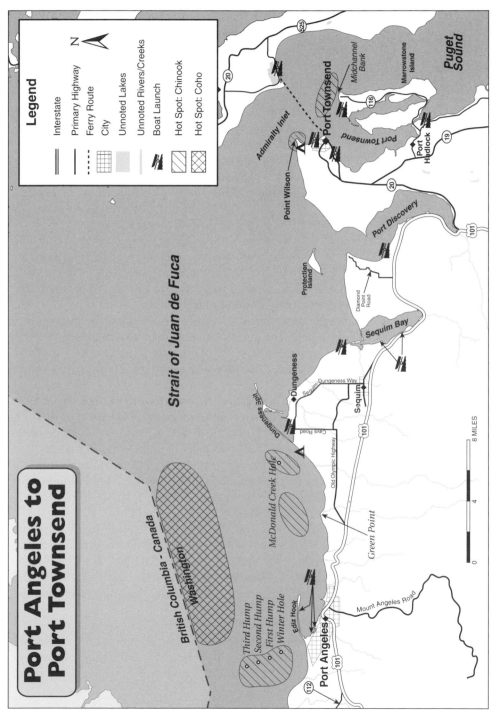

Port Angeles to Port Townsend

Legend

- ||| Interstate
- | Primary Highway
- ⋮ Ferry Route
- ◆ City
- Unnoted Lakes
- Unnoted Rivers/Creeks
- Boat Launch
- Hot Spot: Chinook
- Hot Spot: Coho

N

Puget Sound

Midchannel Bank

Marrowstone Island

Port Townsend

Port Townsend

Port Hadlock

Admiralty Inlet

Point Wilson

Port Discovery

Protection Island

Diamond Point Road

Sequim Bay

Strait of Juan de Fuca

Dungeness

Dungeness Spit

Dungeness Way

Sequim

Sequim River

Cays Road

Old Olympic Highway

McDonald Creek Hole

Green Point

British Columbia - Canada
Washington

Third Hump
Second Hump
First Hump
Winter Hole

Ediz Hook

Port Angeles

Mount Angeles Road

0   4   8 MILES

allowed in waters east of the hook in the year and the season you are fishing, you can run in that direction to Green Point and beyond. Sometimes Green Point is excellent in the summer, and sometimes nothing is happening there at all. It's seldom a compromise. A wide, shallow shelf extends seaward from the point, as it does all along this part of the strait, and you have to move out far enough to find the drop-off, about 3.25 miles off the beach. Salmon, halibut, and lingcod offer a mixed bag for anglers here. On an ebb tide, start your drift about 30 fathoms, and let the current carry you southwest to about 22 fathoms. Take long drifts until you locate the fish, then concentrate on the area where they're feeding. On a flood tide, start about 24 fathoms, and drift northeast to the 32-fathom mark.

A few words of caution: Sea-going freighters steam right through this area to and from the pilot station at Port Angeles, and you have to watch out for them all the time. And, when the wind rises, waves can stack up on the shelf off the point, making it dangerous for small craft.

Beyond the point, eastward up the strait a few miles, is Dungeness Spit. Out from the base of the spit is the McDonald Creek Hole, a deep-water area that pops up onto a flat like the Winter Hole. You fish it for chinook the same as the Winter Hole, providing chinook retention is allowed, dropping your bait down along the ledge. Like the Winter Hole, McDonald Creek is best on the ebb tide.

Port Angeles is a place where some local anglers would rather jig than mooch because dogfish can be such a problem, and the anglers take a lot of big salmon that way. Point Wilson Darts are popular, and so are Dungeness Stingers in candlefish style and in sizes 2-ounce to 6-ounce. Check the size and the color that are working when you're there.

August is when migratory coho start to show in strength and you'll find them out in the rips. Plan on running as many as 5 or 6 miles offshore, and expect to do some prospecting before you zero in on them.

Look for birds and monitor your radio to find out where the schools may be.

Coho fishing here means trolling. Downriggers work well with flasher and fly, and if the fish are feeding near the surface you can take them on a plug-cut herring behind 3 or 4 ounces of lead. Don't overlook planers like the Deep Six, the Pink Lady, or the Dipsy Diver. They work extremely well.

Up the strait beyond Dungeness Spit are Port Townsend and its famous Midchannel Bank. The bank is a lot closer to the Puget Sound metropolitan area than are Port Angeles and the places beyond, and it is a wonderful place to fish for winter blackmouth. Summertime angling is even better than what's available in winter, however, providing that the fishery is open, because in the summer migrating fish stop to feed here.

To find the bank without a chartplotter, follow a compass heading of 60 degrees from the downtown Port Townsend area until, off the northern end of Marrowstone Island, the bottom comes up to 8 or 10 fathoms. Bear north until the bottom drops off, and fish along the eastern edge in 20 to 25 fathoms, preferably starting on a low slack tide and continuing through the flood.

Try to choose a day with mild tidal flows, because the water can move fast here on a big tide.

If the fish aren't hitting, you might try trolling – with a downrigger – northwest along the east side of the bank toward Point Wilson. Try to troll with the tide, rather than against it. At Point Wilson, by the way, anglers do well at times on chinook from the beach. It's one of the few places in western Washington where that's the case.

In late summer, a troller can do very well in waters around Port Townsend on hooknose silvers.

You can launch boats of up to about 16 feet at public ramps at Fort Flagler and Fort Worden state parks, and can launch boats of many sizes at the ramp at the Port of Port Townsend Boat Haven. All have adequate parking.

Among those who contributed information used in this chapter, the author would like to thank:

Walt Blendermann, Dungeness, Washington; John Willits, Port Angeles, Washington; Pete Hanke, Port Townsend, Washington.

Hub City Information
Port Angeles
Population – 18,397 Area Code – 360 County - Clallam

Hotels & Motels

Days Inn, 1510 E. Front St. / 1-877-438-8588

Sportsmen Motel, 2901 Highway 101 E / 457-6196 / www.sportsmenmotel.com

Quality Inn Uptown, 101 E. Second Street / 1-800-858-3812 /
www.qualityinnportangeles.com

Olympic Lodge, 140 Del Guzzi Drive / 1-800-600-2993 / www.olympiclodge.com

Red Lion Hotel – Port Angeles, 221 N. Lincoln / 1-800-Red-Lion /
www.redlion.com/portangeles

Bed & Breakfasts

Inn At Rooster Hill, 112 Reservoir Road / 1-877-221-0837 /
www.innatroosterhill.com

Angeles Inn B&B, 1203 E. Seventh St. / 1-888-552-4263 / www.angelesinn.com

Restaurants

Bella Italia, 118 E. First St. / Italian / 457-5442 / www.bellaitaliapa.com

Bushwhacker, 1527 E. First St. / Steaks, Seafood / 457-4113 /
www.bushwhackerpa.com

Port Angeles Crabhouse Restaurant, 221 North Lincoln / Seafood / 457-0424 /
www.pacrabhouse.com

Launching

Port Angeles Area Launches / www.portofpa.com/marinas/boat-launches

Fishing Tackle

Swain's General Store, 602 E. First St. / 452-2357 / www.swainsinc.com

R & R Marine Supply, 1222 E. Front St. / 452-7062

Hospital

Olympic Medical Center, 939 Caroline St. / 417-7000

Airport

William R. Fairchild International Airport, South Airport Road / Kenmore Air
Provides Several Flights Daily Between Here And Seattle's Boeing Field.

Port Townsend
Population – 8,334 Area Code – 360 County – Jefferson

Hotels & Motels

Aladdin Motor Inn, 2333 Washington St. / 1-800-281-3747 /
www.aladdinmotorinnpt.com

Restaurants

Silverwater Cafe, 237 Taylor St. / Seafood, Meats, Local Beer / 385-6448 /
www.silverwatercafe.com

Sirens Pub, 823 Water St. / Seafood, Pasta, Pizza, Sandwiches / 379-1100 /
www.sirenspub.com

The Public House, 1038 Water St. / Seafood, Meats, Pasta / 385-9706 /
www.thepublichouse.com

Pizza Factory, 1102 Water St. / 385-7223 / www.ptpizzafactory.com

Launching

Port Townsend Area Launches / www.portofpt.com/boat_launches

Fishing Tackle

Swain's Outdoor, 1121 Water St. / 385-1313

Henery Do It Best Hardware, 218 Sims Way / 385-5900 / www.henery.doitbest.com

Hospital

Jefferson General Hospital, 834 Sheridan Ave. / 385-2200

Hood Canal

Few places on earth are as lovely as Hood Canal on a soft, summer day. This is not a canal in the classic sense, so don't let its name fool you. There's nothing artificial about it.

This is a natural finger of Puget Sound, stretching south and then east like a giant fishhook, from its entrance near Foulweather Bluff to its end near Belfair, 80 miles away. Stately Douglas firs press close to its gravel beaches, and the Olympic Mountains tower in snowcapped magnificence over its western shore.

Shellfish abound in the relatively warm waters here. Hardshell clams can be had for the taking, and succulent oysters litter the beaches. Dungeness crabs are easy to catch if you know where to put your pots, and large spot shrimp draw thousands of people here every spring for the sport-shrimping season.

There was a time when this was a paradise for salmon anglers, too. But the canal started to fall on hard times in the late 1970s, when sport catches dropped off dramatically. The Washington Department of Fish and Wildlife said the reasons were complex. Local anglers attributed the decline to burgeoning populations of fish-eating marine mammals and to increased pressure from commercial fishermen. However, recovery has been under way for several years, and the fishery here has begun to regain some of its old luster, making Hood Canal well worth a visit.

Winter blackmouth angling often is good and, when mature ocean fish are migrating, the fishing can be excellent despite competition from commercial beach seiners and gillnetters.

For purposes of discussion, we'll divide the canal into two parts – the northern two-thirds and the southern third, with the dividing line at Ayock Point, a few miles north of Dewatto Bay. The Department of Fish and Wildlife often divides the canal here as well for purposes of season-setting, but check current regulations to be sure.

The northern canal around Seabeck generally is very productive, and this would be a good place for an angler to start. Salmon sometimes are easier to find here than in the south, and dogfish – a major problem in the south – are a little less common here.

A chinook angler will thrill to his first view of Seabeck. The canal widens out here, where Dabob Bay comes in from the northwest to join the main body of water, and points of land abound. Any experienced angler will recognize the opportunities.

Blackmouth are available from about mid-December to the end of March, seasons permitting. A major blackmouth-producer is Hazel Point, on the Toandos Peninsula north of Seabeck, especially on an ebb tide, when nice eddies form just north of the point. Bait often gathers here, attracting feeding chinook. You can mooch

here in close if the dogfish allow it, or you can troll all the way to Brown Point, north of Bangor. But remember: The Navy operates a submarine base at Bangor on the canal's eastern shore, and boaters have to stay on the opposite side.

Oak Head, at the southern end of the Toandos Peninsula, can be fished on either tide, and Tskutsko Point, northwest of Oak on the Dabob Bay side of the peninsula, is good on the flood.

On the eastern shore of the canal, right at the entrance to Seabeck Bay, is Misery Point. Misery sometimes will produce when the others won't.

Big Beef Creek and Little Beef Creek flow into Hood Canal a mile or two northeast of Seabeck, on the eastern shore, and anglers often take winter blackmouth off the mouth of each. South of Misery Point is Stavis Bay, and the entrance to it sometimes is good.

Downrigger trolling with plugs or with flasher and hoochie is popular on the canal in winter. In summer, many anglers prefer to use spoons, such as the Coyote or Coho Killer. At any time of year, using artificials rather than bait tends to discourage dogfish.

Hood Canal, from one end to the other, is definitely an early morning fishery. But there's a twist to it. In much of the canal, you might not find salmon near the surface at the first gray light of day the way you do in other areas. The water's warmer here, and that may be why you sometimes need to go deeper here than you do elsewhere.

Blackmouth move around a lot here, and finding them one day doesn't mean you'll find them at the same place the next. You need to prospect each time by looking for birds and bait, or for schooling fish on your depth sounder.

Ocean chinook begin to show in mid-July, and will be in the area until mid-September, but chinook fishing has been closed in the northern canal in recent years until after mid-October. You fish for them, when you are able, higher in the water column than you do for winter blackmouth, which tend to hang out right on the deck. Hazel is the place to begin, but don't overlook the mouths of the Big Beef and Little Beef Creeks – if regulations allow it – because some mature chinook run up those streams, too.

Ocean silvers start to show toward the end of August, and can provide a fishery through October. They like to school between Tskutsko Point and Hazel Point, and on the inside of Misery Point in Seabeck Bay. Try trolling cut-plug herring, or a flasher and a fly.

Chum, or dog salmon, arrive about October 1 in massive numbers heading for virtually every little creek on the canal, and the fishery for them can continue until mid-December. You'll often find chum cruising in the deep water between Hazel Point and Seabeck Bay. An effective technique is to cast a Buzz Bomb or run an erratic-acting lure such as Hot Shot or Tadpolly from a downrigger about 70 feet down. Green is a favorite color.

In odd-numbered years, pinks usually arrive between August 1 and August 15, and continue to pass through until about the end of September. Many are headed for the Dosewallips and the Hamma Hamma Rivers, although a few go up Big Beef. They sometimes school by the thousands in shallows between Misery Point near Seabeck

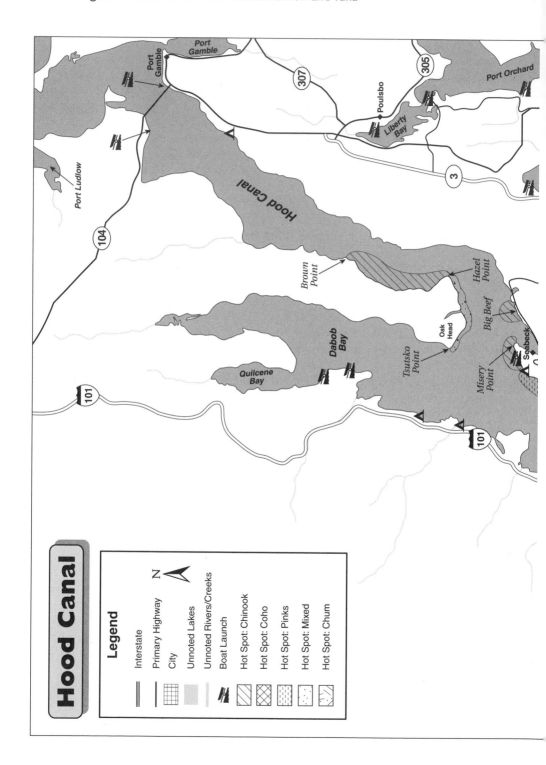

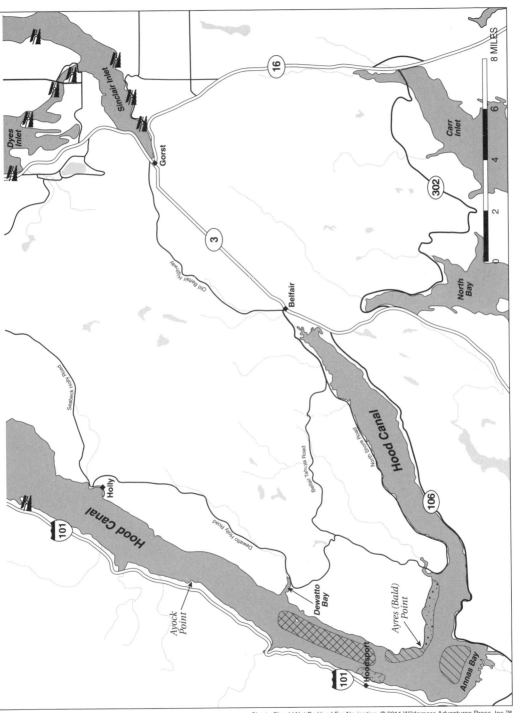

and Scenic Beach State Park just to the southwest, and around the mouth of Pleasant Harbor, directly across the canal from Seabeck. They'll rarely take bait here, but they will go for erratic lures and Buzz Bombs. You'll have to cast to them, mostly, because they're in such shallow water.

Fishing the southern canal is simpler in many ways, because the topography is less varied. The dominant feature here is what anglers call the Great Bend, where the canal makes its fishhook turn to the east. The major landmark on the inside of the bend is Ayres Point, also called Bald Point, where most of the fishing occurs.

Winter blackmouth begin to show in the southern canal between Thanksgiving and the second week of December. As in the north, early morning is by far the best, and direction and stage of tide don't seem to make much of a difference. Speed of the current does, however. The bite will be shorter on a strong tide, lasting as little as 30 minutes after first light. When tidal currents are slow, the fish might feed all morning.

Many local anglers troll at Bald Point, running a route from about a mile north of the point to about 1.5 miles east, near where the Tahuya River enters the canal. White-bodied Tomic or Silver Horde plugs work well in the 3- to 5-inch size. Troll near the bottom, close to the beach, along the 90- to 120-foot line.

Winter blackmouth fishing continues through February, seasons permitting, then begins to taper off in March when many of the fish apparently follow the bait into the northern canal.

About the first week in August, ocean chinook start to arrive. They're headed for the State Fisheries Department hatchery at Hoodsport, a few miles northwest of Bald Point, and for the Skokomish River, which empties into the canal on the outside of the curve at the Great Bend. These fish will move in off Bald Point and, if rain is sparse, will stay there well into September. Many weigh in the 20-pound range, and some scale into the 30s.

Local anglers catch them in ways similar to the way they catch blackmouth, using downriggers to pull a plug or a flasher and hoochie. In summer, however, many anglers switch from plug or flasher-and-hoochie combinations to a spoon, such as a Coyote or a Coho Killer. They also fish shallower for migrating chinook than for blackmouth, often no more than 40 to 60 feet below the surface and often in water ranging from 40 to 100 feet deep.

When a lot of chinook are in, you sometimes find them in the bottom of the fishhook on the canal's south side, right off Alderbrook Inn, following the 90-foot line, and east of there in a place called the Chicken Hole.

Often, the kings will gather in Annas Bay off the mouth of the Skokomish just before going up the river, and you can take them there on Buzz Bombs. Watch for herring balls, watch for birds, and watch your depth finder. Try to cast to the fish. Let the lure drop to the bottom before you start to jig it – a couple of feet at a stroke. Blue pearl and gray pearl, in the 4-inch model, are effective here.

Ocean coho start to arrive around Labor Day. They're headed for the Hoodsport hatchery, for the Skokomish River, for the Tahuya River, for the Union River at the canal's far end, and for Mission Creek, which crosses the northern beach a couple of miles west of Belfair. You must prospect for a school that's waiting to head upriver.

Use a 4-inch Buzz Bomb – pink is good – and cast to them. They're usually easy to find, because they're jumping and rolling.

Anglers catch a lot of nice coho between Dewatto Bay and Bald Point at the Great Bend. An effective technique is to cast a red or orange-red Wiggle Wart toward a school or to troll one slowly, with no weight, close to the beach.

Sometimes returning coho will gather at the Chicken Hole to wait for rain, and you can find them there day after day. Or, they might gather off the north shore of the canal between Bald Point and Sisters Point.

The coho remain until precipitation calls them out of the saltchuck – usually the first good rain in October.

Chums are the last to arrive from the sea, bound for the Hoodsport hatchery and for the Skokomish. You can fish them in the canal itself, casting a 3-inch Buzz Bomb. A white one works well, especially if one side is painted a fluorescent green. A major fishery develops every fall in waters around the Hoodsport hatchery, where anglers cast green corky-and-yarn combinations from the beach.

Launching is easy on Hood Canal. A Fish and Wildlife Department ramp with space to park about 75 vehicles and trailers is located near Seabeck, on the west side of Misery Point. It has no float and no breakwater, however, and a strong south wind can make launching and retrieving impossible. The ramp also has little incline, and large boats – those of about 18 feet and longer – can be floated only a couple of hours either side of high slack tide.

On the west side of the canal is a modern ramp with a float at the Triton Cove trailer park, a few miles south of the Duckabush River.

Anglers may use a ramp at the Department of Fish and Wildlife shellfish laboratory at Point Whitney, although parking there is limited. Another ramp is located inside the Quilcene Boat Basin on the western shore of Quilcene Bay. It is the best protected of all, since it is located inside a breakwater, but launching here may require a four-wheel-drive vehicle because of disrepair to the ramp. This ramp also is farthest from much of the fishing.

On the southern canal, there's a public ramp at Union. Parking is limited, though, and requires leaving your rig on the highway's narrow shoulder. On a low tide, beware of the mud flat that extends from Union around into Annas Bay. A boater returning on a direct course from Bald Point may run aground.

Another public ramp with adequate parking is located at Potlatch, a few miles west of Union, and another, with a float, is located at Twanoh State Park on the canal's south side a few miles west of Belfair.

Among those who contributed information used in this chapter, the author would like to thank:

Larry Alf, Hoodsport, Washington; Rod Huberty, Union, Washington; Doug Nalley, Union, Washington; Dennis McBreen, Port Orchard, Washington; Rick Thomason, Seabeck, Washington.

The San Juans

If I were to design my own version of paradise, it would look a lot like the San Juan Islands in summer – rocky, fir-covered islands in a usually placid sea, hiding hundreds of little harbors and coves. Bald eagles wheel overhead, and hungry fish abound.

On many of the islands sit state marine parks, where you can anchor, tie up to a buoy, or moor to a float and go ashore, if you'd like, to pitch a tent under the trees. Picnic tables, fire rings, and pit toilets are provided, and sometimes piped-in water.

You have found such a place, at the end of a day's fishing. As the dusk thickens you throw some more wood on the fire, then scrape together some coals and set fresh salmon steaks on a grill to broil. Your companions sit by the flames, sharing laughter over the day's events. You look out beyond the flickering light to where your boat rides on its tether in the deepening darkness. It's magic – a moment frozen in time. Life seems full and complete, and you want to be right where you are, doing just what you're doing, more than anything else in the world.

Nobody, if he can help it, goes to the San Juans only once. The place gets under your skin, calls you back again and again. But its beauty is only a part of its lure. The fishing alone makes a visit worthwhile. Rockfish and lingcod prowl its underwater pinnacles. Coho and pink and chinook salmon hunt bait in its tidal rips and off its rocky points.

The San Juans cover a lot of territory. They contain scores of islands, hundreds of bays and coves, thousands of points and drop-offs and rips. Everywhere you look you see salmon-angling potential. And any of these places may produce. Follow your instincts – explore, experiment, and enjoy.

Over the years, however, some of these places have attained, in the lore of the sport, the stature of consistent producers, spots known for giving up certain kinds of fish at certain seasons.

If you're going to fish the San Juans, you have a major decision to make early on. You can launch at Anacortes and run out from there, or you can ferry into the islands with your trailered boat behind your rig, and set up camp at a marine park or at a resort.

If you launch at Anacortes, a good bet is the ramp at Washington Park, a nice facility run by the city. It provides two launch lanes, with a float, and parking in an area that's patrolled. You pay a fee to launch and park. You also can launch on a ramp at Cornet Bay on northern Whidbey Island, and run out through Deception Pass to access the San Juans, or you can launch by means of slings at Cap Sante Boat Haven in downtown Anacortes or at Skyline Marina on Anacortes' west side.

Towing your boat onto a Washington State Ferry can be expensive. But it means you'll be able to return to the mainland whenever you want. Much of the water in the San Juans is quite well protected. But the return to Anacortes, across Rosario Strait, can be tricky if the wind is howling out of the north or the south.

Launch ramps are located on all of the islands with ferry service. Local residents can direct you to them.

Blackmouth begin to show in the San Juans in October, and one of the better spots for them at that time is off Cattle Point, on the southeast corner of San Juan Island, the namesake of the island group. Point Lawrence, on the northeastern tip of Orcas Island, can begin to produce about this time, and so can Tide Point, about two-thirds of the way up the western side of Cypress Island.

The fishing improves there and elsewhere in November, and Thanksgiving through February can be prime time for blackmouth everywhere in the islands, provided that fishing is permitted. As has happened elsewhere on the West Coast, fishing seasons here have shrunk significantly over the years as managers seek to distribute fish among various user groups and to protect declining stocks.

Throughout the winter, one of the more productive blackmouth places is President Channel on the west side of Orcas Island, from Deer Harbor to Point Doughty. Troll in close here, with a downrigger and cut-plug herring, following the 80- to 120-foot line just off the beach.

Blackmouth can be anywhere, but they do move around in the San Juans, and sometimes you have to hunt for them. When you find them, it's generally worth the effort. They run mostly 7 to 10 pounds now, with some into the high teens and the 20s, and every winter a few topping 30 pounds are brought to the boat.

About March, the fishing drops off temporarily, then sometime in April turns again for the better, provided April fishing is permitted. Spring fish are beginning to show now, running mostly 12 to 20 pounds, and Point Lawrence is a prime place to take them. Tide Point, on Cypress, is good once again, and so are Obstruction Pass between Orcas and Blakely Islands and Cattle Point on San Juan Island. Deepwater Bay, on the southeast side of Cypress, can be good at this time, although it's even better in the summer.

Both moochers and trollers fish Lawrence on the ebb, catching the rip off the point and riding it south, then tucking in behind the south side of the point to work the back eddy along the beach. The stronger the ebb, the more likely that bait will wash into the eddy south of the point, attracting salmon to the location. Occasionally, trollers will connect off the island's north shore, north of the point, when the tide is inbound. They may pull a flasher and hoochie or a plug.

When you're fishing the ebb, put your gear right on the bottom, in 80 to 140 feet of water, depending on where you think the fish will be. Some moochers traditionally have fished Canadian-style here, with 10.5-foot rods and a half-pound of lead, backing down against the current, if necessary, to keep their line vertical.

About June, large fall-run chinook start to arrive on the west side of San Juan Island. If fishing is open, Eagle, Pile, and Lime Kiln Points are good places to look. You don't have to fish very far from the beach. You can mooch or dawdle along with a

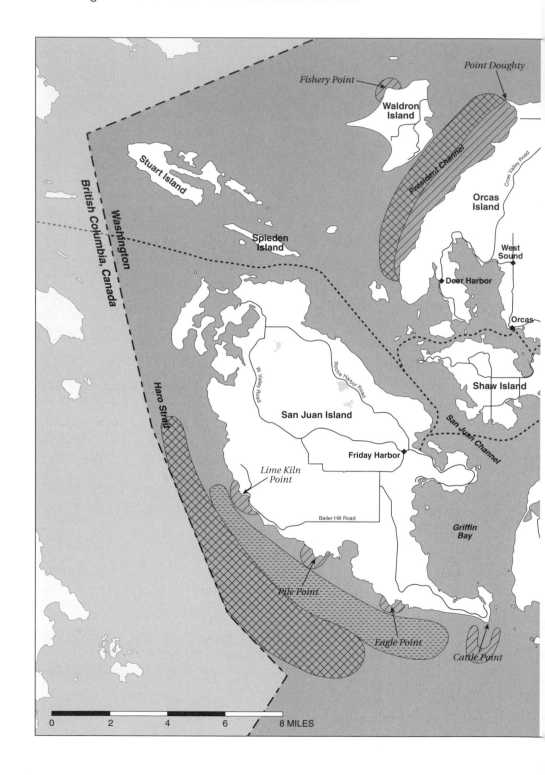

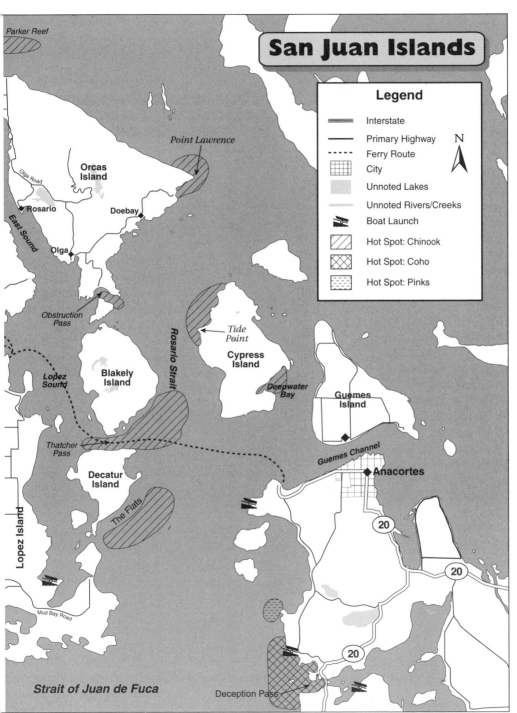

San Juan Islands

Legend

Interstate
Primary Highway
Ferry Route
City
Unnoted Lakes
Unnoted Rivers/Creeks
Boat Launch
Hot Spot: Chinook
Hot Spot: Coho
Hot Spot: Pinks

N

Parker Reef

Point Lawrence

Orcas Island

Olga Road

Rosario

Doebay

East Sound

Olga

Obstruction Pass

Rosario Strait

Tide Point

Cypress Island

Blakely Island

Lopez Sound

Deepwater Bay

Guemes Island

Thatcher Pass

Guemes Channel

Decatur Island

Anacortes

20

The Flats

Lopez Island

20

20

Mud Bay Road

Strait of Juan de Fuca

Deception Pass

downrigger and cut-plug. Look for a rip off a point, and get into the back eddy nearby where a chinook might go to get out of the current. Pile Point is particularly good on the ebb. Eagle also casts a nice shadow when the current moves south and east, but can be fished on the flood as well.

President Channel along the west side of Orcas can be good now, too.

Those old standbys, Tide Point and Lawrence, are churning out fish this time of year. So is Fishery Point on the northwest corner of Waldron Island. And don't overlook waters around Point Doughty, Point Thompson, and Parker Reef on the north side of Orcas.

A prime jig fishery develops in summer at Deepwater Bay. The bay shelters lots of dogfish that wreak havoc on mooched baits, so some anglers troll. But many turn to jigs, such as Point Wilson Darts. When fishing gets hot, lots of boats may crowd the spot.

A big, sandy shoal marks the bay's outer edge. Candlefish get up on the shoal, and chinook go up after them. An evening flood tide gives good fishing here, although you can fish on the ebb. High slack, if it's late in the day, is the best time of all.

Don't overlook the north and south sides of Thatcher Pass, between Blakely and Decatur Islands, just across Rosario Strait from Anacortes, as well as the southeast side of Blakely Island and the flats off the southeast side of Decatur. Downrigger trolling is popular in these places. But watch out for the gear-grabbing hump that lurks midway through Thatcher Pass on its south side.

You can find resident coho in the San Juans most of the year. They tend to stick to the southern part of Georgia Strait, north of Patos and Sucia Islands, and around Alden Bank. By the end of June, they're running maybe 3 pounds apiece, and by the end of summer they'll average 6 to 7.

Ocean coho start to show in early August, and the western side of San Juan Island is the first place to look. By the end of August, the fishery really gets good, and it will stay that way through September. Find a nice tide rip out in Haro Strait, off one of the points that you fished for chinook, and you'll probably get some action there. Like chinook, coho will move up President Channel between Waldron and Orcas, and by the end of August that area can produce good fishing, too.

Sometimes you can catch coho on top, the way you do most other places, with a cut-plug herring or a strip, trolled 20 or 30 feet behind the boat. At other times, especially on the outside of San Juan Island, they're a little harder to please. If you don't find them on top, slow your troll a little and add some weight. Look for them at 60, 70, or 80 feet below the surface. If you have a downrigger, so much the better. Just fish your cut-plug right off that.

You'll usually find plenty of action, especially in September, because thousands of these fish pass through to Bellingham Bay. Additional thousands head for the Fraser River and its tributaries, at Vancouver, B.C., and for other Canadian tributaries on Georgia Strait. Regulations of recent years, however, have required release of wild coho, aimed at least in part at protecting fish from Canada's Thompson River, a Fraser tributary.

A good fall fishery for returning Skagit River coho adults often develops at the entrance to Deception Pass, a few miles south of Anacortes, and in onshore waters just north and just south of the pass.

In odd-numbered years, pink salmon fishing starts about the end of July, and improves as summer progresses. These 5- or 6-pound fish are headed mostly for the Fraser, and you'll find pinks in Haro Strait on the west side of San Juan, in Boundary Pass north of Waldron, in President Channel next to Orcas, and even a few in Rosario Strait off Anacortes, although that's not a hot spot. The best place to catch them is off the west side of San Juan, fairly close to the beach. You won't have too much trouble finding them if they're around, because they'll be jumping. Closer to the mainland, try the waters just south of Deception Pass, which separates Whidbey and Fidalgo Islands, or a bit north of the pass around Biz Point.

The most effective way to catch pinks is with a dodger and a small hoochie in pink, orange, or red, trolled from a downrigger at a depth of 40 to 60 feet.

Among those who contributed information used in this chapter, the author would like to thank:

Chuck Wahtola, former president, Fidalgo Island Chapter of Puget Sound Anglers, Anacortes, Washington; Jay Field, former president, Fidalgo Island Chapter of Puget Sound Anglers, Anacortes; Russ Orrell, La Conner, Washington; Larry Carpenter, Master Marine Services, Inc., Mount Vernon, Washington.

A good spoon can be very effective when dogfish sharks make fishing with bait problematic. Photo courtesy of Tomic Lures.

Hub City Information
Anacortes
Population – About 16,000 Area Code – 360 County – Skagit

Hotels & Motels

Islands Inn, 3401 Commercial Ave. / 1-866-331-3328 / www.islandsinn.com

Anaco Bay Inn, 916 33Rd St. / 1-877-299-3320 / www.anacobayinn.com

Marina Inn Hotel, 3300 Commercial Ave. / 293-1100 / www.marinainnwa.com

Bed & Breakfasts

Autumn Leaves Bed And Breakfast, 2301 21St St. / 1-866-293-4929 /
www.autumn-leaves.com

Heron House Guest Suites, 11110 Marine Drive / 293-4477 /
www.heronhouseguestsuites.com

Restaurants

Brown Lantern Ale House, 412 Commercial Ave. / Soups, sandwiches, burgers,
salads / 293-2544 / www.brownlantern.com

Star Bar, 416 ½ Commercial Ave. / Seafood, meats, extensive wine list / 299-2120 /
www.starbaranacortes.com

Rockfish Grill / Anacortes Brewery, 320 Commercial Ave. / Meats, seafood,
sandwiches, pizzas, beer brewed on-site / 588-1720 /
www.anacortesrockfish.com

Greek Islands Restaurant, 2001 Commercial Ave. / Greek / 293-6911

Village Pizza, 807 Commercial Ave. / 293-7847

Bellissima Ristorante, 904 Commercial Ave. / Italian / 293-1362 /
www.bellissimatrattoria.com

Charters

Catchmore Charters, Departs Skyline Marina, 2011 Skyline Way / 293-7093 /
www.catchmorecharters.com

Anacortes Highliner Charters, Departs Skyline Marina / 770-0341 /
www.highlinercharters.com

R&R Charters, Departs Skyline Marina / 293-2992 / www.rrcharters.com

Dash One Charters, Departs Skyline Marina / 293-6450 /
www.dashonecharters.com

Launching

Public Launch Ramp / At Washington Park. Sling Launching At Cap Sante Boat
Haven Downtown, And Skyline Marina, 2011 Skyline Way

Fishing Tackle

Ace Hardware, 1720 Q Ave. / 293-3535

Holiday Market Sports Center, 680 State Route 20, Burlington / Large Inventory and Expert Advice / 757-4361

Hospital

Island Hospital, 1211 24Th St. / 299-1300

Airport

Bellingham International Airport, 4255 Mitchell Way, Bellingham / 676-2500 / Commuter Flights To Seattle-Tacoma And Regular Service To Las Vegas, Oakland, Palm Springs, Phoenix, Reno, San Diego, San Francisco Bay

North Puget Sound

If you have trouble catching salmon, you're going to love the North Sound – at least in odd-numbered years.

That's when pink salmon often return by the hundreds of thousands, most bound for the Stillaguamish and Snohomish Rivers, with a few headed for the Skagit. They fill the Snohomish, which empties into Puget Sound at Everett, and anglers fill the water in front of the river from Everett all the way to Mukilteo.

That fishery starts in late summer, and it's wild and exciting, both on the water and at the ramps. At the eight-lane ramp in Everett, for instance, some anglers will be coming back with their limits before others in the launching line even have been out.

This is an extremely popular fishery in the Everett and Edmonds areas, and clearly the highest-participation fishery in terms of numbers of boats pursuing salmon in the North Sound. It's not unusual, for example, to find 500 boats on the water between Everett and Edmonds on a Saturday morning when the pinks are running. And fishery managers say the highest "catch per unit effort" among all Washington salmon anglers occurs during the pink salmon fishery in August of odd-numbered years. In regular English, that means pinks produce the most productive fishing.

Pinks are easy to catch, and one way to do it is with an 8-inch Hot Spot flasher in white or glow white, or a white No. 0 or No. 1 dodger, pulling a squid or a mini squid. The size of the squid may be optional, but color is not. Use pink or red. Some of those who do best use a translucent, hot-pink model, and they fish it very slowly. They don't even turn the dodger – just let it swing back and forth.

You can fish right off the river, in 80 to 90 feet of water, even right up into its mouth. But the hottest location is a place known as Humpy Hollow, which lies along the beach between the town of Mukilteo and Picnic Point to the south.

An item of interest: In recent times, more and more pink salmon, or "humpies", have returned to the Snohomish in even-numbered years. Recent even-year returns have been so large, in fact, that anglers have shown up specifically to target them.

There's a lot more to North Sound fishing than pinks, however. And there's a whole different feel to the fishing. You'll find it by running southwest, leaving Everett awash in your wake. There, a dozen miles from the cityscape, the melancholy sound of a bell buoy rolls out to greet you, coming across the water like a layer of oil, the way a train whistle wails across the empty reaches of the high plains.

There's a haunting quality to the sound, especially on a gentle day when the buoy rolls easily in the swells, clanging with a measured, funereal beat. It's a sound you'll come to know well if you fish Possession Bar.

But the sound is all that's melancholy at Possession, because for much of the year this vast underwater reef at the southern end of Whidbey Island is a gathering place for salmon from all over Puget Sound. That's both a blessing and a curse. Traditionally, anglers flocked here from miles away to take part in some of the finest and most enjoyable fishing to be had anywhere east of the Pacific Ocean. They came in large numbers, because Possession's location between Everett and Seattle put it within easy range of the major population centers of Washington, which happens to be – after California – the most densely populated of all the western states.

In recent years, however, this area has been closed to fishing much of the time precisely because it is such a mixed-stock area and some of those stocks require protection.

The fish that move through here are headed from the ocean to a variety of places: some are southbound for the Green River or the Lake Washington system in central Puget Sound, others for the Puyallup River system near Tacoma, and others are on their way to Minter Creek, Chambers Creek, the Nisqually River or other locations in southern Puget Sound. Still others round the corner at Possession and go north, through Possession Sound to spawning areas on the Snohomish or the Stillaguamish river systems. Some turn the corner and then bear left up Saratoga Passage, all the way to the Skagit, preferring to round Possession Point rather than go straight across the northern end of Whidbey through Deception Pass.

The bar itself extends as much as 1.5 miles south from the southern end of Whidbey Island, lying between Possession Point on the east and Scatchet Head on the west.

As good as the fishing here can be, however, it's not a year-round thing. January through March, the baitfish go elsewhere, and the salmon follow. About April, the

Lots of chinook are caught in South Puget Sound on plugs. Photo courtesy of Tomic Lures.

herring return, and the blackmouth come with them, like wolves following caribou. By the middle of April, big spring chinook are arriving. April through June can provide some of the finest fishing of the entire year, but often fishing is closed at that time to protect depressed stocks.

July starts off a little slower, but that turns out to be just a valley between the peaks. By the end of July, the first fall chinook start to arrive from the ocean in a run that will peak around the end of the first week in August, although in some years regulations require release of chinook sometimes from July all the way through October.

Ocean silvers start to show as early as July, but typically don't arrive in any real numbers until about the last week in August.

Most years, excellent silver fishing continues through September, depending on the weather. Too much rain can send the silvers directly up the rivers.

By October the blackmouth fishery has resumed, regulations permitting, and usually is excellent until about the first of the year. Blackmouth commonly tip the scale at 3 to 8 pounds, sometimes in the teens, and occasionally surpass 20 pounds. Not only is the fishing good, but you'll find the waters here a lot less crowded in the fall, when many sportsmen are off hunting and others simply are waiting for spring.

Chum salmon runs vary from year to year, and chums never make up a very large part of the sport catch. But they're usually available at Possession from mid-October through about Thanksgiving, and hooking a bright chum salmon is like tying into a Clydesdale. Plan on watching a chum strip a lot of line from your reel.

You can choose any style of fishing you prefer at Possession Bar. Some anglers mooch, and some even jig with Point Wilson Darts for chinook or Buzz Bombs for coho. But there's a whole lot of water to cover here, so most anglers troll with downriggers for chinook, either with plugs, flasher and hoochie, flasher and spoon, or with a spoon by itself.

You should check the tide, then head for the lee side of the bar. Try to fish along its edges at 90 to 200 feet, exploring until you find the depth at which the fish are feeding.

Silvers, of course, are a different story. They have little affinity for bottom structure, and may be up against the kelp one day and out in the shipping lanes the next. You fish for them here the way you do in the Strait of Juan de Fuca. You get out in the rips and look for birds. When you find the birds you'll probably find the fish.

How do you get to Possession Bar? That's a problem. You can launch at several places on the mainland, including Seattle, and run north or south. It's a long run north from Seattle, though, about 15 miles from Shilshole Bay. And the wind usually blows out of the south, making for an even longer run back.

You can use the sling at the Port of Edmonds, cutting the run by more than half.

Closest to Possession is Mukilteo, which has a city-owned ramp, usually equipped with a small float from May through October. But the ramp is exposed to wind and waves, making it a difficult and sometimes dangerous place to launch and retrieve.

Farther north is Everett, and its excellent Port of Everett ramp on West Marine View Drive. This ramp is located on the Snohomish River, protected from the elements, and will handle as many as eight boats at a time. However, Possession Bar is more than a dozen miles to the south.

Across Puget Sound, west of Possession Point, lies Point No Point on the northern end of the Kitsap Peninsula. Angling here can be as good as at Possession, and sometimes better.

Anglers do well at No Point at the start of the year, finding winter blackmouth from 4 to 10 pounds, with a few into the teens, January through March, regulations permitting. But that's not the only thing that makes it different from Possession. Most of the people here are moochers, and they seem to do best near bottom in 100 to 150 feet of water. In winter, in fact, the fish seem to be closer to the bottom than at any other time.

As at Possession, the tide determines where you will fish, although it's not as important here in winter as it is the rest of the year. You might find fish right off the point or, in winter, straight out in front of the town of Hansville, just north of the point.

Another good area, just south of Point No Point, is known as "the flats". It's shallows that extend out from the beach, deepening very gradually to about 100 feet. To fish it, you get out on the edge where it starts to drop off, and put your cut-plug herring near bottom in 120 to 150 feet. You can fish the flats on either tide.

In April, a few spring chinook begin to show. Resident coho, about a pound apiece, are also here now, but most anglers ignore them. The month of May might provide good fishing for spring chinook, if fishing is permitted.

About this time, the last couple of hours of an ebb become a good time to fish, and that will hold true through the summer. Many anglers gravitate now toward the eddy that's found right off the light at the tip of the point.

A nice boat for use in protected waters. Photo courtesy of Lund Boats.

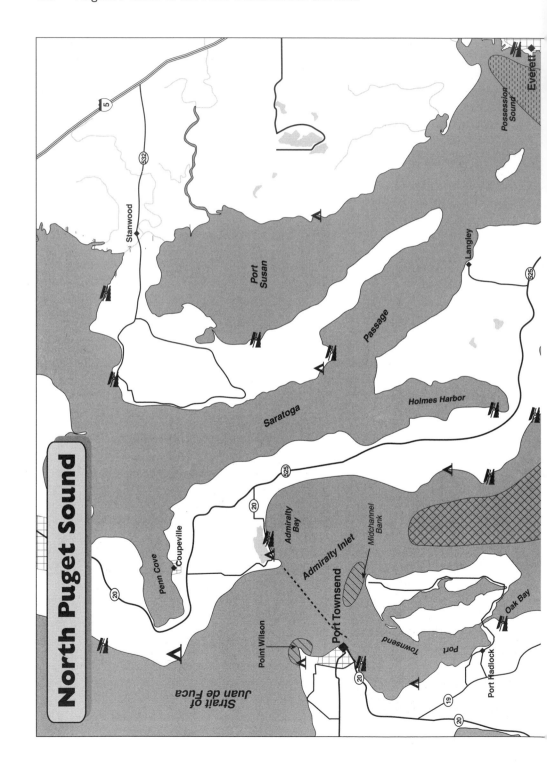

North Puget Sound

Everett

Possession Sound

Langley

525

Port Susan

Saratoga

Passage

Holmes Harbor

Stanwood

532

5

525

20

Penn Cove

Coupeville

20

Admiralty Bay

Admiralty Inlet

Midchannel Bank

Port Townsend

Point Wilson

Strait of Juan de Fuca

Port Townsend

Oak Bay

Port Hadlock

20

19

20

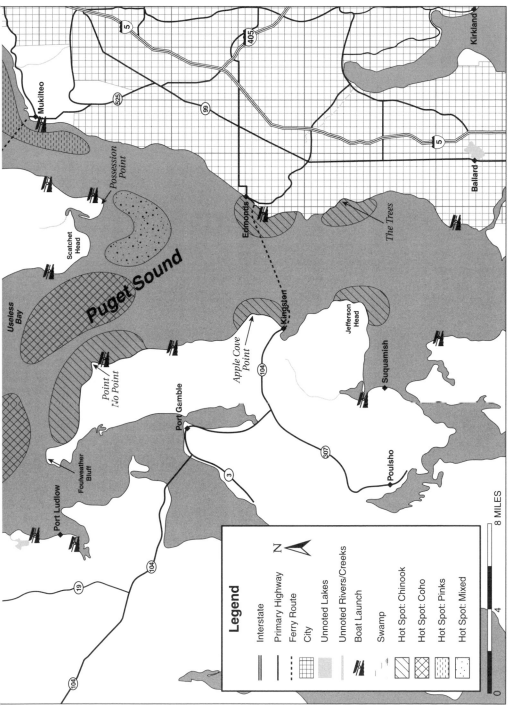

Legend

N

Interstate
Primary Highway
Ferry Route
City
Unnoted Lakes
Unnoted Rivers/Creeks
Boat Launch
Swamp
Hot Spot: Chinook
Hot Spot: Coho
Hot Spot: Pinks
Hot Spot: Mixed

0   4   8 MILES

In June, July, and August mature kings are rounding Point No Point, with the peak of the run passing through from about mid-July to mid-August, but fishing – or at least chinook retention – often is prohibited now to protect these mixed-stock fish. If you can fish, the last two hours of the ebb definitely are best now, as well as the first hour of the flood.

The time of day is less important than the stage of the tide, but a midmorning or late-morning low seems to be best of all. A good bite also may develop right around high slack, especially if the slack occurs in the evening.

South of the point on the flats, you often find fish on the last couple of hours of the flood and at high slack.

When the silvers show in the first part of September, you can take them by mooching right off the point, as though you were fishing for kings. They seem to favor deeper water here than in most places, and you should be fishing 60 to 80 feet deep. If that fails, you can troll out in the rips, just as you would anywhere else.

For silvers, early morning is best, no matter what the stage of the tide, although lesser bites generally occur on high and low slacks, as well.

Kings usually are gone by the end of the third week of August, and silvers provide good fishing until about the middle of October. In November and December, Point No Point will produce blackmouth again, and tides are not quite as important now as they were.

Some years, the chums bite fairly well here sometime between late October and the end of November. It will last only a week or so, and seems to be best from about an hour before low slack to about an hour after.

As it is on the other side of the sound, launching here can be a problem. You can launch at the Port of Kingston, which is about 8 miles south of No Point, or at the Hood Canal Bridge on the opposite side of the Kitsap Peninsula.

The Port of Kingston provides a two-lane ramp with float, and 18 nearby vehicle/trailer parking stalls, with additional parking located farther away. Persons launching boats here larger than 18 or 19 feet will have to keep an eye on the tides, however, because a minus tide could make the ramp temporarily unusable.

The bridge launch on Hood Canal can be tricky, because to reach Point No Point from there, a boat must round Foulweather Bluff, which is appropriately named.

An angler who has been fishing at the point could find a strong south wind roaring up Hood Canal, meeting him head-on as he rounds the bluff on his return to the ramp. A wind from the north could be even worse, because it will hit the bluff before it reaches Point No Point. An angler trying to round the bluff to get back to the ramp on Hood Canal could find waves stacking up there.

Among those who contributed information used in this chapter, the author would like to thank:

Mike Chamberlain, Ted's Sports Center, Lynnwood, Washington; Gary Krein, All Star Fishing Charters, Seattle and Everett, Washington; Vic Nelson, Hansville, Washington.

Hub City Information
Everett
Population – 103,500 Area code – 425 County – Snohomish

Hotels & Motels

Quality Inn & Suites, 101 128th St. S.E. / 609-4550 /
www.qualityinn.com/hotel-everett-washington
Best Western Cascadia Inn, 2800 Pacific Ave. / 258-4141 /
www.bestwesternwashington.com/hotels/best-western-cascadia-inn
Holiday Inn Downtown Everett, 3105 Pine St. / 1-888-465-4329 /
www.ichotelsgroup.com/h/d/hi/1/en/hotel/PAEWashington

Bed & Breakfasts

Gaylord House B&B, 3301 Grand Ave. / 1-888-507-7177 / www.gaylordhouse.com

Restaurants

The Irishmen, 2923 Colby Ave. / Irish / 374-5783
The Scuttlebutt Brewing Co., 1524 W. Marine View Drive / Soups, salads,
sandwiches, burgers / 257-9316 / www.scuttlebuttbrewing.com
Anthony's Home Port, 1725 W. Marine View Drive/ Seafood / 252-3333 /
www.anthonys.com

Charters

All Star Fishing Charters / Departs Port of Everett, 1726 W. Marine View Drive /
1-800-214-1595 / www.allstarfishing.com
Possession Point Fishing Charters / Departs Port of Everett / 1-866-652-3797 /
www.possessionpointfishing.com
AAA Fishing Charters / Departs Port of Everett / 1-800-783-6581 /
www.aaafishingcharters.com

Launching

Tenth Street Marina / On Tenth Street off West Marine View Drive / 13 lanes,
parking for 300-plus vehicles and trailers, one of the largest public launch areas
on the U.S. West Coast / www.portofeverett.com

Fishing Tackle

John's Sporting Goods, 1913 Broadway / Large inventory and lots of expertise /
259-3056 / www.johnssportinggoods.com
Jerry's Surplus, 2031 Broadway / 252-1176

Hepman's Big Fish Bait, 307 W. Mukilteo Boulevard / 252-7920

Ted's Sports Center, 15526 Highway 99, Lynnwood / Large inventory and good advice available / 743-9505

Hospital

Providence Regional Medical Center, 1321 Colby Ave. / 261-2000

Seattle and Central Puget Sound

Central Puget Sound is a beacon of hope – and a pit of despair – for people who love the Pacific salmon. It provides a peek into the future that reveals a sophisticated urban environment and, right along with it, a glimpse of nature at its most enthralling.

The contrast is immediately apparent to anyone who takes to Puget Sound here with rod in hand. In the east towers Seattle's high-rise skyline, its futuristic Space Needle putting a Northwest stamp on the scene. To the left and the right, super ferries, grain ships, and container ships ply into and out of Elliott Bay, churning up wakes in the slate-gray water. Overhead, jumbo jets hang low in the sky, flaps down, lining up with runways at Seattle-Tacoma International Airport.

But that isn't all. Below the ruffled surface of the sound, just out of sight of this urban anthill, schools of sockeye and pink and coho and chinook salmon respond to the same elemental forces that have driven them for eons. They fight their way back to their rivers of origin in this busy inland sea.

It's a thrilling thing to experience, this meeting of the old and the new. The fisheries that remain offer some promise that if we place a high enough value on the fish, if we pay enough attention to their needs, they may continue to rebound against some of the changes we have wrought in their environment. But the fisheries that are gone serve as a warning: If we continue on the path that we followed in the latter half of the 20th century, thoughtlessly exploiting fish and destroying their essential freshwater habitat, no amount of effort on their part will be able to overcome our negligence.

Salmon fishing, what is left of it, is at its best here in the summer and the fall, when ocean-grown fish return as adults. But winter angling also is available, with blackmouth making up that portion of the catch.

For anglers launching in Seattle, this often means a cross-sound run, because some of the best winter fishing is outside of Elliott Bay. Blake Island is a good place to start. It's located southwest of West Seattle's Alki Point and northwest of the northernmost point of Vashon Island. Troll a triangle from the southern tip of Blake to the northern tip of Vashon, then west to the ferry dock at Southworth on the Kitsap Peninsula, and back to Blake. If that does not produce, you can troll between Southworth and Manchester, on a southeast-northwest line west of Blake Island. A flasher and hoochie fished off a downrigger can be very effective here.

North of Blake Island past Restoration Point on the southeast tip of Bainbridge Island is Blakely Rock. It lies off the entrance to Bainbridge's Blakely Harbor, and is another good place for winter blackmouth, which feed among the nearby tidal rips.

Off the northern end of Bainbridge Island, across Port Madison, lies Jefferson Head, a popular blackmouth area on the northern Kitsap Peninsula. Early morning fishing can be excellent here, especially on a tide change and on the ebb.

These fisheries all peak between February and May, when spawning herring school around Blake and Bainbridge Islands and at Jefferson Head, but regulations may not permit fishing at that time.

North of Jefferson on the Kitsap Peninsula is a place called Apple Cove Point. It often produces nice blackmouth.

Directly across Puget Sound from Jefferson Head, on the mainland north of Seattle, is an area just north of Carkeek Park called the Trees. The actual trees are long since gone, but a black can buoy marks the spot where three big cottonwoods grew along an old railroad right-of-way, and it provides good spring and summer fishing for kings, regulations permitting. You can mooch here or you can troll, with the 100- to 120-foot depths generally the most productive.

North of the Trees on the mainland side of the sound opposite Apple Cove Point is Edmonds. It can provide some excellent blackmouth fishing from November through January, regulations permitting. February and March can be hot or cold. You generally find either good fishing then or none at all.

Fishing is very concentrated here in winter, and most of it takes place right in front of the Edmonds oil tanks. Fish in 90 to 200 feet of water, making a circle in front of the tanks.

Tomic plugs are popular here. So are Apex lures, which are plastic spoons with a bend in the forward end. Coho Killer and Coyote spoons fished behind flashers also have many advocates, and many anglers like to pull a Grand Slam Bucktail fly behind a flasher. Fish your lures 30 to 60 feet behind a downrigger.

Point Monroe, on the northeast tip of Bainbridge Island can be every bit as good as Jefferson Head. Fish it the way you would Jeff, on the ebb through low slack.

As you make the turn around the northern end of Bainbridge Island, you enter Agate Pass, once well known for its Pacific cod fishery in February. That fishery collapsed years ago. What's never been as well known is that some nice blackmouth feed here in the spring, and they'll hammer a trolled lure or a flasher and hoochie if fishing is permitted then.

About a third of the way down the west side of Bainbridge Island is Battle Point, where a good spring blackmouth fishery often can be found. South of there on the southwest tip of Bainbridge sits Point White. Waters south of White can provide very good winter and spring fishing for chinook. Troll deep – 120 to 130 feet.

About May, resident coho sometimes start to school in Elliott Bay, off Duwamish Head, and can provide a productive fishery in many places around Seattle during July and early August. You should fish them differently, however, than you would mature coho, because – while these smaller resident fish feed ravenously and bite well – they are feeding primarily on shrimp and krill rather than herring. It's often late July before their diet switches to herring. So during that early period, your lure must be smaller. A flasher-and-hoochie combination still is effective, but use a smaller squid than you

would when your target is feeding on herring, and troll it a bit slower. As the coho switch to a baitfish diet, you should switch to a larger squid, and pull it faster.

About the middle of June, big kings start to move in, a few weighing 30 pounds or more. Anglers begin to pick them up off West Seattle between Alki Point and Duwamish Head, if they are allowed to fish that area. The fishery gradually works its way into the inner bay, peaking there about the Fourth of July.

With the middle of July comes another run of kings and, from then into September, kings will come through fairly steadily, headed up the Duwamish Waterway into the Green River.

You should fish along the beach, trolling a plug or a hoochie or a cut-plug herring along the 120-foot line, working your way farther and farther into the bay as summer gets older. By late in the season, if regulations allow it, you should be fishing right off the river mouth.

Early in the 21st century, a major run of pink salmon established itself in odd-numbered years in the Green River as a result of colonization of that river by the fish without any encouragement by managing agencies. In good years, the run might number in the hundreds of thousands, a potential recreational mother lode. Managers allowed virtually no directed fishing on the run, however, despite its abundance, because of an effort to curtail sport fishing on Green River fall chinook that returned about the same time.

Meanwhile, another run of kings moves in about the same time just north of Elliott Bay. It's the Lake Washington run, which comes in across the Ballard Flats, through the Hiram M. Chittenden Locks and the Lake Washington Ship Canal into Lake Union, then moves from there to Lake Washington and beyond. It will begin to show about the first week of June, and will continue to come through into September. The best way to take these fish, if regulations allow it, is on the flats just outside the canal, with trolled herring and a few ounces of lead.

Sockeye returning to the Cedar River move through the Ship Canal and into Lake Washington in early summer, with run size peaking at the locks about the Fourth of July. If the size of the run permits, the state Department of Fish and Wildlife allows a sport fishery on sockeye in Lake Washington, where anglers successfully slow-troll bare, colored hooks behind a dodger.

Ocean silvers start to show about the last week of August. You'll generally find them first well out in the sound, and anglers will run out to fish for them offshore. They have a tendency to come straight down Admiralty Inlet, hit the shoreline around Edmonds, then split into groups and go north or south. Chinook like to move along the shoreline, but adult coho often come down the middle of the sound, and anglers often catch them in mid-channel. As the fish work their way into Elliott Bay, anglers follow, trolling near the surface, sometimes with just herring and 3 or 4 ounces of lead. These fish stay away from the beach even after they've moved into the bay, and you have to be alert to where you are and what's going on around you, because ferry and freighter traffic can be heavy here at times.

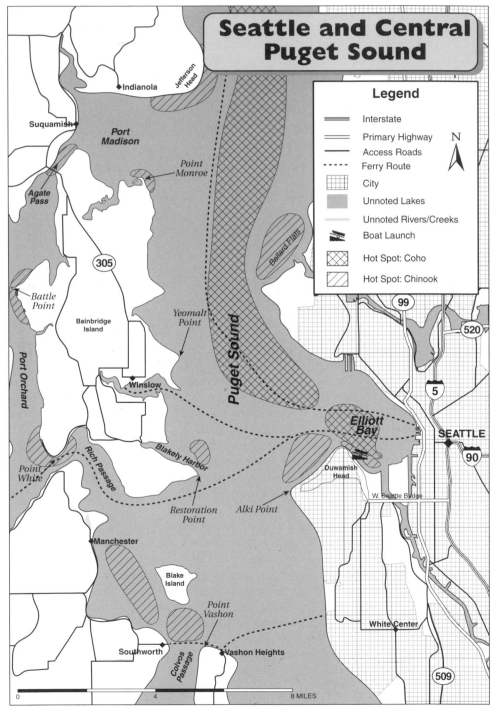

Seattle and Central Puget Sound

Legend

☰	Interstate
☰	Primary Highway
—	Access Roads
- - -	Ferry Route
⊞	City
▨	Unnoted Lakes
	Unnoted Rivers/Creeks
⚓	Boat Launch
⊠	Hot Spot: Coho
⧄	Hot Spot: Chinook

N

Indianola

Jefferson Head

Suquamish

Port Madison

Point Monroe

Agate Pass

Ballard Flats

305

Battle Point

Bainbridge Island

Yeomalt Point

Puget Sound

99

520

5

Winslow

Elliott Bay

SEATTLE

90

Port Orchard

Blakely Harbor

Rich Passage

Duwamish Head

Point White

Restoration Point

Alki Point

W. Seattle Bridge

Manchester

Blake Island

Point Vashon

White Center

Southworth

Colvos Passage

Vashon Heights

509

| 0 | 4 | 8 MILES |

These ocean fish seem more intent on traveling than on feeding, unlike the immature resident fish, and so antagonizing them with a hoochie is often just as effective – or even more so – than offering them a nice plug-cut herring.

Depending on commercial fishing pressure, these silvers may continue to show in good numbers well into October.

Spring usually is the best time to fish Blake Island, but a fair number of silvers show here, too, in the fall. The old triangle, from the south tip of Blake to Vashon to the Southworth ferry dock can be productive. Look for birds working the water, and fish where they do.

Restoration Point, at the south tip of Bainbridge Island, can be good for silvers in the fall, and so can Blakely Rock above that. Yeomalt Point, about halfway up the island on its eastern side, can produce from time to time, and it's worth a check if you're in the neighborhood.

Seattle has numerous launch ramps on Lake Washington, which lies along the city's eastern boundary, but an angler launching there has to travel through the locks to get to Puget Sound. On a beautiful summer weekend, that can mean a delay of hours as traffic backs up.

Launching in the sound makes more sense, but facilities are fewer. One ramp is located in West Seattle, near Duwamish Head, and another near the Ship Canal, at the north end of Shilshole Bay Marina. On the western side of the sound, ramps are available at Manchester and Kingston.

Among those who contributed information used in this chapter, the author would like to thank:

Tom Pollock, Auburn Sports & Marine, Auburn, Washington; Gary Krein, All Star Fishing Charters, Seattle and Everett, Washington; David Nelson, Edmonds, Washington; Dave P. Nelson, Seattle.

Hub City Information
Seattle
Population – 602,000 Area Code – 206 County – King

Hotels & Motels

Best Western Executive Inn, 200 Taylor Ave. N. / 448-9444 /
www.book.bestwestern.com

Comfort Suites Downtown Seattle Center, 601 Roy St. / 282-2600 /
www.comfortsuites-seattle.com

Mayflower Park Hotel, 405 Olive Way / 11-800-426-5100 /
www.mayflowerpark.com

Inn at Queen Anne, 505 First Ave. N. / 1-800-952-5043 / www.innatqueenanne.com

Silver Cloud Inn Lake Union, 1150 Fairview Ave. N. / 1-800-330-5812 /
www.scinns.com

Restaurants

Metropolitan Grill, 820 Second Ave. / Steaks / 624-3287 /
www.themetropolitangrill.com

Elliott's Oyster House, 1201 Alaskan Way, Pier 56 / Seafood / 623-4340 /
www.elliottsoysterhouse.com

Mamma's Mexican Kitchen, 2234 Second Ave. / Purportedly Seattle's oldest
Mexican restaurant / 728-6262 / www.mammas.com

Pike Place Chowder, 1530 Post Alley / Seafood and chowders / 267-2537 /
www.pikeplacechowder.com

La Isla Seattle, 2320 N. Market St. / Puerto-Rican-style / 789-0516 /
www.laislaseattle.com

Charters

All Star Fishing Charters / Departs Shilshole Marina, 7001 Seaview Ave. N.W. /
1-800-214-1595 / www.allstarfishing.com

Fish Finders Private Charters / Departs Shilshole Marina / 632-2611 /
www.fishingseattle.com

A Spot Tail Salmon Guide / Departs Shilshole Marina / 295-7031 /
www.salmonguide.com

Adventure Charters / Departs Shilshole Marina / 789-8245 /
www.seattlesalmoncharters.com

Launching

Seattle Parks Department launches / www.seattle.gov/parks/Boats

Fishing Tackle

Linc's Fishing Tackle & Honda, 501 Rainier Ave. S. / 324-7600

Outdoor Emporium, 1701 Fourth Ave. S / 624-6550 / www.sportco.com

Seattle Marine & Fishing Supply Co., 2121 W. Commodore Way / 285-7925 / www.seamar.com

Hospital

Harborview Medical Center, 325 Ninth Ave. / 744-3000

Airport

Seattle – Tacoma International Airport, 17801 International Boulevard (Pacific Highway South) between Seattle and Tacoma / 787-5388

Tacoma and South Puget Sound

It was as unlikely a salmon-angling scene as you could imagine. Big smokestacks belched effluent into the late-summer sky from the sprawling Tacoma industrial area that lined both sides of the river. Just outside the river's mouth, freighters rode at anchor in Commencement Bay, awaiting their turns to take on cargo for the other side of the Pacific. Burly tugboats plied the waters, towing barges and pushing ocean-going vessels into and out of crowded berths.

Around and through it all buzzed a mosquito fleet of tiny boats, 14-, 15- and 16-footers, some a little larger, weaving in and out among the commercial vessels and back and forth across the mouth of the Puyallup River.

The little boats were trolling for silver salmon, bright hooknose fish that were returning to the river from the sea. These fish arrive from late August through September, and anglers turn out in droves to intercept them near Brown's Point, where the silvers round the corner into the bay, and along the north side of the bay all the way to the Puyallup River itself.

Deep Sixes are particularly effective here, especially when pulling a fresh plug-cut herring. A good place to use them is right off the mouth of the Puyallup, preferably on a flood tide, where the milky waters of the glacial river empty into the bay.

The murky freshwater, being lighter, rides atop the saltwater upon entering the bay. Let out about 15 pulls of line. That will be enough to take your trolled bait down through the glacial silt and into the clear saltwater beneath. And that's right where the feeding coho will be, in the clear water beneath the ceiling of silt.

Another good place to look for silvers at this time is to the west, away from the river mouth, toward Gig Harbor. Troll the rips on an ebb tide over the shelf that lies between Tacoma's Point Defiance and Vashon Island's Point Dalco. A flasher-and-hoochie combination is effective here, or a flasher and herring. You can troll off a downrigger, although some local anglers like to troll here with meatlines. In either case, depths of 30 to 60 feet are productive. Occasionally you'll find the silvers deeper, and once in a while they'll be at the surface, and you can toss out a monofilament line weighted with a 2- or 3-ounce crescent sinker, and catch them right on top.

You also can look for ocean silvers near Point Fosdick at the southwest entrance to the Tacoma Narrows, at the concrete dock on the southeastern side of Fox Island, and at Day Island, which lies off the eastern shore of the sound just south of the narrows.

Farther south, look for hooknose silvers in September around Johnson Point and near the saltwater net pens that traditionally have produced coho at Squaxin Island. Gull Harbor, near the northern end of Budd Inlet, is another good place to check. A combination of wild stock and Squaxin stock mills there before making the final push

home. Trolled flies, Buzz Bombs and Blue Fox spinners all are popular coho-takers in South Puget Sound.

Tacoma-area fishing is more than just a late-summer thing, though. Winter blackmouth angling usually begins about Thanksgiving, and can continue strong through February and even March, seasons permitting. Point Defiance can be productive on an ebb tide for anglers mooching right off the light or trolling a plug or a squid parallel to the clay banks and near the bottom in 90 to 180 feet of water. The point can be mooched on a flood tide, as well, in the eddy inside the rip, right at the head of the Tacoma Narrows. That's where the fish are, up close to the light.

Point Evans on the northwestern shore of the narrows is another good place to mooch in the winter. It's usually fished on the ebb or on a small flood. On the ebb, you drift from Evans north, 300 to 400 yards. On big tides, a large back eddy forms north of the point, where baitfish mill about. That's where the salmon will be. On smaller ebbs, the bait and the salmon stay farther from the beach, closer to the middle of the channel. On small flood tides you drift south, from the overhead power lines to the Narrows Bridges.

The entrance to Quartermaster Harbor, at the south end of Vashon Island, is a good winter blackmouth area. Anglers usually troll around the buoy at Quartermaster's entrance or back along the beach to the west of the buoy. Watch your depth finder, and stay in no less than 90 feet of water. The last of the flood tide and the first of the ebb generally are best there.

Point Dalco, to the west of the harbor entrance, is traditionally a flood-tide fishery, usually best from low slack through the start of the flood. But it also can be fished on a small ebb. An angler can troll big figure-eights off the point, or he can move in close and troll right off the retaining wall. The bottom drops steeply here, and you should stay fairly close to the beach.

Point Fosdick, which produces silvers in September, can provide some good winter blackmouth fishing on the flood. A big back eddy forms just around the corner from the Narrows Bridges, and a lot of anglers find productive fishing here, especially on a big tide.

Waters off the Fox Island concrete dock are a popular winter blackmouth spot. They're usually fished on the ebb, but can be good on a small flood.

Farther south, winter blackmouth fishing can be productive at Eagle Island, at Ketron Island, off the south end of Anderson Island, at Johnson Point, and at Devils Head. Tide changes are popular at Anderson, Johnson, and Devils Head. Over the long run, it doesn't seem to matter whether it's high ebb or low ebb, although differences can be apparent from day to day.

Anderson generally is mooched. The most popular drift is from its southeast corner along the edges of the rip. On a flood tide, the area known as the staircase can be good. It's about 0.25 mile northwest of the southeast corner, and often produces blackmouth fairly close to the beach.

Blackmouth anglers like to troll the east side of Johnson Point in 60 to 80 feet of water with downriggers, from about Zittel's Marina to the end of the point. Flasher-and-hoochie combinations are effective here, particularly with a herring strip on the leading hook.

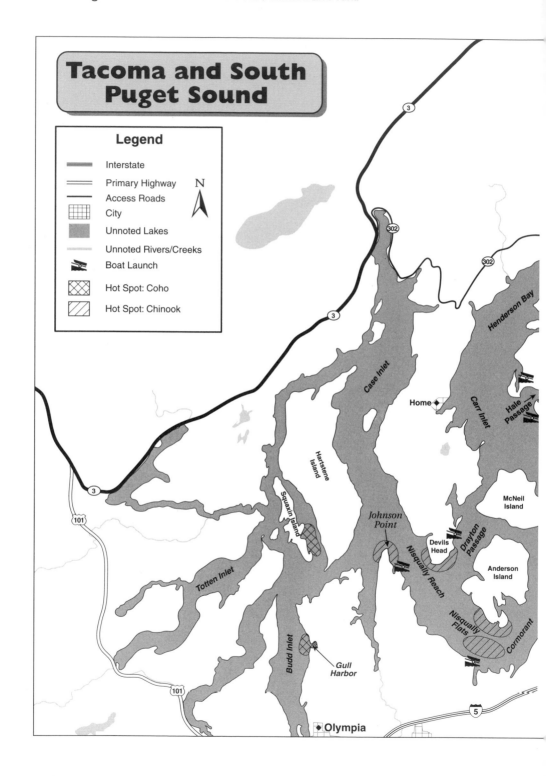

Tacoma and South Puget Sound

Legend

- Interstate
- Primary Highway
- Access Roads
- City
- Unnoted Lakes
- Unnoted Rivers/Creeks
- Boat Launch
- Hot Spot: Coho
- Hot Spot: Chinook

N

302

302

3

3

3

101

101

5

Case Inlet

Henderson Bay

Carr Inlet

Hale Passage

Home

Hartstene Island

Squaxin Island

McNeil Island

Johnson Point

Devils Head

Drayton Passage

Anderson Island

Nisqually Reach

Totten Inlet

Nisqually Flats

Cormorant

Budd Inlet

Gull Harbor

Olympia

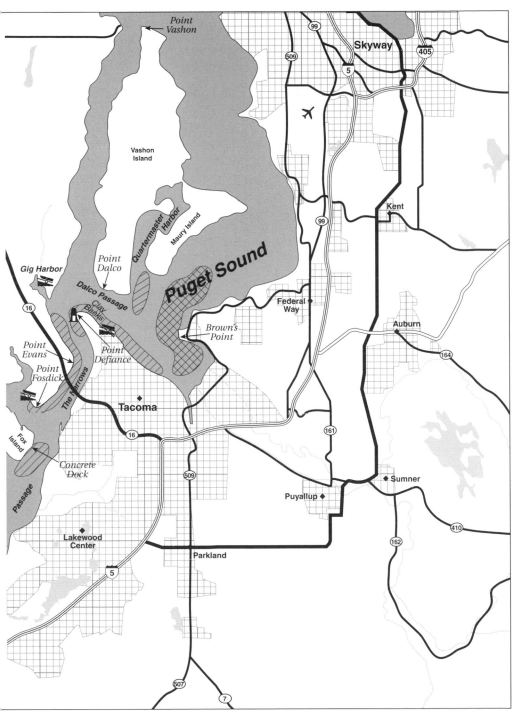

Johnson also can be mooched, and can be quite productive on the ebb, drifting from the point to the southeast.

Resident coho aren't usually very numerous in waters just north of the narrows, but some years they provide a major fishery in waters to the south. Some anglers like to take them on cast flies in April and May in Hale Passage and along the eastern side of Johnson Point. Coho also gather off the south end of Anderson and at Devils Head where small, trolled lures will take them.

Fall chinook begin to show in June, gathering at the usual places – near the Point Defiance clay banks, at Point Dalco, and at Day Island, Point Fosdick, and Anderson Island.

Day Island provides a good mooch fishery for big chinook in July and August. Look for a big flood tide – late afternoon usually is best – and drift south along Day Island's western side. You start on a shelf, in about 90 feet of water, and when you hit 200 to 240 feet you run back up and start another drift.

By August, chinook are piling up off the mouth of the Puyallup River and just outside the railroad trestle at the mouth of Chambers Creek. They're not feeding very actively now, and they can be hard to catch.

Near the sound's south end, a popular and productive chinook fishery develops about the end of July and continues through August around the green buoy on the Nisqually flats off the mouth of the Nisqually River. Some anglers like to jig there and some like to troll, usually pulling a flasher and hoochie.

Another good chinook producer during the same period lies off the mouths of Big Fish Trap and Little Fish Trap Bays on Dana Passage between Boston Harbor and Johnson Point. Fish outside the bays in 30 to 70 feet of water. The most effective method is to jig, sometimes with candlefish-style jigs, sometimes with herring-style jigs.

In recent odd-numbered years, pink salmon have returned in large numbers to the Puyallup, a river they have colonized with little encouragement from fishery managers. The number of anglers who turn out to intercept the pinks off the river mouth has grown likewise. Pink Buzz Bombs have been particularly effective for this purpose there.

Launch facilities in the Tacoma area are good, although crowding can be a problem when fishing is hot.

At Tacoma, boaters can take advantage of a modern, multi-lane public ramp at Point Defiance Park. A smaller, privately operated ramp is located at Narrows Marina at the south end of the Tacoma Narrows on the eastern shore. Public ramps also are located at Gig Harbor, in Wollochet Bay, at the Fox Island bridge, at Home (a community on the Key Peninsula) and near Devils Head on the Longbranch Peninsula, and at Luhr Beach on the Nisqually Delta. Privately operated launching also is available at Zittel's Marina on Johnson Point and at Boston Harbor on Budd Inlet.

Among those who contributed information used in this chapter, the author would like to thank:

Tom Cromie, Point Defiance Boathouse & Marina, Tacoma; Mike Zittel, Zittel's Marina on Johnson Point, Olympia, Washington; Nick Zittel, Zittel's Marina, Olympia.

Hub City Information
Tacoma
Population – 197,181 Area Code – 253 County – Pierce

Hotels & Motels

Silver Cloud Inn – Tacoma, 2317 N. Ruston Way / 1-866-820-8448 / www.silvercloud.com/tacoma.php
Courtyard Marriott, 1515 Commerce St. / 591-9100 / www.marriott.com
Holiday Inn Express Hotel & Suites, 8601 S. Hosmer St. / 1-877-863-4780 / www.hiexpress.com
La Quinta Inn & Suites, 1425 E. 27th St. / 383-0146 / www.lq.com

Bed & Breakfasts

Branch Colonial House, 2420 N. 21st St. / 1-877-752-3565 / www.branchcolonialhouse.com
Chinaberry Hill, 302 Tacoma Ave. N. / 272-1282 / www.chinaberryhill.com
The Green Cape Cod Bed & Breakfast, 2711 N. Warner / 1-866-752-1977 / www.greencapecod.com

Restaurants

Katie Downs Waterfront Tavern & Eatery, 3211 Ruston Way / Soup, salad, seafood, pizza, steak / 756-0771 / www.katiedowns.com
Harbor Lights, 2761 N. Ruston Way / Seafood / 752-8600 / www.anthonys.com/restaurants/info/harborlights.html
Southern Kitchen, 1716 Sixth Ave. / Authentic Southern cooking / 627-4285
Il Fiasco, 2717 Sixth Ave. / Italian / 272-6688 / www.ilfiasco.com

Charters

Captain Jerry's Charters, departs 1101 Dock St. / 752-1100 / www.tacomasportfishing.com

Launching

Point Defiance Marina, 5912 N. Waterfront Drive / Ramp
Narrows Marina, 9001 S. 19th St. / Ramp
Foss Harbor Marina, 821 Dock St. / Sling
Ole & Charlie's Marinas, 4224 Marine View Drive / Sling

Fishing Tackle

Point Defiance Marina, 5912 N. Waterfront Drive / Hottest lures and good advice available here / 591-5325 / www.metroparkstacoma.org
Narrows Marina, 9001 S. 19th St. / 564-3473 / www.narrowsmarina.com

Sportco Warehouse Sporting Goods, 4602 20th St. E., Fife / 922-2222 / www.sportco.com

Hospital

Tacoma General Hospital, 315 Martin Luther King Jr. Way / 403-1000

Olympia
Population – 42,514 Area code – 360 County –Thurston

Hotels

Red Lion Hotel Olympia, 2300 Evergreen Park Drive S.W. / 943-4000 / www.redlion.rdln.com
Governor Hotel, 621 Capitol Way S. / 1-877-352-7701 / www.olywagov.com
Quality Inn, 1211 Quince St. S.E. / 943-4710 / www.qualityinn.com
Comfort Inn, 4700 Park Center N.E., Lacey / 456-6300 / www.comfortinn.com

Restaurants

Anthony's Home Port, 704 Columbia St. N.W. / Seafood / 357-9700 / www.anthonys.com/restaurants/info/olympia
Oyster House, 320 Fourth Ave. W. / Seafood, chowder, beef / 753-7000
Urban Onion Restaurant and Lounge, 116 Legion Way / Salads, deli sandwiches, chicken, beef, pasta / 943-9242 / www.theurbanonion.com
Old School Pizzeria, 108 Franklin St. / Pizza, calzones, salads / 786-9640 / www.oldschoolpizzeria.net

Launching

Zittel's Marina on Johnson Point, 9144 Gallea St. / Sling and ramp / 459-1950 / www.zittelsmarina.com

Fishing Tackle

Tom's Outboard, 221 East Bay Drive N.E. / 754-3882 / www.tomsoutboard.com
Tumwater Sports Center, 6200 Capitol Way S.E., Tumwater /' 352-5161 / www.tumwatersports.com
Cabela's, 1600 Gateway Boulevard N.E., Lacey / 252-3500 / www.cabelas.com

Hospital

Providence St. Peter Hospital, 413 Lilly Road N.E. / 491-9480

Crossing the Bar

The U.S. Coast Guard describes the Pacific Northwest as "home to some of the roughest bars in the world", and it isn't talking about places a person goes to sip suds and listen to honky tonk music. It is talking about those treacherous shallow areas where swift-flowing rivers meet the Pacific Ocean, and where many a careless or unlucky seafarer has met his maker. Once an angler leaves the relatively protected "inland" waters of Puget Sound and its environs, he faces a whole new set of conditions. In order to survive the experience, he's got to understand the potential hazards of crossing the bar.

Many boaters are unaware of the special dangers associated with West Coast locations where river and sea collide, often creating steep, standing waves. Unfortunately, the penalty for ignorance can be death, and that penalty has been invoked many times up and down the coast.

An example of how wrong things can go on a bar occurred June 14, 2003 at Tillamook Bay, Oregon. Ten-foot waves were breaking on the Tillamook Bay Bar that morning. The skipper of the 32-foot-long charter fishing vessel Taki-Tooo decided to leave the safety of the bay and follow three other charter fishing boats out to sea. He didn't make it.

For reasons still not understood, the Taki-Tooo turned broadside to the waves. A large one capsized the boat, throwing its occupants into water so violent that it tore the vessel's fly bridge off.

Rescuers managed to save eight people. Eleven died, including the Taki-Tooo's skipper and mate.

The Coast Guard had issued a small craft advisory that morning, had posted a warning about rough conditions on the bar, and had ordered recreational boats and certain other vessels not to attempt a crossing. The Taki-Tooo and the others that left the harbor that day were of a class of vessel not subject to the order, however.

The National Transportation Safety Board found that the skipper had not been impaired in any way, and that his boat had not experienced any mechanical problems. It attributed the tragedy to the skipper's decision to attempt a crossing of the bar despite the rough conditions, and said more of the boat's occupants might have survived if they had put on life jackets before the crossing.

To reduce the danger of such crossings as much as possible, a small-boat skipper must understand what a bar is, how it works and what its particular characteristics are at every location he plans to fish. In fact, the characteristics vary at every location.

A bar is a shallow area caused by siltation at the mouth of a river or bay where incoming ocean swells may turn into breaking waves. Bars are most dangerous on an ebb tide, when water is flowing seaward. Particularly when the ebb is supplemented by a river current, the outward flow of water can be tremendous, and when it collides with incoming surf, huge waves can stack up.

Talk to experienced anglers where you plan to fish, and consider following their example. If bar conditions are rough, stay inside until they improve. If you're fishing outside, pay attention to the stage of the tide, and get back inside before the ebb begins. If you are caught outside on the ebb, consider heaving-to and waiting until the tidal current reverses course.

Remember, all things being equal, it's easier to get out over a rough bar than it is to get in. Going out, you're headed into the seas, and you have better control of your boat. Coming in, the seas are astern, which reduces your maneuverability. Keep in mind also that it's easier to judge a bar from the landward side, where you can more easily see any breakers. From seaward, breakers may not be visible, and the bar may look calmer than it is.

If you get into trouble coming in, try to keep the incoming seas squarely astern. Keep one hand on the throttle, and try to ride the back of a swell, keeping clear of the following wave. Do not allow your boat to overtake a breaking wave and plunge down its face, however. If the wave is high enough and steep enough, the boat can submerge its entire bow deep in the water at the bottom of the wave and then pitch-pole, flipping stern-over-bow. And do not allow your boat to turn sideways to the seas. That's called a broach, and it's what happened to the Taki-Tooo.

The Coast Guard monitors bars from before dawn to sundown each day during boating and fishing seasons, and Coast Guard stations along the coast broadcast bar conditions on VHF Channel 16. They also provided a recorded report at each station, which boaters can access by telephone.

In Washington, such reports are available for the Quillayute River at La Push, for the Grays Harbor Bar at Westport, and for the Columbia River.

In Oregon, in addition to the Columbia, they are available for the Nehalem River, Tillamook Bay, Depoe Bay, Yaquina Bay, Siuslaw River, Umpqua River, Coos Bay, and the Coquille, Rogue and Chetco Rivers.

In California, bar reports are available for Humboldt Bay and for the Noyo River at Fort Bragg.

Telephone numbers and other hazardous-bar information for Washington and Oregon are available on the 13th U.S. Coast Guard District's web site at www. uscg.mil/d13/bar/default.htm.

A rich source of information on Oregon bars is available on-line from the Oregon State Marine Board at www.marinebd.osmb.state.or.us/safety/. Click on "Coastal Waters Guide".

For California, telephone numbers for Coast Guard stations at Humboldt Bay and Noyo River are available at www.uscg.mil/d11. Click on "Shore Commands".

Among those who contributed information used in this chapter, the author would like to thank:

The U.S. Coast Guard; the Oregon State Marine Board, Dave Yarger, Sebastopol, CA.

Lower Columbia River and Washington Coast

It's a wonderful, exhilarating, dangerous fishery – thousands of boats crammed into the mouth of the mighty Columbia River, pitching and rolling in the slop, competing for space and for migrating ocean silvers and kings.

The name of the game is intimidation. Big boats bear down upon smaller ones in the strong tidal current, and skippers hurl warnings and challenges as line crosses line and whirling props threaten taut monofilament.

Anglers flock to this fishery – known as "the Buoy 10 fishery" – from both sides of the Columbia. It takes place right inside the river mouth, and is named for the numbered buoy that marks the seaward boundary of the area in which fishing occurs. It's not uncommon for more than a million salmon to enter the Columbia during a summer, but obviously the fishery isn't for everyone. For those who prefer the security of a larger boat, a thriving charter industry operates out of both the Washington and Oregon sides of the river. For those who want to fish from their own trailered boat, caution is the watchword.

The water can be exceedingly rough when the wind rises here, and the south jetty area in particular can be treacherous with breaking waves. Usually the danger is visible, but a flood tide can push you right into it if you aren't alert, so it's a good idea to stay north of the red buoy line for safety.

How crowded does this river get? In years gone by, traffic might back up from the launch ramp at Fort Canby State Park on the Washington side of the river – an efficient, modern facility with good floats – literally for miles. Nearby, a sling launch at the Port of Ilwaco would work late into the night to accommodate arriving anglers, then resume before first light the next day.

In recent years the pace has slowed, but only to a degree. Ilwaco and its fellow cities on the opposite shore in Oregon still host an annual influx of anglers when the salmon return. The Port of Ilwaco now operates two slings and a two-lane ramp, and provides parking for 75 vehicle/trailer combinations. If that parking is full, an angler can unhook his trailer and park it in the port's trailer-storage area, which accommodates about 200 unattached trailers, then leave his tow rig in the port's 500-space vehicle lot. Guest moorage is available here, among the more than 800 slips the port operates, but the port accepts no reservations.

Both Fort Canby and downtown Ilwaco are convenient to the fishery, which you reach through a channel behind Sand Island. But follow the channel markers, because it's easy to run aground here.

On the Oregon side, launch ramps are a longer run from Buoy 10. Astoria has one ramp – a modern, two-lane facility in its East Boat Basin that performs well at all stages of the tide. The Columbia is, in fact, a tidal river here in its lower reaches. The Port of Astoria also operates a sling launch in its West Basin, and provides parking for 120 vehicles with trailers in its West Basin and for 200 vehicle-trailer combinations in the East Basin.

Better facilities are located just downstream at Warrenton, however, where a two-lane ramp is available at the Warrenton Boat Basin, about a mile from the Columbia on the Skipanon River, with parking for about 150 rigs. Hammond, even farther downstream, boasts a four-lane ramp right on the Columbia, with parking for as many as 600 rigs, but you still face about a 7-mile run to Buoy 10.

Don't expect to avoid crowds by launching in Oregon. During the height of the fishery, trailered boats sometimes line up for several miles on the Oregon side. Hammond might launch 400 or 500 boats per day on a weekend, while Warrenton's smaller ramp might handle 100 or 125. If you plan to launch just once and then moor for a while in Oregon, try to make your arrangements well in advance, because much of the moorage sells out ahead of time.

If you think fishing is about peace and solitude and gentle nourishment for the soul, Buoy 10 probably is not for you. But if you're confident with rough water and tough competition, this hotbed of salmon activity can provide an angling experience you'll never forget.

Fall chinook hit the river about the middle of August. These are primarily tules (lower Columbia River hatchery chinook) headed for hatcheries on the lower Columbia. Coho usually are mixed among them, and fishing can be good well into September.

Use fresh bait. Anchovies seem to work better than herring here, and usually are fished whole. Fish the incoming tide from low slack through high. You can find fish anywhere between Buoy10 and Astoria, but many anglers like to push right into the crowd near Buoy 10, in the rips near where the river meets the ocean, to be among the first to greet the fish. Bait usually is plentiful here, and ocean fish may drift in and out with the tide many times, gorging on baitfish before finally heading upriver for good.

The water usually is no more than 60 feet deep, an ideal place for planers. Start with about 10 pulls of line, then strip out some more if you don't find fish quickly. Point your bow toward the ocean and troll against the incoming current, letting the tide back you slowly upriver.

Charter captains, who often like to hold their place in the river through low-speed use of their engines, complain that small-boat operators often drift upriver dangerously fast on the tide as they put out their gear, turning their backs on other boats while they work with their tackle. This creates a hazard for everyone.

In a mix as volatile as this, where the current runs as fast as the Columbia's often does, it's good policy to designate one member of a small-boat party to keep constant watch for danger while others ready their gear. The person on watch can alert the skipper in time to avoid a mishap.

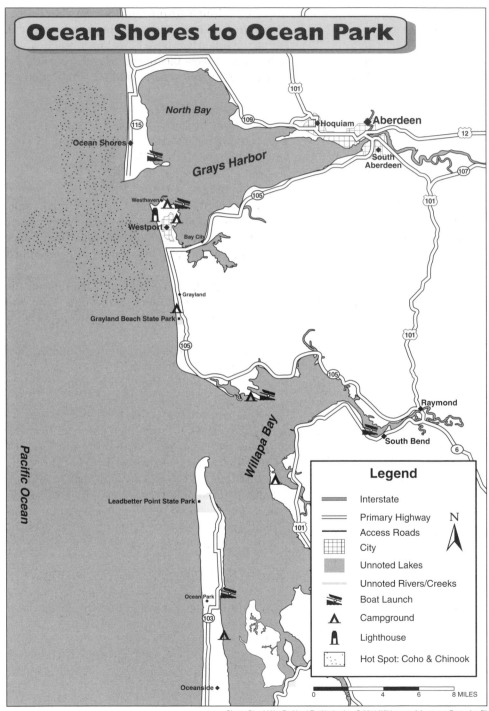

Ocean Shores to Ocean Park

North Bay

Aberdeen

Hoquiam

Ocean Shores

Grays Harbor

South Aberdeen

Westhaven

Westport

Bay City

Grayland

Grayland Beach State Park

Raymond

South Bend

Willapa Bay

Pacific Ocean

Leadbetter Point State Park

Ocean Park

Oceanside

Legend

≡≡≡	Interstate
═══	Primary Highway
───	Access Roads
⊞	City
▨	Unnoted Lakes
───	Unnoted Rivers/Creeks
⛵	Boat Launch
⛺	Campground
⬢	Lighthouse
⠒⠒	Hot Spot: Coho & Chinook

N

0   4   6   8 MILES

Charts Should Not Be Used For Navigation. © 2011 Wilderness Adventures Press, Inc.™

Watch out also for the wing dams located on the south sides of Upper and Lower Sand Island. Each island has two, constructed of pilings and extending a couple of hundred yards into the river. Water runs between the pilings. The purpose of the dams is to prevent river-caused erosion to the islands' shorelines, but the strong current can pin a boat against a dam and overturn the craft. An angler pitched into the water here also can be pinned against the dam with little chance of escape, like a kayaker pressed fatally against a fallen tree in the current of an inland river. Stay well clear of the structures if the current is moving you in their direction.

Actually there's no need to fight the crowd at Buoy 10 for salmon unless you wish to. You can fish instead at Buoy 11, the next marker upriver from 10, and have the area mostly to yourself, then fish along the river's edge all the way to the town of Chinook with little competition. Some experienced anglers say the fishing between Buoy 11 and Chinook can be very productive, lacking only the frenetic angler activity one encounters around Buoy 10. You'll find the water about 60 feet deep around Buoy 11, shallowing to as little as 24 feet along the river's edge as you let the current carry you upriver. Fish this area the same way you would Buoy 10, running a planer and anchovy behind your boat.

When ocean fishing is open, small boats from Ilwaco and the Oregon river ports generally turn south beyond the Columbia River bar and fish along the Oregon coast. But sometimes the fish gather to the north, on the Washington side of the river mouth, and in that case the fleet will fish there.

Anglers interested in fishing the central and northern Washington coast have two options, aside from Neah Bay at the northwest corner of the state. One is Westport and the other is La Push, on the Quileute Indian Reservation between Westport and Neah Bay. Both locations offer charter services, and many anglers opt to fish aboard charters from those locations.

If you plan to trailer your own boat to the coast, it's crucial that you have sound boating experience and utilize good judgment. At Westport, your whole focus must be the formidable bar. You will want to cross it on a flood tide, although you can cross on an ebb if the ocean is flat. With any swell at all, however, the ebbing tide running against the swell will create steep, often breaking, waves.

Even on the flood, the bar can be unpredictable depending on the direction of the swell, and a cross-wave can put a lot of water over your gunwale.

You should obtain a local chart and a good tide book, and know how to use them. Sometimes you'll have a half-hour's grace on the tail end of the high, when the water over the bar remains slack. The worst time of all is three or four hours after the high – the period of maximum ebb – when the bar is the nastiest.

You'll see boats of many sizes on the ocean around here if the day is calm, but many knowledgeable locals are reluctant to attempt the bar in anything smaller than an 18-footer. Channel 13 is the local citizens' band radio channel. An angler in trouble and without VHF can use it to call for assistance and hope that someone will relay his message to the Coast Guard inside the harbor.

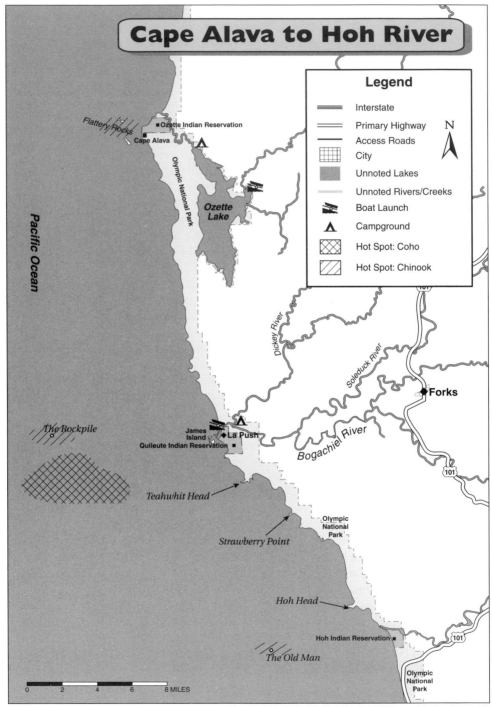

Cape Alava to Hoh River

Legend

Interstate
Primary Highway
Access Roads
City
Unnoted Lakes
Unnoted Rivers/Creeks
Boat Launch
Campground
Hot Spot: Coho
Hot Spot: Chinook

N

Flattery Rocks
Ozette Indian Reservation
Cape Alava

Olympic National Park

Ozette Lake

Pacific Ocean

Dickey River

Soleduck River

Forks

The Rockpile

James Island
La Push
Quileute Indian Reservation

Bogachiel River

101

Teahwhit Head

Strawberry Point

Olympic National Park

Hoh Head

Hoh Indian Reservation

The Old Man

101

Olympic National Park

0   2   4   6   8 MILES

Once you've crossed the bar, you often can find good fishing right in front of it, particularly for bigger chinook during afternoon tides. Often an angler will turn north or south, because the middle waters tend to remain fairly rough for two or three hours after the ebb.

The north beach off Ocean Shores is a productive place for chinook. The 25- to 30-fathom line (150 to 180 feet) has been the most productive during the past few years, but start at the 10-fathom line and work your way gradually deeper if the inshore areas are not productive. Be aware that with any swell at all, the north spit can be very dangerous because of the many commercial crab pots here. A lot of the heavy pots are buried immovably in the sandy ocean floor. Should a crab pot line wrap around your prop, a large swell can pick you up and flip you like a piece of balsa. It's happened more than once, sometimes with tragic results.

A lot of anglers like to follow the red buoy line southwesterly from the harbor mouth. The first buoy in the line actually is yellow, and is marked with an "SJ". It locates the end of a sunken jetty, and from there along the south beach is a prime area for larger fish. Again, 10 fathoms is a good place to begin.

Beyond the SJ buoy are buoys 8, 6, 4, 2 and finally the GH buoy, which is about 3 miles from the harbor. It's a good idea for an angler who's inexperienced here always to keep a buoy in view, for help getting home if a fog comes down. Most small boats fish between the beach and the GH, and they catch both species of salmon here. The closer to shore you fish, the more likely you are to find bigger chinook. If you're targeting coho exclusively, you might consider running beyond the GH toward the 6-mile line, which is at 25 fathoms. But remember, you're dealing with a big ocean.

Nearly all of the small-boat anglers here troll, rather than mooch, and a Deep Six or a Pink Lady is very effective, even for chinook. Sometimes, in fact, a big fish may hit while you actually can see the planer fishing just below the surface in only 20 or 30 feet of water.

Chinook always are feeding in the waters off Westport, but a major migration comes down the coast between mid-July and mid-August, and peaks in the Columbia River in about the third week of August. Coho usually arrive from mid-June to early July, and also peak in the Columbia River in late August. Runs of pink salmon come through in odd-numbered years, but anglers have not traditionally targeted them here.

La Push, long popular with both small-boat and charter anglers, fell out of favor with fishermen in the latter part of the 20th century, but by the early years of the 21st century had regained much of its old cachet. A handful of charter skippers operate here, and a good launch ramp is available on the east side of the La Push marina for trailered boats. The marina office in La Push carries herring, but might not open early enough to suit many anglers, so it's wise to be prepared with bait if you want it.

July typically is an excellent month for chinook, although exceptionally warm ocean water has been known to delay the arrival of the fish from Canada. Coho usually begin to show in the catch in late August. They are present earlier, but don't usually attain much size until about the middle of August.

Many anglers run in July to an area they call Umatilla Reef off Cape Alava, an area about 20 miles north-northwest of La Push. A buoy about 3 miles off the beach warns ships to steer clear of the shallow water. The place that anglers fish actually is listed on marine charts as Flattery Rocks. It's an east-west formation whose outer edge, which culminates in Umatilla Reef, lies about 2 miles offshore. The inner edge lies within 0.25 mile of the beach. Chinook traveling down the coast tend to pile up on the north side of the rocks. There's a spot on the inside portion of the formation, in 40 to 50 feet of water and surrounded by rocks, that local anglers like to fish in the early mornings for kings. You can jig, mooch, or troll there, but most of the time jigging candlefish imitations is productive. Later in the day, the kings, and the anglers, move deeper.

Some anglers run to a place called "the rock pile", about 10 miles west of La Push, where most people troll for kings. The bottom typically is 220 feet all around the rock pile, but it comes up to 150 feet in places here. Anglers typically fish 50 or 60 feet deep, sometimes a little deeper. A flasher-and-hoochie combination with herring strip works well.

Sometimes, anglers run south toward the mouth of the Hoh River, about 13 miles from La Push. Trolling is effective here for kings, but a lot of people mooch. They use either technique about 6 miles west of the river mouth, over a little formation the locals call "the old man", where the bottom comes up just 20 or 25 feet from 200. The change isn't much, but it's enough to create a little upwelling of the water, and the fishing here can be good at times.

For coho, the rips about 2 miles south of the rock pile provide one of the most productive spots. You can fish a flasher and hoochie in the top 40 or 50 feet of water, either off a downrigger or with a planer. Sometimes, just a few ounces of lead ahead of a cut-plug herring, fished within a few feet of the surface can be very productive here.

The river-mouth bar at La Push is not usually considered formidable, and locals say a small boat usually can get in and out of the harbor on any tide. Fog is a big factor here in summer, however, and you want to have radar and a good GPS chartplotter to help guide you in. Often, anglers will run out a couple of miles in pea-soup fog and then break into the open under blue skies. Heat from the land and moisture from the sea often create a bank of fog that hangs right along the shore.

Among those who contributed information used in this chapter, the author would like to thank:

Max Gentry, Sea Breeze Charters, Ilwaco, Washington; Perry VanOver, charterboat skipper, Ilwaco; Mack Funk, manager, Port of Ilwaco; Neil Kennedy, Ilwaco; Mark Cedergreen, executive director, Westport Charterboat Association and 2010-11 president, Pacific Fishery Management Council, Westport, Washington; Chuck Towslee, Westport; Randy Lato, charterboat skipper, Forks, Washington; Dave Churchill, assistant harbormaster, City of Warrenton Marinas, Warrenton, Oregon.

Hub City Information
La Push

Located on the Quileute Indian Reservation
Population – 371 Area Code – 360 County – Clallam

Hotels & Motels

Quillayute River Resort, 473 Mora Road, Forks / 374-7447 / www.qriverresort.com
Oceanside Resort, 330 Ocean Drive / Tribally operated / 374-5267 /
  www.quileutenation.org/business/resort

Restaurants

Stewart Gray Restaurant, 41 Main St. / American / 374-0777
Forks Coffee Shop, 241 S. Forks Ave., Forks / Family restaurant / 374-6769 /
  www.forkscoffeeshop.com

Charters

Top Notch Ocean Charters, departs La Push Marina / 1-888-501-5887 /
  www.forks-web.com/jim/salt
All-Ways Fishing, departs La Push Marina / 374-2052 / www.allwaysfishing.com

Launching

La Push Marina / Ramp

Fishing Tackle

Olympic Sporting Goods, 190 S. Forks Ave., Forks / 374-6330
Forks Outfitters, 950 S. Forks Ave., Forks / 374-6161 / www.forksthriftway.com

Hospital

Forks Community Hospital, 530 Bogachiel Way, Forks / 374-6271

Westport
Population - 2,137 Area Code – 360 County – Grays Harbor

Hotels & Motels

The Islander Resort, 421 E. Neddie Rose Drive / 1-800-322-1740 /
  www.westport-islander.com
Harbor Resort, 871 Neddie Rose Drive / 268-0169 / www.harborresort.com
Chateau Westport, 710 Hancock / 1-800-255-9101 / www.chateauwestport.com
Windjammer Motel, 461 E. Pacific Ave. / 1-866-208-7371 /
  www.windjammermotel.net

Restaurants

Half Moon Bay Bar & Grill, 421 E. Neddie Rose Drive / American / 1-800-322-1740 / www.halfmoonbaybarandgrill.com
Anthony's Restaurant, 260 E. Dock St. / Italian and Greek / 268-1609
One Eyed Crab, 2309 Westhaven Drive / Seafood / 268-0891
The Fog Cutter Cafe II, 1155 Ocean Ave. W. / 268-6097
Mermaid Deli & Pub, 200 E. Patterson / Sandwiches, soups / 612-0435 / www.mermaiddeli.com

Charters

Westport Charterboat Association / www.charterwestport.com
Westport Charters, 2411 Westhaven Drive / 1-800-562-0157 / www.westportcharters.com
Deep Sea Charters, Opposite Float 6 / 1-800-562-0151 / www.deepseacharters.biz
Cachalot Charters, 2511 N. Westhaven Drive / 1-800-356-0323 / www.cachalotcharters.com

Launching

Westport Marina, at foot of Wilson Street, next to Coast Guard station / ramp with three lanes, 2 floats

Fishing Tackle

Englund Marine & Industrial Supply, 280 E. Wilson Ave. / 268-9311 / www.englundmarine.com
Hungry Whale Enterprises, 1680 S. Montesano St. / 268-0136

Hospital

Grays Harbor Community Hospital, 801 N. Montesano St. / 268-0725

Ilwaco
Population – 986 Area Code – 360 County – Pacific

Hotels & Motels

Coho Charters & Motel / 1-800-339-2646 / www.cohocharters.com
Col-Pacific Motel, First and Main / 642-3177 / www.colpacificmotel.com
Harbor Lights Motel, Restaurant and Lounge, 147 Howerton Way S.E. / 642-3196
Heidi's Inn, 126 Spruce St. / 1-800-576-1032 / www.heidisinnmotel.com
Long Beach Super 8 Motel, 500 Ocean Beach Boulevard S., Long Beach / 1-888-478-3297 / www.longbeachsuper8.com
Discovery Coast Cottage Inn, 401 Ocean Beach Boulevard N., Long Beach / 1-877-642-2613 / www.discoverycoastonline.com

Our Place at the Beach, 1309 S. Ocean Beach Boulevard, Long Beach / 1-800-538-5107 / www.ourplacelongbeach.com

The Breakers, Highway 103 at 26th Street, Long Beach / 1-800-219-9833 / www.breakerslongbeach.com

Bed & Breakfasts

Inn at Harbour Village, 120 Williams Ave. N.E. / 1-888-642-0087 / www.innatharbourvillage.com

China Beach Retreat, 222 Robert Gray Drive / 642-5660 / www.chinabeachretreat.com

Restaurants

Port Bistro, 235 Howerton Way / www.portbistro.com

Pelicano Restaurant, 177 Howerton Way S.E. / Mediterranean-influenced seafood, meats / 642-4034 / www.pelicanorestaurant.com

Harbor Lights Restaurant, 147 Howerton Way / Seafood / 642-3196 / www.harbor-lights-ilwaco.com

Tuscany Café, 161 Howerton Way / Italian / 642-4899

Don's Portside Café, 303 First Ave. S. / Seafood, pizza / 642-3477

Charters

Sea Breeze Charters / 1-800-204-9125 / www.seabreezecharters.net

Coho Charters & Motel / 1-800-339-2646 / www.cohocharters.com

Pacific Salmon Charters, 191 Howerton Way / 1-800-831-2695 / www.pacificsalmoncharters.com

Beacon Charters, 332 Elizabeth St. / 642-2138 / www.fishbeacon.com

Sea Sport Fishing Charters, 221 Howerton Way / 1-866-211-6611 / www.seasportfishingcharters.com

Launching

Port of Ilwaco, 165 Howerton Ave. / 642-3143 /800-slip marina located just inside the Columbia River bar with ramp and two slings / www.portofilwaco.com

Fishing Tackle

Englund Marine & Industrial Supply, 123 Howerton Way / 642-2308 / www.englundmarine.com

Hospital

Ocean Beach Hospital, 174 First Ave. N. / 642-3181

Airport

Portland International Airport, 7000 N.E. Airport Way, Portland, Ore. / 1-877-739-4636

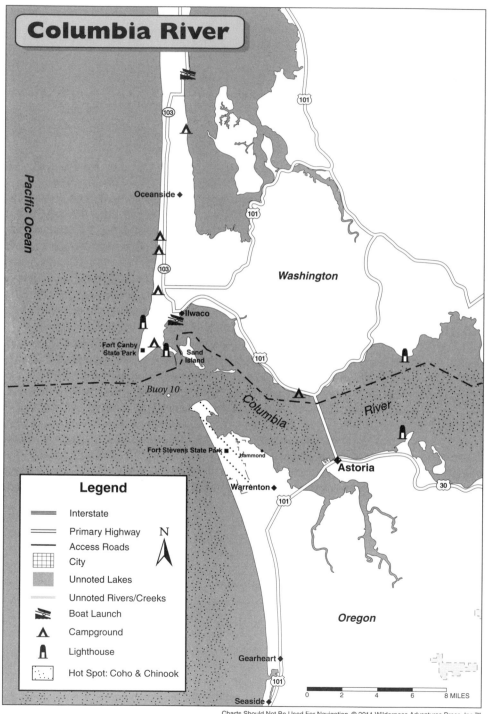

Columbia River

Pacific Ocean

Washington

Oregon

Oceanside ◆

Ilwaco

Fort Canby State Park

Sand Island

Buoy 10

Columbia

River

Fort Stevens State Park

Hammond

Astoria

Warrenton ◆

Gearheart ◆

Seaside ◆

Legend

═══	Interstate
──	Primary Highway
──	Access Roads
▦	City
	Unnoted Lakes
──	Unnoted Rivers/Creeks
⛵	Boat Launch
⛺	Campground
⛴	Lighthouse
⋰	Hot Spot: Coho & Chinook

N

0   2   4   6   8 MILES

Charts Should Not Be Used For Navigation. © 2011 Wilderness Adventures Press, Inc.™

Oregon Coast

Fisheries Management

Salmon anglers have a couple of wonderful things going for them in Oregon – excellent fishing in the ocean and in the many coastal bays, and one of the most beautiful coastlines in the world on which to enjoy it.

A wealth of angling opportunity exists here for small-boat fishermen, from the ports on the Columbia River just across the water boundary from Washington, to Brookings, near the California line.

In Oregon, fishery managers have long recognized the need to identify hatchery fish so they can be distinguished from wild fish and, when necessary, managed differently than wild ones. For example, managers understand the desirability of releasing hatchery fish in the lower portions of their rivers when possible so they will tend to linger there on their return from the ocean. Meanwhile, wild fish move through to the upper river where they may not be as much subject to fishing pressure, and this enhances the opportunity for managers to allow anglers to fish selectively on the hatchery stocks.

Selective fishing here, as elsewhere, often is important, and often is driven as it is elsewhere – by its impacts on the "bycatch". During the first years of this century, for example, the entire non-Indian spring chinook fishery on the Columbia River, both sport and commercial combined, permitted – on average – just a two percent impact on the wild portion of the run. So in order to fish, anglers and netters had to be able to identify wild fish and release them. When the handling of wild fish in that selective fishery was estimated to have killed two percent of the wild total, the entire fishery shut down, even though thousands of hatchery chinook continued to pass into the river.

In the ocean, all of the salmon fisheries off the Oregon coast are divided into geographical zones and are tightly restricted. Where once they traditionally ran Memorial Day through Labor Day and fishing was unselective, it became unusual through the early part of the 21st century if coho seasons lasted more than two or three months. Selective-fishing rules for coho became the norm, and the old three-fish daily bag limit was reduced, as it was in Washington. You had to know the area in which you were fishing, and you had to know which day of the week it was, because north of Cape Falcon, you got only a five-day-a-week fishery, as you did on

the Washington coast. South of Cape Falcon, fishing usually ran seven days a week, but when the quota was reached, fishing shut down.

In Oregon waters north of Cape Falcon, closures on certain days of the week also governed the chinook fishery. South of Cape Falcon, chinook fishing generally ran seven days per week, and most ocean chinook fishing was managed on a season basis without a quota. Seasons sometimes ran from March or May through October, although chinook fishing closed entirely in most south-of-Falcon waters to protect California's Sacramento River fall chinook run after it fell on hard times a few years into the 21st century.

South of Humbug Mountain, which is located between Port Orford and Gold Beach on the southern Oregon coast, coho fishing sometimes was entirely prohibited to protect ESA-listed wild Oregon coastal coho, which tend to distribute themselves in a southerly direction. Wild coastal coho don't mix with as many hatchery fish in the south as they do in the north, since most of the hatchery coho in Oregon are produced in the Columbia. So, any fishery tends to become harder on the wild coastal fish as you move south and the ratio of wild fish to hatchery fish increases. However, while federal Endangered Species Act limitations are generally more restrictive for southern Oregon and northern California stocks, managers have authorized coho seasons in that area in recent years. Impacts to those stocks have been managed to stay within guidelines provided by the National Marine Fisheries Service.

Oregon Fishing Licenses

Annual fishing, resident $33
Annual fishing, nonresident $106.25
Annual tag to fish for salmon, steelhead, sturgeon, and Pacific halibut, resident and
    nonresident $26.50
One-day fishing, resident and nonresident $16.75
Two-day fishing, resident and nonresident $31.50
Three-day fishing, resident and non-resident $46.25
Four-day fishing, resident and nonresident $58.00
Seven-day fishing, nonresident only $59.75
Daily licenses include tag to fish for salmon, steelhead, sturgeon, and Pacific halibut
Hatchery harvest tag, resident and nonresident $16.50 (which, along with tag to
    fish for salmon, steelhead, sturgeon, and Pacific halibut, authorizes harvest of 10
    fin-clipped hatchery salmon)

Oregon Information Sources

National Association of Charterboat Operators / www.nacocharters.org
Oregon Coast Sportfishing Association / www.oregoncoastalfishing.net

Columbia River

The northern end of the coast is dominated, of course, by the Columbia, which at its peak was probably the greatest salmon-producing river in the history of the world. It still produces its share, and anglers fish out of the Columbia ports virtually all summer long.

When the ocean is open under state and Pacific Fishery Management Council regulations, many small-boat anglers cross the Columbia River bar, one of the most dangerous on the coast. Like all bars, it's usually worse on an ebbing tide, when boaters face the additional hazard of being swept out to sea if anything goes wrong. Each boat operator must decide for him- or herself whether to attempt the crossing, depending on water conditions, weather, the seaworthiness of his boat, and his own ability as a skipper. Low slack and high slack usually provide the best bar conditions, with a flood tide the next-best time to try to cross. Sometimes the bar will be too rough even on an incoming tide, and the Coast Guard will close it to some or all recreational boats, and will announce the decision on Channel 16 VHF. It also will patrol the bar to turn back small craft.

The entrance to the Columbia isn't always rough, but it is unpredictable. And you can't judge conditions by what you see where you launch. The day may be calm in the harbor, but when you get to the bar you may find it ugly. Clatsop Spit, inside the river's south jetty, can be particularly unpredictable, especially on an ebb tide, spawning dangerous breakers and directing them toward the shipping channel to its north. Stay north of the red buoys here, especially around ebb tide.

Likewise, Peacock Spit, which is outside the river's north jetty on the Washington side, can produce waves that break in a variety of directions. If you should lose power, an ebb current is apt to carry you into this area and put you in danger of capsizing. When leaving the river, never proceed north of the green-buoy line. And if you round the spit on its seaward side, give it wide clearance, because even on calm days it can produce breakers in unexpected locations without warning.

Most chinook are caught within 3 miles of the beach off the Columbia, regulations permitting, although you may run several miles along the coast before you start fishing.

For coho, you may want to run out to the navigational buoy, then steer a southwesterly course of about 200 degrees. Troll for both species, a little deeper for chinook, with a fresh or frozen anchovy. Planers are popular for silvers, but rarely are used for chinook in this area. Many anglers here prefer 5 to 7 ounces of lead, and try to fish 20 to 30 feet below the surface.

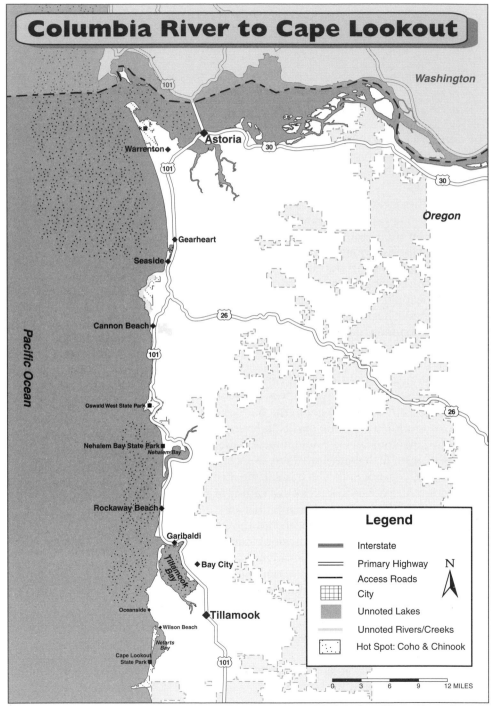

Columbia River to Cape Lookout

Washington

101

Warrenton ◆ ◆ Astoria   30

101   30

Oregon

◆ Gearheart

Seaside ◆

26

Cannon Beach ◆

101

26

Oswald West State Park ■

Nehalem Bay State Park ■
Nehalem Bay

Rockaway Beach ◆

Garibaldi ◆

Tillamook Bay   ◆ Bay City

Oceanside ◆

◆ Wilson Beach

◆ Tillamook

Netarts Bay

Cape Lookout State Park ■   101

Pacific Ocean

Legend

═══	Interstate
──	Primary Highway
──	Access Roads
⊞	City
▓	Unnoted Lakes
▒	Unnoted Rivers/Creeks
⋮	Hot Spot: Coho & Chinook

N

0   3   6   9   12 MILES

Charts Should Not Be Used For Navigation. © 2011 Wilderness Adventures Press, Inc.™

Tillamook Bay

A few miles south of the Columbia on the Oregon coast is Tillamook Bay, which is fed by five rivers – the Miami, Kilchis, Wilson, Trask, and Tillamook. All support salmon. The Wilson and Trask are the biggest and by far the most productive.

Spring chinook start funneling into the bay about Mother's Day, headed mostly for the Trask. Coho become fairly numerous the middle of June, and stay that way through Labor Day; and fall chinook start to show late in July or the first part of August. Both species are bound for all five rivers. Many of the fall chinook are very large, and several 50-pounders usually are caught each season, as well as – occasionally – a 60.

Anglers here fish in the ocean primarily for chinook during the summer, then fish for chinook in the bay starting about Labor Day. An in-bay fishery for coho is not as extensive as the one for chinook, apparently because anglers prefer to target the larger species, and because coho don't bite quite as well as chinook in the bay.

On the ocean, anglers use planers for both species, although downriggers have been gaining popularity. Chinook stick closer to the beach, and anglers will seek them from the mouth of the bay to just north of Nehalem, from about the 10-fathom line inward. For coho you fish farther out, starting at the 40- or 50-fathom line.

Inside the bay, a spreader and dropper is used for chinook – a sort of three-way swivel with one leg about 3 inches long, and the other 1.5 inches long, with a weight on the short leg and a 6-foot leader on the other. Cut the leader in half and insert a bead chain swivel, then bait up with cut-plug herring.

Bay anglers here don't use the term "mooch", but that's what they do. They dangle their herring over the side of the boat, kicking their motors in and out of gear at very low speed. It's a crowded fishery, and your terminal tackle must be as nearly as possible directly under the boat, so sinkers of 4 to 6 ounces are common, and 12 ounces are not unusual, depending on the size of the tide.

It's important to fish deep. You want your bait suspended above the bottom of the bay, but when you lower your rod you should tap bottom.

The Tillamook bar can be tough, with breaking water on an ebb tide, although it's frequently good in the summer when it sometimes can be crossed on an ebb as long as it's not a big ebb. In September and October, especially, the bar can get ugly. Check the Coast Guard tower near the harbor entrance. The Coast Guard will post a "rough bar" warning there when conditions warrant.

About the last 100 yards of the north jetty on the seaward end are submerged, and conditions there can be dangerous. Avoid that part of the jetty and use extreme caution in the channel just south of it. Also, remember that the channel changes often from natural silting and scouring, so navigate with care. Likewise, the last 100 yards of the south jetty on the seaward end also are submerged, and boaters must avoid

that area when entering or exiting. The area behind the end of the south jetty also can be hazardous, and boats capsize there nearly every season. The bottom of the bay is mostly sand or mud. Rocks are a hazard only in one place, which is well marked.

The bell buoy and the whistler buoy outside the bay moved to new locations in 2006, so be sure to input new coordinates for them in your GPS if the material it now contains is outdated.

Most ocean anglers launch at the Port of Garibaldi ramp or at the Old Mill Marina in Garibaldi. A couple of other ramps are located farther from the mouth, and are popular for in-the-bay fishing.

Hub City Information
Portland
Population – 557,706 Area Code – 503 County – Multnomah

Hotels & Motels

The Paramount Hotel, 808 S.W. Taylor St. / 1-800-716-6199 /
www.portlandparamount.com

Hotel de Luxe, 729 S.W. 15th Ave. / 1-866-986-8085 /
www.hoteldeluxeportland.com

Marriott Portland-City Center, 520 W.W. Broadway / 226-6300 /
www.marriottportland.com

River Place, 1510 S.W. Harbor Way / 1-800-227-1333 /
www.larkspurhotels.com/collection/riverplace

Holiday Inn Express Jantzen Beach, 2300 N. Hayden Island Drive / 1-800-315-2621
/ www.ichotelsgroup.com

Best Western Pony Soldier Portland Airport, 9901 N.E. Sandy Boulevard /
1-800-634-7669 / www.book.bestwestern.com

Hampton Inn Portland Airport, 8633 N.E. Airport Way / 288-2423 /
www.hamptoninn.com/en/hp/hotels/index.jhtml?ctyhocn=PDXAPHX

Restaurants

Mother's Bistro & Bar, 212 S.W. Stark St. / Upscale home cooking / 464-1122 /
www.mothersbistro.com

Kells Irish Restaurant & Pub, 112 S.W. Second Ave. / 227-4057 /
www.kellsirish.com/portland

Rock Bottom Restaurant & Brewery, 206 S.W. Morrison St. / 796-2739 /
www.rockbottom.com

Escape From New York Pizza, 622 N.W. 23rd Ave. / 227-5423

Besaw's, 2301 N.W. Savier St. / American / 228-2619 / www.besaws.com

Fishing Tackle

Fisherman's Marine & Outdoor, 1120 N. Hayden Meadows Drive / 283-0044 /
www.fishermans-marine.com

Sports Authority, 10245 N.E. Cascades Parkway / 493-7374 /
www.sportsauthority.com

Hospital

Legacy Good Samaritan Medical Center, 1015 N.W. 22nd Ave. / 413-7711

Airport

Portland International Airport, 7000 N.E. Airport Way / 1-877-739-4636

Astoria - Warrenton
**Population – Astoria 10,045, Warrenton 4,096 Area Code – 503
County – Clatsop**

Hotels & Motels

Holiday Inn Express Hotel & Suites, 204 W. Marine Drive, Astoria / 1-877-863-4780 / www.hiexpress.com

Red Lion Inn Astoria, 400 Industry St., Astoria / 325-7373 / www.redlion.com

Best Western Lincoln Inn, 555 Hamburg Ave., Astoria / 325-2205 / www.bestwesternoregon.com\

Shilo Inns Suites Hotel, 1609 E. Harbor Drive, Warrenton / 861-2181 / www.shiloinns.com

Bed & Breakfasts

Rose River Inn Bed and Breakfast, 1510 Franklin Ave., Astoria / 1-888-876-0028 / www.roseriverinn.com

Clementine's Bed & Breakfast, 847 Exchange St., Astoria / 1-800-521-6801 / www.clementines-bb.com

Restaurants

Dooger's Seafood & Grill, 103 U.S. 101, Warrenton / 861-2839

Baked Alaska Fine Dining & Public House, 1 Twelfth St., Astoria / Seafood, meats / 325-7414 / www.bakedak.com

Silver Salmon Grille, 1105 Commercial, Astoria / Seafood, steaks, pasta / 338-6640 / www.silversalmongrille.com

Ship Inn British Pub & Restaurant, 1 Second St., Astoria / Seafood, pub food / 325-0033

Gunderson's Cannery Café, 1 Sixth St., Astoria / Seafood, meats, pasta / 325-8642 / www.cannerycafe.com

Wet Dog Café and Astoria Brewing Co., 144 11th St., Astoria / Soup, sandwiches, burgers, seafood, meats / 325-6975 / www.wetdogcafe.com

Charters

Todd Dielman Fishing, 91120 Youngs River Road, Astoria / 338-7467 / www.dielmansguides.com

Tiki Charters, 350 Industry St., Astoria / 325-7818 / www.tikicharter.com

Charlton Charters, 470 N.E. Skipanon Drive, Warrenton / 861-2429 / www.charltoncharters.com

Defiance Charters, departs from Hammond Marina / 440-2413 / www.defiancecharters.com

Perry's Fishing Adventures, 84647Junction Road, Seaside / 1-866-738-6991 / www.fishingwithval.com

Tackle Time Charters, 530 E. Harbor St., Warrenton / 861-3693 /
www.tackletime.net

Merrin Fisheries Thunderbird, 45 N.E. Harbor Place, Warrenton / 861-1270

Launching

John Day County Park, on Columbia River off U.S. 30 about 5 miles east of Astoria

Westport Boat Launch, about 0.5 mile north of Westport on Columbia River

Port of Astoria East Basin, Two-lane ramp, downtown / 325-4521

Warrenton Marina, 550 N.E. Harbor Place / Two-lane ramp, generous parking /
861-3822

Hammond Bay Marina, on Lake Drive, Warrenton / multi-lane ramp

Fishing Tackle

Tackle Time Bait Shop, 530 E. Harbor St., Warrenton / 861-3693 /
www.tackletime.net/baitshop

Englund Marine & Industrial Supply, 95 Hamburg Ave., Astoria / 325-4341 /
www.englundmarine.com

Hospital

Columbia Memorial Hospital, 2111 Exchange St., Astoria / 325-4321

Tillamook
Population – 4,675 Area Code – 503 County – Tillamook

Hotels & Motels

Shilo Inn Suites Hotel – Tillamook, 2515 N. Main / 842-7971 / www.shiloinns.com

Best Western Inn & Suites, 1722 Makinster Road / 842-7599 /
www.bestwestern.com/hotels

Terimore Lodging by the Sea, 5105 Crab Ave. W., Netarts / 1-800-635-1821 /
www.oregoncoast.com/terimore

Comfort Inn, 502 Garibaldi Ave., Garibaldi / 322-3338 / www.comfortinn.com

Harborview Inn & RV Park, 302 S. Seventh St., Garibaldi / 322-3521 /
www.harborviewfun.com

Ocean Front Cabins, 1610 Pacific Ave., Tillamook / 1-888-845-8470 /
www.oceanfrontcabins.com

Bed & Breakfasts

Thyme and Tide Bed and Breakfast, 5015 Grand Ave., Oceanside / 842-5227 /
www.thyme-and-tide.com

Restaurants

Pacific House Restaurant, 2102 First St., Tillamook / Seafood, Northwest cuisine, Mexican / 354-2211

Roseanna's Café, 1490 Pacific Ave., Oceanside / Seafood, chicken, pasta / 842-7351 / www.roseannascafe.com

Blue Heron French Cheese Co., 2001 Blue Heron Drive, Tillamook / Deli foods / 842-8281 / www.blueheronoregon.com

The River Edge Grill, 12140 Wilson River Highway, Tillamook / Local seafoods / 842-3474

La Mexicana, 2203 Third St., Tillamook / Mexican / 842-2101

Charters

Garibaldi Charters, Seventh and Highway 101, Garibaldi / 1-800-900-4665 / www.garibaldicharters.com

SIGGI – G Ocean Charters, 611 S. Commercial, Garibaldi / 322-3285 / www.siggig.com

Kerri Lyn Charters, 611 Commercial, Garibaldi / 355-2439

Troller Deep Sea Charter, 304 Mooring Basin, Garibaldi / 322-3666

Fishing Oregon, Tillamook / 842-5171 / www.fish-oregon.com

Sidewinder Charters, Departs Garibaldi Marina / 360-740-7888 / www.sidewindercharters.com

Launching

Tillamook County Launch Ramps / www.co.tillamook.or.us/gov/Parks/BoatLaunches

Port of Garibaldi Marina Launch Ramp, 402 S. Seventh St., Garibaldi / 355-3292 / (North Tillamook Bay)

Memaloose Launch Ramp, (South Tillamook Bay)

Old Mill Marina, 210 S. Third St., Garibaldi / 322-0322 / www.oldmill.us/html/park

Fishing Tackle

Tillamook Sporting Goods, 2207 Main Ave. N., Suite B, Tillamook / 842-4334 / www.tillamooksportinggoods.com

Hospital

Tillamook County General Hospital, 1000 Third St., Tillamook / 842-4444

Newport and Depoe Bay

Chinook become more prevalent as you move south on the Oregon coast, although on the central part of the coast much of the fishery centers on coho. Much of the fishing here is done with a planer, and many anglers run a dodger or – less commonly – a flasher behind it, followed by a herring for chinook or a hoochie for coho. You can plug-cut your herring, or utilize strips, but whole herring is common when fishing for chinook, and many coho anglers will add a chunk or strip of herring to their hoochie.

South of Tillamook Bay, the next real concentration of small-boat fishing takes place around Newport, which is located on Yaquina Bay. Heading seaward from the bay, you can start to fish around the whistle buoy, about 3 miles from the beach. Anglers target coho here, although they'll occasionally pick up chinook. Some anglers run all the way to Stonewall Banks, about 18 miles offshore, which is a productive area for both coho and chinook.

The season usually opens in early spring, and typically closes about the end of October. Coho fishing often opens between mid-June and early July, and its closing date often depends on the number of fish caught and the size of the coho sportfishing quota.

Tides don't make much difference here in when and how you fish. However, under some conditions an ebbing tide can make for a sloppy bar, even though small-boat anglers consider Yaquina Bay to have one of the three most boater-friendly bars in Oregon, along with Coos Bay and Brookings. Submerged rocks along the inside length of both the south and north jetties pose some danger for boaters who approach too close, and submerged rocks also are located near the tip of the north jetty.

Don't cut corners. Remain in the channel leaving the bay, all the way to Buoy No. 1. Enter the channel there on your return. Yaquina Reef lies parallel to the beach outside the north jetty, and always is dangerous even in light winds. A large swell can cause a destructive breaker here with no warning, even in calm seas, and you never should fish near the reef. South Reef, which parallels the beach south of the south jetty, is an extension of Yaquina Reef, and is equally dangerous.

The Port of Newport operates one ramp, and it will accommodate several boats at a time.

A small-boat fleet also fishes out of Depoe Bay, about 13 miles to the north. It has a very narrow and hazardous channel, and it's important that you talk to knowledgeable local skippers before you attempt it. A boat clearing the entrance should proceed directly seaward until reaching the red bell buoy. Landward of

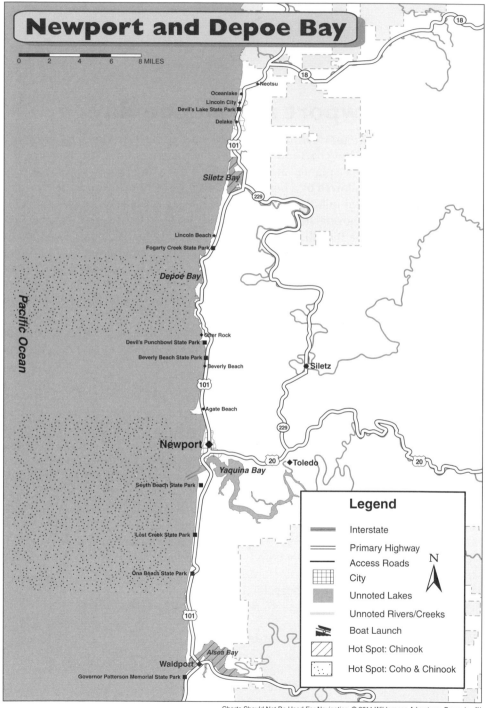

Newport and Depoe Bay

0   2   4   6   8 MILES

Neotsu

Oceanlake
Lincoln City
Devil's Lake State Park
Delake

101

Siletz Bay

229

Lincoln Beach
Fogarty Creek State Park

Depoe Bay

Otter Rock
Devil's Punchbowl State Park
Beverly Beach State Park
Beverly Beach

Siletz

Agate Beach

101

Pacific Ocean

Newport

20   Toledo   20

Yaquina Bay

South Beach State Park

Lost Creek State Park

Ona Beach State Park

101

Alsea Bay

Waldport
Governor Patterson Memorial State Park

Legend

	Interstate
	Primary Highway
	Access Roads
	City
	Unnoted Lakes
	Unnoted Rivers/Creeks
	Boat Launch
	Hot Spot: Chinook
	Hot Spot: Coho & Chinook

N

that buoy to the north is North Reef. Seas can break over it from the northwest and southwest simultaneously, and you never should take a boat near it. South of the entrance is South Reef, also known as Flat Rock, and waves almost always are breaking here. Returning home, always run first to the bell buoy, then in from there.

Both North Reef and South Reef are unusually close to the channel, and in bad weather, breakers from North Reef may break right across the channel, making the harbor inaccessible.

All boats are required to sound a prolonged blast of the horn when entering or leaving Depoe Bay. Custom awards the right-of-way to inbound vessels.

Upwelling of the Pacific can bring cold water onto the beach anywhere along this coast, and that can result in fog at any time. Often the fog will burn off in the morning, but sometimes it might not lift for a week. Under these conditions, some anglers will follow a charter boat out. Others will navigate with GPS chartplotter, but many anglers stay in their moorages then, not wanting to risk it.

In September and October, in-bay fisheries for chinook also occur at Siletz and Alsea Bays. Trolled baitfish is standard, although some anglers take fish with eggs under bobbers. Both bays have launching facilities, but neither has an entrance jetty, and the mouths of both are very dangerous.

Hub City Information
Depoe Bay
Population – 1,355 Area Code – 541 County – Lincoln

City officials maintain that Depoe Bay, at six acres, is the smallest harbor in the world, with moorage for 137 boats. The harbor entrance, directly from the Pacific Ocean, is 30 feet wide and 8 feet deep.

Hotels And Motels

Crown Pacific Inn, Highway 101 and Northeast Bechill Street / 765-7773 / www.crownpacificinn.com

Inn at Arch Rock, 70 N.W. Sunset St. / 1-800-767-1835 / www.innatarchrock.com

Bed & Breakfasts

The Harbor Lights Inn, 235 S.E. Bay View Ave. / 1-800-228-0448 / www.theharborlightsinn.com

Whale Cove Inn, 2345 S. Highway 101 / 1-800-628-3409 / www.whalecoveinn.net

Restaurants

Gracie's Sea Hag Restaurant and Lounge, 58 N. Highway 101 / Seafood, steak, pasta / 765-2734 / www.theseahag.com

Wing Wa Restaurant & Lounge, 330 U.S. 101 / Asian / 765-2288

Jack's Steaks & Seafood, 3245 U.S. 101 / 764-4222

Italian Riviera Restaurant and Piano Bar, 3400 N. Highway 101 / Chicken, steak, pasta, pizza / 764-3400 / www.italriv.com

Charters

Dockside Charters, 270 Coast Guard Place / 1-800-733-8915 / www.docksidedepoebay.com

Tradewinds Charters, Highway 101 downtown / 1-800-445-8730 / www.tradewindscharters.com

The Mariner at Depoe Bay, Dock 1, Depoe Bay Harbor / 270-6163 / www.depoebaymariner.com

Newport
Population – 10,240 Area Code – 541 County – Lincoln

Hotels & Motels

The Sylvia Beach Hotel, 267 N.W. Cliff / (A reading retreat, with no TVs, no radios, no phones) / 265-5428 / www.sylviabeachhotel.com

Elizabeth Street Inn, 232 S.W. Elizabeth St. / 1-877-265-9400 / www.elizabethstreetinn.com

Hallmark Resort, 744 S.W. Elizabeth St. / 1-888-448-4449 / www.hallmarkinns.com

Comfort Inn Newport Hotel, 531 S.W. Fall St. / 265-6203 / www.newporthotel.com

La Quinta Inn & Suites, 45 S.E. 32nd St. / 867-7727 / www.lq.com

Bed & Breakfasts

Newport Belle Bed and Breakfast, 2126 S.E. OSU Drive / 1-800-348-1922 / www.newportbelle.com

Restaurants

Mo's, 622 S.W. Bay Boulevard / The original location, and perhaps the most famous chowder house on the Oregon coast / 265-2979 / www.moschowder.com

Mo's Annex, 657 S.W. Bay Boulevard / (Across street from original, with a view of Yaquina Bay)

Quimby's Restaurant, 740 W. Olive St. / Seafood / 265-9919 / www.quimbysrestaurant.com

Saffron Salmon, 859 S.W. Bay Boulevard / Seafood / 265-8921 / www.saffronsalmon.com

Charters

Newport Tradewinds Deep Sea Fishing, 653 S.W. Bay Boulevard / 1-800-676-7819 / www.newporttradewinds.com

Newport Marina Store and Charters, 2128 S.E. Marine Science Drive / 867-4470 / www.nmscharters.com

Yaquina Bay Charters, 1000 S.E. Bay Boulevard / 1-866-465-6801 / www.yaquinabaycharters.com

Captain's Charters, 343 S.W. Bay Boulevard / 1-800-865-7441 / www.captainsreel.com

Launching

Sawyer's Landing RV Park and Marina, 4098 Yaquina Bay Road / 1-888-216-3907

Port of Newport Marina & RV Park, 2120 S.E. Marine Science Drive, Southbeach / Three lanes, parking for about 200 vehicles with trailers / 867-3321 / www.portofnewport.com

Fishing Tackle

Englund Marine & Industrial Supply, 880 S.E. Bay Boulevard / 265-9275 / www.englundmarine.com

Hospital

Samaritan Pacific Communities Hospital, 930 S.W. Abbey / 265-2244

Florence and Reedsport

Farther down the coast beyond Alsea Bay lie Florence, at the mouth of the Siuslaw River, and Reedsport, near the mouth of the Umpqua River on Winchester Bay. Both areas offer excellent summer salmon angling.

The quality of the chinook fishing in both areas depends on the year, but the bar at the mouth of the Siuslaw River is dangerous, and not a lot of small-boat sport fishing occurs out of there. The Siuslaw offers only a narrow channel extending past the jetties, and even a moderate swell may prevent small boats from crossing the bar, especially on an ebb. Breakers may occur on the south side of the channel inside the jetties with even a small swell, and at the outer ends of both the north and south jetties.

At Winchester Bay near Reedsport, boaters should run along the inside of the south jetty leaving and entering. The area near the north jetty can be dangerous, because it develops small breakers when a swell is running, and large breakers may come in from the outside. From the end of the north jetty to the black bell buoy, a little swell can result in breakers large enough to capsize a boat.

Generally, coho fishing always is good in this part of Oregon. The fish tend to arrive toward the end of June, and remain in these waters well into August, although the fishery may actually close earlier. In fact, Winchester Bay has one of the most consistently productive coho catches throughout the season on the entire Oregon coast.

The top-notch action for silvers will begin to wind down in both areas no later than the middle to latter part of August, providing regulations allow it to remain open that long, and more chinook will begin to show in the catch then. The coho that anglers are catching here – as elsewhere on the Oregon coast – tend to be predominately Columbia River fish, which are working their way northward to the river mouth, so the fishing tends to last a little later in the season as you proceed north.

Anglers who fish off the coast here use a planer with flasher and hoochie for coho. Some use a downrigger. For chinook, they'll generally use a planer or a downrigger, and will troll a whole baitfish.

The Reedsport area supports a substantial chinook fishery in the bay each fall, which typically starts about mid-August, and in late August an in-river fishery begins near Florence. Both usually continue through October.

Launching at Florence is confined to the Port of Siuslaw ramp, a two-laner. Near Reedsport, most saltwater anglers launch at the town of Winchester Bay, where county-operated Salmon Harbor Marina provides one two-lane ramp and one four-lane. The marina offers 550 moorages with daily, weekly, monthly, or annual rates, and a county-operated fuel dock.

A one-lane ramp is available in Reedsport on the Umpqua River, and another is located in Gardiner, a few miles north, although this county-operated ramp is not usable at low tides and is not well maintained. Both are utilized mostly by river fishermen and by clam diggers.

Hub City Information
Reedsport
Population – 4,378 Area Code – 541 County – Douglas

Hotels & Motels

Economy Inn, 1593 Highway 101 / 1-800-799-9970 /
www.economyinnreedsport.com
Anchor Bay Inn, 1821 Winchester Ave. / 1-800-767-1821
Winchester Bay Inn, 390 Broadway, Winchester Bay / 1-800-246-1462 /
www.winbayinn.com
Harbor View Motel, 540 Beach Boulevard, Winchester Bay / 271-3352

Restaurants

Waterfront Restaurant & Lounge, 351 River Front Way / 271-1080
Schooner Inn Café, 423 River Front Way / 271-3945
Harbor Light Family Restaurant, 930 Highway 101 S. / 271-3848
Giff's on the Bay Restaurant, 142 Bayfront Loop, Winchester Bay / 271-2512

Charters

Strike Zone Charters, 465 Beach Boulevard, Winchester Bay / 1-800-230-5350
Rivers End Guide Service, 3421 Ridgeway Drive / 1-888-388-3125
www.umpquafishing.com
Krista Jay Charters, 182 Bay Loop, Winchester Bay / 271-5698
Salmon Harbor Charters, 495 Beach Boulevard, Winchester Bay / 271-2010 /
www.salmonharborcharters.com

Launching

Salmon Harbor Marina, Winchester Bay / Two launch ramps here in one of the
largest recreational marinas on the Oregon coast, with 550 slips

Fishing Tackle

Turman Tackle, 139 N. Third St. / 271-0586 / www.turman-tackle.com
Reedsport Outdoor Store, 2049 Winchester Ave. / 271-2311
Stockade Market & Tackle Shop, 350 Beach Boulevard, Winchester Bay / 271-3800

Hospital

Lower Umpqua Hospital, 600 Ranch Road / 271-2171

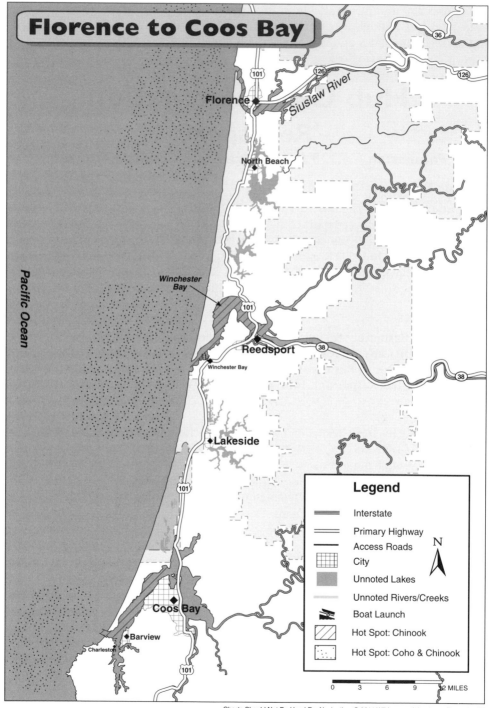

Florence to Coos Bay

Pacific Ocean

Florence

Siuslaw River

North Beach

Winchester Bay

Reedsport

Winchester Bay

Lakeside

Coos Bay

Barview

Charleston

Legend

Interstate
Primary Highway
Access Roads
City
Unnoted Lakes
Unnoted Rivers/Creeks
Boat Launch
Hot Spot: Chinook
Hot Spot: Coho & Chinook

N

0   3   6   9   12 MILES

Charts Should Not Be Used For Navigation. © 2011 Wilderness Adventures Press, Inc.™

Coos Bay

Farther down the coast, around Coos Bay, large runs of coho start passing through about the middle to the end of June. They'll continue to come through at least a couple of weeks into August and then will begin to taper off.

The chinook fishery here can be good at times. Fish close to the beach for them. Many anglers mooch near the bar for returning fall fish.

On the ocean, it's mostly a trolling scene, however. A typical angler uses a planer, about 3 feet of leader between it and a flasher, then 8 to 20 inches of leader tied to a hoochie with a herring chunk or strip. Some anglers use a whole herring instead of a hoochie, in which case they'll sometimes eliminate the flasher.

Anglers pick up chinook out of Coos Bay the entire season, often inside the 25-fathom line, which is 2 to 3 miles from the beach, but local anglers favor some deepwater spots as well. Coho usually are outside of 50 fathoms, although not always.

The Coos Bay Bar is one of the gentler on the coast. The channel is deep and, usually, the water is fairly calm. Steep swells may build on the bar, but usually they won't break clear across. Sometimes, anglers can even cross on an ebbing tide, although not when the ocean is rough.

Some words of warning, however: Watch out for commercial traffic in the channel that could push you into dangerous areas. Avoid the shoals that extend toward the channel from inside the south jetty, where breakers often occur. And when departing the bay, be sure to clear Buoy No. 3 before turning north. The north jetty extends about 200 yards, submerged, past its visible terminus, and waves break in this area much of the time.

Launching facilities here are good. There's a six-lane ramp in the hamlet of Charleston, near the harbor's mouth. Other ramps are available farther inland.

Bandon

Large numbers of coho pass through the ocean here in the summer, and anglers who operate out of Bandon – many of them fishing from charter vessels – do well on chinook. A fairly large in-river fishery takes place here, too, in the Coquille. However, bar conditions here often are dangerous for small-boat operators, much like those at Florence on the Siuslaw River.

Port Orford

South of Bandon is Port Orford. There is no real harbor here, and sport effort out of Port Orford targeting salmon is minimal.

Hub City Information
Coos Bay
Population – 16,210 Area Code – 541 County – Coos

Hotels & Motels

Best Western Holiday Motel, 411 N. Bayshore Drive / 269-5111 / www.bestwesternoregon.com

Red Lion Hotel Coos Bay, 1313 N. Bayshore Drive / 267-4141

Edgewater Inn Coos Bay, 275 E. Johnson Ave. / 1-800-233-0423

Bed & Breakfasts

This Olde House Bed & Breakfast, 202 Alder Ave. / 267-5224 / www.thisoldehousebb.com

Coos Bay Manor Bed & Breakfast Inn, 955 S. Fifth St. / 1-800-269-1224 / www.coosbaymanor.com

Restaurants

Benetti's Italian Restaurant, 260 S., Broadway / 267-6066 / www.benettis.com

Blue Heron Bistro, 100 Commercial Ave. / Seafood, German / 267-3933 / www.blueheronbistro.com

Abby's Legendary Pizza, 997 S. First / 267-5839 / www.abbys.com

Charters

Betty Kay Charters / 888-9021 / www.bettykaycharters.com

Prowler Charters, 325 First St. S.E., Bandon / 1-888-347-1901 / www.prowlercharters.com

Launching

Charleston Marina, 63534 Kingfisher Road, Charleston / Six-lane ramp, tackle, bait, marine supplies / 888-2548 / www.charlestonmarina.com

Fishing Tackle

Basin Tackle Shop, 63510 Kingfisher Road, Charleston / 888-3811

Bite's On Bait & Tackle, 750 Newmark Ave. / 888-4015

Englund Marine & Industrial Supply, 91146 Cape Arago Highway / 888-6623 / www.englundmarine.com

Hospital

Bay Area Hospital, 1775 Thompson Road / 269-8111

Airport

Southwest Oregon Regional Airport, 2348 Colorado St., North Bend / The only commercial airport on the Oregon coast, served by United, with service to San Francisco Bay and Portland.

Gold Beach and Brookings

Farther south on the coast is Gold Beach, where the fabled Rogue River spills into the Pacific, and south of there is Brookings and the mouth of the Chetco River. The two are a study in contrasts.

The Port of Brookings has the largest number of bar crossings in Oregon, after the Columbia River, but the bar is so kind you can hardly tell when you get to the ocean. In the Chetco River, inside the bar, are several modern ramps.

At Gold Beach, however, conditions can be dangerous. Many a boat has capsized in the surf here, and many an angler has drowned. Although annual dredging has tamed the bar to some extent, and the Coast Guard monitors conditions there in the summer, exercise plenty of caution here during periods of large ocean swells.

Some anglers fish only in the river at Gold Beach, inside the bar. A public ramp that provides four lanes and two floats is located here at the Port of Gold Beach. Jot's Resort provides a ramp for the use of its guests, but it can be problematic at some stages of the tide. The in-river fishery occurs mostly in August and early September, and can attract a couple of hundred boats per day.

If you can get over the bar, ocean fishing often can be excellent, but most salmon angling in recent years has occurred inside the bar in the lower reaches of the river. Fishing there has been effective, not to mention safer and nearly immune to bad weather, and in-river seasons have been more dependable, commonly running from July into October, while ocean seasons have tended to be virtually unpredictable.

Anglers who fish the tidal waters inside the bar rig almost exclusively with anchovies, occasionally with a sardine, and fish it on what they call a "Rogue bait rig". It consists of a few beads on a monofilament leader followed by a spinner blade in front of the hooks. The anchovy is fished head-toward-the-angler, with the spinner blade in front of its nose. The leader, of 4 to 6 feet, is tied to a small spreader, typically weighted with 2 to 3 ounces of lead, sometimes more.

Anglers who do head over the bar lean toward large boats with lots of horsepower. Tides are important, and wind is a factor, too. You must go in and out on the slack or the flood. Ebb tides can be lethal.

"But you hardly ever see any boats on the ocean for salmon anymore," one local guide observed. "Just for bottom fish."

Inside the channel itself – between the jetties – gravel bars and shoals on the south side can create breakers to 6 feet when a heavy swell is running, and prevailing northwest summer winds can push you into them if you're not paying attention. Trolling by small-boat operators inside the jetties often becomes crowded, and

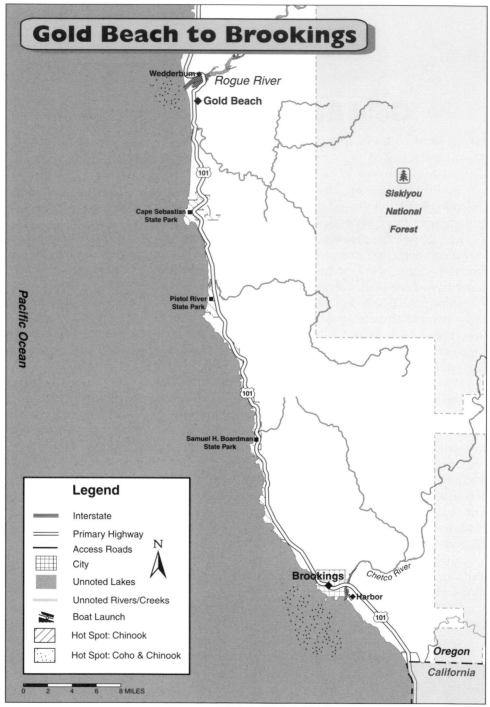

Gold Beach to Brookings

Wedderburn
Rogue River
◆ Gold Beach

101

Siskiyou National Forest

Cape Sebastian State Park

Pacific Ocean

Pistol River State Park

101

Samuel H. Boardman State Park

Legend

Interstate	
Primary Highway	
Access Roads	
City	
Unnoted Lakes	
Unnoted Rivers/Creeks	
Boat Launch	
Hot Spot: Chinook	
Hot Spot: Coho & Chinook	

N

Brookings
Chetco River
◆ Harbor

101

Oregon
California

0 2 4 6 8 MILES

creates the possibility for trolling lines to get wrapped around a prop. If this or any other mishap should disable your boat here, be prepared to anchor immediately, otherwise prevailing winds and tidal currents are likely to carry you quickly onto the hazardous shoal.

At the outer ends of both jetties almost always are breakers, and when the sea is running from the west or the southwest, particularly, they can be very dangerous. The worst winds are from the south, which make the bar especially rough. You can preview bar conditions, by the way, by driving out on the north jetty from the community of Wedderburn.

Trolled frozen anchovies and frozen herring are popular bait for those who fish the ocean near Gold Beach, and generally are pulled behind a dodger or a flasher and fished with a Pink Lady or Deep Six. Twenty to 30 pulls of line will get you to the right depth. Occasionally, a sinker of 2.5 to 5 ounces is substituted for the planer.

Usually the first 3 miles from the beach are where you find chinook. They gather off the river mouth, where they strike readily at baits or lures. The fish here are big. Expect chinook to run 12 to 30 pounds, with a few to 40, and the average 22 to 27 pounds.

Anglers target chinook off Brookings, too, catching primarily Sacramento River stocks from California, along with some fish from the Klamath and the Rogue. Some Rogue stocks are south-turning, so anglers at Brookings are the beneficiaries.

Fishing starts usually around Memorial Day off the southern Oregon coast, and Labor Day weekend generally finds it open, too. But occasionally managers close it at times between those holidays. Sometimes regulations provide for some extended sport seasons to continue through October off the Chetco and off the Elk River, which is farther north near Cape Blanco, usually in a narrow coastal strip.

Like the Rogue, the Chetco offers fishing inside the bar, mainly in the fall. Anglers take some huge fish here then, with the ten largest each fall often in the 50- to 60-pound range. September and October are peak in-river months here, a little later than in the Rogue. Good fishing continues until the first heavy fall rains, when the fish move upriver. A shallow area inside the harbor entrance here, known as the West Jetty Rock Area, is covered at high tide and may appear to be navigable, but it is not.

Among those who contributed information used in the Oregon chapter, the author would like to thank:

Jim Martin, former fishery chief, Oregon Department of Fish and Wildlife; Tony Nigro, ocean salmon and Columbia River program manager, Oregon Department of Fish and Wildlife; Jack Zimmerman, Warrenton, Oregon; Steve Morris, Garibaldi, Oregon; Sherry Lyster, Lyster's Bait & Tackle, Barview, Oregon; Eric Schindler, fisheries biologist, Oregon Department of Fish and Wildlife, Newport, Oregon; Gary Hettman, Newport; Jeff Vander Kley, Harbor Manager, Salmon Harbor Marina, Winchester Bay, Oregon; Sam Waller, guide, Jot's Resort, Gold Beach, Oregon; Oregon State Marine Board.

Hub City Information
Gold Beach
Population – 1,897 Area Code – 541 County – Curry

Hotels & Motels

Ireland's Rustic Lodge, 29346 Ellensburg Ave. / 1-877-447-3526 /
www.irelandsrusticlodges.com

Gold Beach Inn, 29346 Ellensburg Ave. /1-888-663-0608 / www.goldbeachinn.com

Jot's Resort, 94360 Wedderburn Loop Road / Contains one of the largest tackle shops on the Oregon coast. Can book you with a guide or on a charter boat. Provides a marina with dock space for resort guests. A south-coast angling institution. / 1-800-367-5687 / www.jotsresort.com

Gold Beach Resort, 29232 Ellensburg Ave. / 1-800-541-0947 / www.gbresort.com

Restaurants

Sea Star Bar & Grill, 29745 Ellensburg Ave. / Soup, ribs, burgers, fish & chips / 247-9759 / www.seastarbar.com

Barnacle Bistro, 29805 Ellensburg Ave. / Soup, sandwiches, fish & chips / 247-7799 / www.barnaclebistro.com

Port Hole Café, on the harbor in the red cannery building / Seafood, steaks, sandwiches / 247-7411 /www.portholecafe.com

Indian Creek Café, 94682 Jerrys Flat Road / 247-0680

Charters

Five Star Charters, Port of Gold Beach / 1-888-301-6480 /
www.goldbeachadventures.com

Fishboss Guide Service, 28379 Mateer Road / 1-800-263-4351 /
www.fishchinook.com

Launching

Port of Gold Beach / Four lanes, two floats
Jot's Resort / Ramp for use of resort guests

Fishing Tackle

Jot's Resort Tackle Shop
Gold Coast Products, 94180 Seventh St. / 247-5706

Hospital

Curry General Hospital, 94220 Fourth St. / 247-3000

Brookings
Population – 6,455 Area Code – 541 County – Curry

Hotels & Motels

Ocean Suites, 16045 Lower Harbor Road / 1-866-520-9768 /
www.oceansuitesmotel.com
Best Western Beachfront Inn, 16008 Boat Basin Road / 469-7779 /
www.bestwesternoregon.com
Wild Rivers Motor Lodge, 437 Chetco Ave. / 1-877-469-5361 /
www.wildriversmotorlodge.com
Pacific Sunset Inn, 1144 Chetco Ave. / 1-800-469-2141 /
www.pacificsunsetinn.com

Bed & Breakfasts

South Coast Inn Bed and Breakfast, 516 Redwood St. / 1-800-525-9273 /
www.southcoastinn.com
By the Sea Bed & Breakfast, 1545 Beach Ave. / 1-877-469-4692 /
www.brookingsbythesea.com

Restaurants

O'Holleran's Restaurant & Lounge, 1210 Chetco Ave. / Steaks, seafood / 469-9907
Suzie Q's Bistro, 613 Chetco Ave. / Steaks, pasta, chicken, seafood / 412-7444 /
www.suzieqsbistro.com
Bella Italia Ristorante, 1025 Chetco Ave. / 469-6647
Rancho Viejo Mexican Restaurant, 1025 Chetco Ave. / 412-0184

Charters

Tidewind Sport Fishing & Whale Watching, 16368 Lower Harbor Road / 469-0337 /
www.tidewindsportfishing.com
Wild Rivers Fishing / 813-1082
Strictly Salmon / 1-866-682-6394
Chartle Charters / 251-4562 / www.chartlecharters.com

Launching

Port of Brookings Harbor, 16408 Lower Harbor Road / Complete launch services
with six-lane ramp and sling, lots of trailer parking. Moorage. Purportedly the
busiest recreational port on the Oregon coast. / 469-2218

Fishing Tackle

Sporthaven Marina, 16374 Lower Harbor Road / 469-3301
Chetco Riverside Market, 98877 N. Bank Chetco River Road / 469-4496 /
www.chetcoriversidemarket.com
Harborview Enterprises, 222 Cove Road / 469-8890

California Coast
Fisheries Management

The commercial salmon cannery that claimed to be the first on the U.S. Pacific coast opened in 1864. Not in Alaska. Not in Washington or Oregon. But on the Sacramento River in California.

And that historical fact speaks volumes about what you find in the West even today. You might think that as an angler moved south along the coast, out of the Pacific Northwest and into California, the fishing would decline. Nonsense.

If anything, it often gets better. The Sacramento, which enters saltwater in San Pablo Bay inside the Golden Gate, held its own through most of the 20th century as one of the most prolific chinook-producing rivers in the world. And the rugged California coastline from Crescent City near the Oregon border all the way to Monterey Bay, between San Francisco and Los Angeles, offered excellent opportunity for small-boat salmon angling. Here, they call it "skiff fishing".

In the last 15 or 20 years, however, the California sport fishery has undergone an evolution so extensive that in hindsight it appears to have been almost a revolution. The location of most fishing effort has changed significantly. And the techniques employed in catching salmon also have changed.

Managing California fish is complicated by some of the same factors that apply to salmon management elsewhere, one of which is how far salmon range, across how many political boundaries, and how many fisheries they contribute to in far-flung places.

The driver of the California coast in the early years of the 21st century was Klamath River fall chinook. It's a stock that often suffers because the federal government allows so much water to be diverted from the river for agriculture that not enough remains for fish. Some years, however, south-migrating Oregon coastal wild coho have been more restrictive to the California fishery than have the Klamath chinook, and more recently, Sacramento River fall chinook have been the driver of the coastal fishery.

Meanwhile, California's own coho stocks have grown so weak that managers here prohibit retention of coho everywhere in the state. While anglers often may fish for chinook, they must turn loose all coho, whatever their origin, in the ocean and in the rivers as well.

By the end of the first decade of the 21st century, Sacramento River fall chinook – despite their illustrious history – had come to drive the ocean fishery, necessitating

a 2009 closure of all ocean salmon fishing south of Horse Mountain, which is located between Eureka and Fort Bragg.

Until that closure, stocks primarily targeted for harvest in ocean mixed-stock fisheries off California were those same Sacramento River fall chinook (which often contributed more than 80 percent of the salmon caught off the California coast), and to a lesser extent, fall chinook from the Klamath. Ocean harvests of the Klamath River fish usually were the more constrained, not only to meet the need for spawning escapement but also to provide salmon for an in-river commercial gillnet fishery by the Yurok and Hoopa Valley Indian tribes. The U.S. Department of the Interior maintains that the tribes have a right to half the harvestable Klamath Basin salmon.

Managers imposed a 35,000-fish floor for wild spawners in the Klamath Basin, which includes the Klamath and Trinity Rivers and their tributaries. In addition, no more than two-thirds of the expected run was allowed to be harvested in any year. Managers estimate abundance of the stock for an approaching year, in a manner similar to that employed by managers in Oregon and Washington, and estimate the impacts of various potential fisheries on it based on historical harvest data. The Klamath fall chinook then may or may not become the driver that constrains fisheries, in some years affecting harvests nearly everywhere south of Cape Falcon in Oregon.

Sacramento River fall chinook, meanwhile, comprised a major presence on the southern coast in a normal year. To put their impact in perspective, managers established spawning-escapement goals for the Sacramento fish of 122,000 to 180,000 annually through the early part of the 21st century, but in the first five years of the century, escapement never dropped below 500,000. The stock is supported by several large hatcheries and by a river system that drains the entire central California area, both northern and southern, and managers tried to target harvest on it as much as possible while avoiding the Klamath stocks.

That changed dramatically, however, in 2008 when only about 66,200 fall chinook adults returned to spawn in the Sacramento system, the lowest such return ever recorded until that time. Managers predicted an increase in returns for 2009, but in 2009 the estimated return plunged even further to 39,530. This was expected to result in severe constraints on ocean salmon fisheries in California and possibly as far north as Cape Falcon in Oregon.

Managers attribute the precipitous decline to several things that happened in concert. A multiagency group which looked into the matter concluded that the immediate cause was poor ocean conditions. However, the ultimate cause, the group concluded, involved operation of the Sacramento system's hatcheries, which had been built in an effort to ameliorate the fish-blocking impact of dams on the Sacramento system. Hatchery management practices, and integration of the hatchery strain of chinook into wild spawning areas, had degraded the stock itself, the group said, causing the stock to lose the genetic diversity and physical resiliency it needed to deal with marginal ocean conditions.

Several other factors also came into play about the same time. One was flooding in the Sacramento system that could have had an impact on smolts, followed by

severe drought that likewise could have affected them. Also, apparently because of budget constraints, California Fish and Game trucked its smolts to release points one year and turned them loose directly rather than confining them first in net pens to acclimatize them before release.

Normally, Central Valley fall stocks distribute themselves widely in the ocean from Santa Barbara in the south to Vancouver Island in the north. Sometimes – like Washington stocks – they contribute significantly to fisheries off the west coast of Vancouver Island. They're also a mainstay of the Oregon and California commercial troll fisheries in a normal year.

Meanwhile, south of Point Arena, which is located a few miles south of Fort Bragg, an Endangered Species Act constraint has prevented expansion of early-season ocean fisheries in order to protect a chronically weak race of winter-run chinook to the Sacramento River. Winter-run chinook in California reproduce only in the Sacramento River system. They arrive on the spawning grounds between the middle of December and early August the following year, peaking in March, and spawn primarily in May and June in the upper river mainstem not far below Shasta Dam. It was Shasta Dam, by the way, that cut off their access to traditional spawning grounds – and caused their population to crash – as a result of its construction in 1945.

Other management considerations here involve protection for California coastal fall chinook, which spawn in coastal streams south of the Klamath River and north of the Golden Gate, and coastal and Central Valley spring chinook. All of those stocks are in jeopardy, and have been for some time. Coastal fall chinook, in particular, often constrain ocean fishing.

California Fishing Licenses

Annual fishing, resident $43.46
Annual fishing, nonresident $116.90
One-day fishing, resident and nonresident $14.04
Two-day fishing, resident and nonresident $21.86
Ten-day fishing, nonresident-only $43.43
Ocean Enhancement Validation (for ocean south of Point Arguello in Santa Barbara County) $4.89

California Information Sources

National Association of Charterboat Operators / www.nacocharters.org
San Francisco Bay Sportfishing Fleet / www.sfsportfishing.com/fleet_page.html

Crescent City and Eureka

For most of the 20th century, California's saltwater salmon anglers tended not to mooch. It simply wasn't the fashion. Trolling was the name of the game almost exclusively. That began to change in the late 1980s. By the turn of the century, mooching had become so popular here that it brought with it a whole new set of issues and, ultimately, a ban on the use of standard "J" hooks for mooching. More on that later.

Also beginning in the late 1980s, another groundswell of change began. This involved the areas of greatest fishing effort. In the '80s, Crescent City – about 20 miles south of the Oregon line – was a hub of angling action for big chinook salmon. Fishermen flocked to the port from all over California when the bite got hot, and whopper kings that took two arms to lift were pulled into skiffs every season. However, regulations here and around Eureka on California's far-northern coast were growing so restrictive, primarily to protect Klamath River chinook, that angling effort began to drop off sharply. Ports to the south, such as San Francisco and Monterey, essentially maintained their levels of angler participation, and the effect was to shift effort and catch, in relative terms, southward.

In the late 1970s, for example, all California coastal waters north of Tomales Point, a few miles north of San Francisco, were open year round. Waters south of Tomales Point were open for about nine months. By 2004, seasons had contracted to various periods between mid-May and mid-September in the Crescent City-Eureka area, mid-February to mid-November around Fort Bragg, mid-April to mid-November around San Francisco and early April to early October around Monterey. As recently as 1990, Crescent City recorded nearly 42,700 salmon angler trips for the season, and Eureka 38,650. By 2004, with allowable fishing time just a fraction of what it formerly was, the number of salmon angler trips at Crescent City had fallen to less than 7.5 percent of the 1990 level, hitting about 3,150. At Eureka, during the same period, the number of salmon angler trips dropped by more than 40 percent, to fewer than 22,500. Some of the old fishing pressure shifted south past Cape Mendocino to Fort Bragg on the sparsely populated coast between Eureka and San Francisco Bay. Because of the more liberal seasons there, angler effort at Fort Bragg more than doubled to about 30,575 in 2004 from about 14,650 in 1990.

Despite diminished participation, however, fishing does continue out of Crescent City. Anglers there like to pull a planer (which Californians often call a "diver") ahead of a flasher, followed by a fresh or frozen anchovy or herring. Often, instead of using a planer, they'll run their rig off a downrigger. Sometimes they will take their offering to the desired depth by means of a breakaway sinker – a uniquely California technique

that employs a weight rigged to detach itself from the line and fall away when a fish strikes. Some anglers use a hoochie behind the flasher, with a baitfish strip on the leading hook, and others will troll a lure, such as the Apex, with or without the flasher.

The middle of July to the middle of August usually produces the best fishing for chinook here, providing regulations allow fishing at that time, and many of the fish run to 40 pounds and more.

A single three-lane launching ramp in Crescent City is adequate, but can become busy on a summer morning.

One of the things that traditionally contributed to Crescent City's popularity, besides its proximity to salmon-rich waters, was its good harbor and the absence of a bar at its mouth, making it an ideal place to launch small boats. Often, anglers here can be into salmon as little as 300 yards off the jetty, and 6 or 8 miles is about as far as anyone ever has to run – not out into the ocean, but south and a little west from the harbor mouth. Anglers often fish in as little as 60 feet of water, and it hardly ever is necessary to go beyond the 40-fathom mark. Fog can be a problem here, as it can anywhere along the coast, but GPS chartplotters have taken a lot of the menace out of fog.

Eureka, about 70 miles south of Crescent City by sea, was always a tougher place to fish, because a formidable bar lies here at the mouth of Humboldt Bay. As a rule, boaters judge many of the bay and river mouths in California to be less treacherous than most of those on the Oregon and Washington coasts because of several factors, including the milder tides experienced in California compared to the other states. In fact, the bar at Eureka is one of only two in California that mariners deem to be serious. The other is at the mouth of the Noyo River near Fort Bragg.

At Eureka, tides sometimes control the activities of skiff fishermen in that an ebb tide may be capable of creating a dangerous crossing on the bar, although the worst bar conditions customarily occur in winter. Bar conditions often remain mild during the part of the year that salmon fishing is open, regardless of the stage of the tide. But even on a flood tide in summer, an angler should watch the weather because the water can get rough in a hurry.

Salmon inhabit this area spring through fall, so finding them is no problem within seasons set by the Pacific Fishery Management Council. By the first of June, the ocean usually settles down enough to become fishable, and June into September is when the bulk of the fishing takes place. It's important to keep in mind that you may have only a six- or seven-hour fishing day, however. You can cross the bar at low slack going out, but you might want to be back by high slack or there's a possibility you could have a long wait at sea for the bar to settle down.

As at Crescent City, anchovies are the preferred bait here, fished whole on a two-hook rig and often pulled behind a planer and a flasher. Many anglers use Dipsy Diver planers, which can be set to take a line to the left or the right of the boat as well as down. That permits anglers to run more lines than they can with divers that fish directly off the stern. Downriggers also have become popular here, and many other anglers troll with breakaway weights.

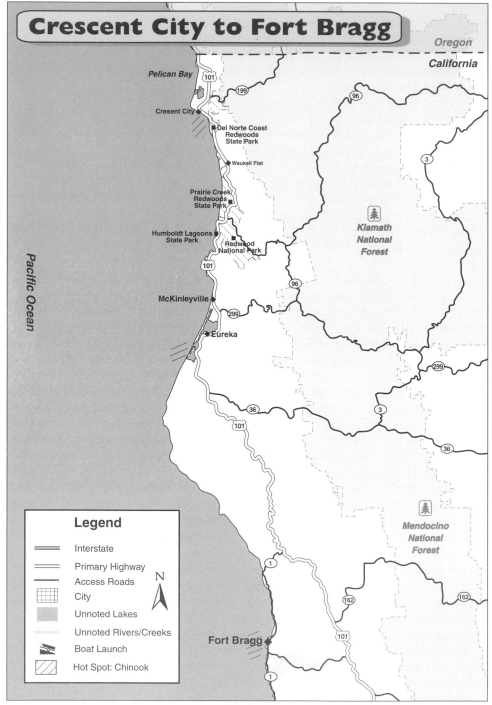

Crescent City to Fort Bragg

Oregon
California

Pelican Bay
101
199
96
Cresent City
Del Norte Coast
Redwoods
State Park
3
Waukell Flat
Prairie Creek
Redwoods
State Park
Klamath
National
Forest
Humboldt Lagoons
State Park
Redwood
National Park
101
96
McKinleyville
299
Eureka
299
36
3
101
36
Pacific Ocean
Mendocino
National
Forest
1
162
162
Fort Bragg
101
1

Legend

═══	Interstate
───	Primary Highway
───	Access Roads
▦	City
▨	Unnoted Lakes
───	Unnoted Rivers/Creeks
⚓	Boat Launch
▨	Hot Spot: Chinook

N

Chinook usually are available right out front, between imaginary points about a mile north and a mile south of the harbor. The bulk of the fishing takes place within a couple of miles of the beach, much of it around the whistler buoy a mile from the harbor entrance, although anglers sometimes run 3 or 4 miles to find the schools.

Launching is adequate in Humboldt Bay, with several public ramps and several private ones.

Cape Mendocino, which juts into the Pacific south of Eureka, divides federal salmon-management areas, and south of the cape the rules are more liberal, providing the Sacramento River stock is strong. When it has been, fishing has run from mid-February to mid-November in the Fort Bragg area, a somewhat shorter time around San Francisco Bay and somewhat shorter yet around Monterrey Bay, although still more liberal near Monterrey than in the Crescent City-Eureka area. Most of the sport catch from Cape Mendocino all the way to the southern limits of the fishery, near Santa Barbara, is Sacramento River stock.

Hub City Information
Crescent City
Population – 7,300 Area Code – 707 County – Del Norte

Hotels & Motels

Hampton Inn& Suites, 100 A St. / 465-5400 / www.hamptoninn.com

Quality Inn & Suites Redwood Coast, 100 Walton St. / 1-877-424-6423 / www.qualityinn.com

Best Western Northwoods Inn, 655 Highway 101 S. / 1-800-485-0134 / www.bwnorthwoodsinn.com

Lighthouse Inn, 681 Highway 101 S. / 1-877-464-3993 / www.crescentcitylighthouseinn.com

Bed & Breakfasts

Anna Wulf House Bed & Breakfast, 622 J St. / 464-5340 / www.annawulfhousebedandbreakfast.com

Restaurants

Chart Room, 130 Anchor Way / Seafood, steaks / 464-5993 / www.chartroomcrescentcity.com

Northwoods Restaurant and Lounge, 655 Highway 101 S. / 464-9461 / www.bwnorthwoodsinn.com/html/bed-breakfast-crescent-city.asp#s1

Denny's, 1225 Fifth St. / 464-2656

Harbor View Grotto Restaurant & Lounge, 150 Starfish Way / Seafood, steaks / 464-3815

Beachcomber Restaurant, 1400 Highway 101 St. / Seafood / 464-2205

Charters

Golden Bear Fishing Charters, departs Crescent City's Inner Harbor / 951-0119 / www.goldenbearfishingcharters.com
Chartle Charters, 541-251-4562 / www.chartlecharters.com

Launching

Crescent City Harbor District / Ramp at Inner Boat Basin Dock E, 101 Citizens Dock Road / 464-6174

Fishing Tackle

Englund Marine & Industrial Supply, 201 Citizens Dock Road / 464-1650 / www.englundmarine.com
Lunker Fish Trips Bait & Tackle, 2095 Highway 199 / 458-4704
Sandie's Marine & Sport, 110 Anchor Way / 465-6499

Hospital

Sutter Coast Hospital, 800 E. Washington Boulevard / 464-8511

Airport

Jack McNamara Field, 700 Fifth St. / 464-7229 / United Express scheduled service to San Francisco, Sacramento

Eureka
Population – 26,097 Area Code – 707 County – Humboldt

Hotels & Motels

Red Lion Hotel Eureka, 1929 Fourth St. / 445-0844 / www.redlion.rdln.com
Carter House Inns & Restaurant, 301, 301 L St. / 1-800-404-1390 / www.carterhouse.com
Best Western Humboldt Bay Inn, 232 W. Fifth St. / 443-2234 / www.bestwesterncalifornia.com
Super 8 Eureka, 1304 Fourth St. / 443-3193 / www.super8.com
Clarion Hotel, 2223 Fourth St. / 1-877-424-6423 / www.clarionhotel.com

Bed & Breakfasts

Ship's Inn, 821 D St. / 1-877-443-7583 / www.shipsinn.net
The Daly Inn, 1125 H St. / 1-800-321-9656 / www.dalyinn.com

Restaurants

Lost Coast Brewery & Café, 617 Fourth St. / Pub food / 445-4480 / www.lostcoast.com
Hurricane Kate's, 511 Second St. / Eclectic / 444-1405 / www.hurricanekates.com
Carter House Inns & Restaurant, 303, 301 L St. / Upscale dining / 444-8062 / www.carterhouse.com

Mazzotti's Ristorante Italiano, 301 F St. / 445-1912 / www.mazzottis.com
Samoa Cookhouse, Cookhouse Road in Samoa / Family-style / 442-1659 /
www.samoacookhouse.net

Charters

Full Throttle Sportfishing, 601 Startare Drive / 498-7473 /
www.fullthrottlesportfishing.com

Launching

Eureka City Marina, two-lane ramp / www.ci.eureka.ca.gov
Samoa Boat Ramp County Park, off New Navy Base Road on Samoa Peninsula
Fields Landing Boat Ramp, in town of Fields Landing
Woodley Island Marina, ramp and sling

Fishing Tackle

Englund Marine & Industrial Supply, 2 Commercial St. / 444-9266 /
www.englundmarine.com
Bucksport Sporting Goods, 3650 Broadway / 442-1832

Hospital

St. Joseph Hospital, 2700 Dolbeer St. / 445-8121

Airport

Arcata-Eureka Airport, in McKinleyville / Scheduled service to Los Angeles,
Sacramento, San Francisco, Salt Lake City

Fort Bragg to Tomales Bay

Two ramps, one of them one-lane and one two-lane and operated by Noyo Harbor
District, are available at Fort Bragg between Eureka and San Francisco. Two other
ramps are located at Albion River Campground near Albion, about 18 miles south
of Fort Bragg. A hoist-type launch is available at Point Arena, about 30 miles south
of Albion, but boaters must provide their own lifting straps there. Usual hours
of operation at Point Arena are 7am to 4pm, but the Point Arena Harbor Master
recommends calling ahead to be sure the facility is open. Telephone number is 707-
882-2583.

Between Point Arena and Bodega Bay there's virtually no place to launch, but
Bodega Bay provides three launch sites, and Tomales Bay, just south of Bodega Bay,
contains two cement ramps.

Hub City Information
Fort Bragg
Population – 7,026 Area Code – 707 County – Mendocino

Hotels & Motels

Quality Inn & Suites Tradewinds, 400 S. Main St. / 1-877-424-6423 / www.qualityinn.com

Ocean View Lodging, 1141 N. Main St. / 1-800-643-5482 / www.oceanviewlodging.com

Super 8 Fort Bragg, 888 S. Main St. / 964-4003 / www.super8.com

Seabird Lodge, 191 South St. / 1-800-345-0022 / www.seabirdlodge.com

Bed & Breakfasts

Rendezvous Inn & Restaurant, 647 N. Main St. / 1-800-491-8142 / www.rendezvousinn.com

Atrium Bed & Breakfast, 700 N. Main St. / 1-800-287-8392 / www.atriumbnb.com

Restaurants

Mendo Bistro, 301 N. Main St. / Seafood, pasta, meats / 964-4974 / www.mendobistro.com

North Coast Brewing Co., 455 N. Main St. / Seafood, steak, pasta / 964-2739 / www.northcoastbrewing.com

D'Aurelio's Italian Restaurant & Bar, 450 S. Franklin St. / 964-4227 / www.daureliosrestaurant.com

The Restaurant, 418 N. Main St. / 964-9800 / www.therestaurantfortbragg.com

Charters

Anchor Charter Boats, Noyo Harbor / 964-4550 / www.anchorcharterboats.com

All Aboard Adventures, Noyo Harbor / 964-1881 / www.allaboardadventures.com

Telstar Charters, 32390 N. Harbor Drive, Noyo Harbor / 964-8770 / www.gooceanfishing.com

Fort Bragg Sport Fishing, Noyo Harbor / 961-9692 / www.fortbraggsportfishing.com

Launching

Noyo Harbor District, two public ramps and 10,000-pound sling

Albion River Campground, near Albion / two privately owned ramps

Hospital

Mendocino Coast Hospital, 700 River Drive / 961-1234

San Francisco

South of Point Reyes, expect to see a lot of San Francisco-based party boats on the water in a normal year. California charter skippers operate out of ports all the way from Monterey to Oregon, but the biggest concentration of them occurs around San Francisco, where they operate primarily out of four ports inside the Golden Gate – San Francisco, Sausalito, Berkeley, and Emeryville. They venture north along the Marin County coast, south as far as Half Moon Bay, and seaward about 20 miles to the Farallon Islands, due west of San Francisco Bay. The whole area is known as the Gulf of the Farallones, and is very productive, because anglers here don't have to wait for migratory fish. They target two-year-old resident fish that feed here all year long, and pick up significant numbers of migrants as well.

A vigorous small-boat fishery operates out of San Francisco Bay, but it has its drawbacks. It's a fairly long run to the ocean from launching areas inside, through heavy marine traffic, unpredictable winds and dangerous currents. Fog can come down in an instant and can be especially dangerous in an area as heavily traveled as this, and shoals outside the Golden Gate can pose a rough-water danger to small boats under certain wind and current conditions. Anglers can launch at Half Moon Bay, but heavy highway tourist traffic there, especially on weekends, can make for an aggravating day.

The season here typically runs mid-April to mid-November, and it targets primarily Sacramento River chinook. Anglers here have some contact, usually minimal, with coho, but in recent years have not been allowed to keep them.

Almost all salmon fishing here occurs outside the bay, although on rare occasions – very late in the season – anglers will fish inside the bay. During April, May, and June, fishing typically takes place 10 to 20 miles offshore, and it is feed rather than structure that attracts salmon to that area, where the water runs 150 to 300 feet deep. July through the end of the season, anglers usually fish within 6 or 8 miles of the beach, and sometimes virtually on the beach.

Where anglers fish depends on where salmon have been feeding lately.

"A lot of it is word of mouth – what happened the day before," one California angler said. "And some guys go out just seeking bait. Where there's bait, they fish."

Weather also plays a role, of course, and so do regulations.

"Sometimes we can get out in small boats and sometimes we can't," a recreational angling spokesman said. "Plus, we often have fathom restrictions on how deep we can fish. One year it was 120 feet, another time 180 feet. Sometimes the fish are in really deep water, and we can't get them. They're not in an area we can fish."

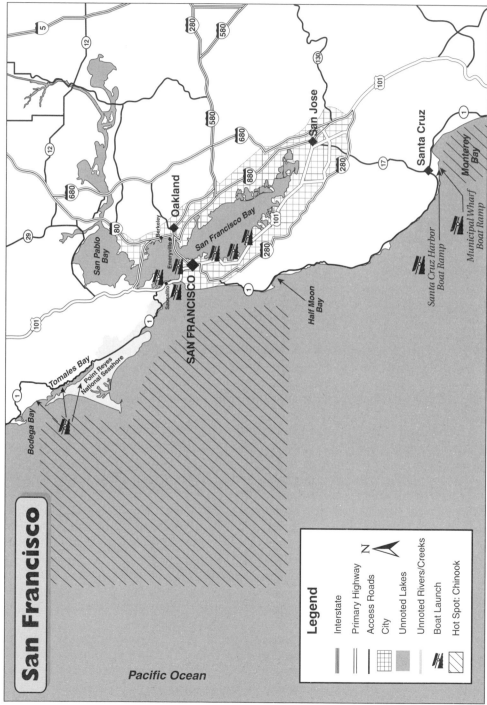

San Francisco

Pacific Ocean

Legend

Interstate
Primary Highway
Access Roads
City
Unnoted Lakes
Unnoted Rivers/Creeks
Boat Launch
Hot Spot: Chinook

5
12
280
580
130
101
12
580
680
680
29
880
17
1
101
80
280
280
1
1
1

San Jose
Santa Cruz
Oakland
Berkeley
Emeryville
Sausalito
SAN FRANCISCO

San Pablo Bay
San Francisco Bay
Monterey Bay
Half Moon Bay
Tomales Bay
Bodega Bay
Point Reyes National Seashore

Municipal Wharf Boat Ramp
Santa Cruz Harbor Boat Ramp

Those rules, he said, generally are aimed at protecting California's weak coho runs and sometimes also Klamath fall chinook.

Fishing techniques are essentially the same whether anglers fish from a charter boat or a skiff. They often troll anchovies here, sometimes sardines, rigging the bait head-toward-the-angler on what Californians call a "crowbar" hook. This is a "J"-style hook with a long shank and a bend in the shank so it spins when it goes through the water. The shank of the hook is threaded through the bait, from tail to mouth, positioning the point of the hook at the tail.

Few anglers in this part of California troll with planers. A lot of trolling, however, particularly aboard charter boats, is done with sinker-release mechanisms and weights of as much as 2 or 3 pounds. The gear is commonly fished at depths of 20 to 80 feet. The weights, which can cost several dollars apiece, fall away when the angler hooks a fish, and are not retrievable.

Skiff fishermen sometimes use the same weight-release technique, but downrigger trolling is more popular aboard skiffs. Anglers commonly pull anchovies or sardines or – when they're available – herring.

Californians also troll here with hoochies or spoons behind a flasher.

"We figure the more junk in the water, the more attractive it is," one experienced angler said.

While trolling continues to find its traditional favor among California anglers, mooching has grown increasingly popular. Most of the mooching, if it occurs, takes place from July through the end of the season. It depends on whether the salmon will take mooched bait.

"We would like to mooch from start to finish," one fishing industry spokesman said, "because it uses lighter tackle and there's more fight in the fish. But a lot of times they won't bite mooching gear. They want a moving bait."

Anglers mooch with a variety of sizes of lead weights, depending on depth and current speed.

"I fish as light as 2 ounces and as heavy as 10, depending on where the fish are and what kind of a drift I have," one angler said.

Mooching became so popular in California during the past decade or two, and the impact of it so alarming to managers, that the Pacific Fishery Management Council adopted a special regulation in 1997 to reduce its impact. The rule requires anglers to use barbless circle hooks when fishing for salmon anywhere in the ocean off California by any method other than trolling.

During mooching, the California Department of Fish and Game said, line is fed out to the salmon when it strikes "to encourage the salmon to swallow the bait and hook." While most troll-caught salmon are hooked in the mouth, it said, many mooched salmon "are gut hooked."

Observations conducted on charter boats by the department's Ocean Salmon Project found that more than 60 percent of salmon under the legal size limit that were caught by means of mooching with standard "J" hooks were hooked in the gut or the gills. Studies have found that 80 to 90 percent of such fish die as a result.

The department's Ocean Salmon Program decided to test three kinds of terminal gear to try to find a way to reduce gut hooking: "J" hooks, so-called "gut-blocker" hooks designed by the California charterboat industry, and circle hooks. "J" hooks are those shaped essentially like the letter for which they are named. Gut-blocker hooks are "J" hooks modified with a thin piece of wire attached to the shank near the eye of the hook. The wire projects away from the shank at a 45-degree angle on the side of the shank opposite the point of the hook. Circle hooks are shaped more like an exaggerated letter "C" than a "J", with the hook making nearly a complete circle and the point terminating nearly back at the shank.

The California study determined that fishing with gut-blocker hooks did not prevent salmon from swallowing them. In fact, it found that the wire attached to the shank often created an additional hazard to the salmon by cutting its gills, which also was fatal. The study found that circle hooks, however, reduced gut hooking from 60 percent to 9.5 percent for sub-legal fish, those shorter than 20 inches, and to 14.6 percent for fish 26 inches or less.

Researchers also tested mooching with the bait threaded in three different positions – head down (or away from the angler, which was the normal position for California mooching), head up (which is the usual method for trolling), and pierced through the nose as though it were live bait. They determined that using circle hooks with the bait threaded head-up reduced gut hooking to the greatest degree. It found that in fish shorter than 26 inches, less than 1 percent caught on hooks rigged in this manner were gut-hooked (compared to 60 percent caught on "J" hooks). Among fish shorter than 20 inches caught in this manner, none was hooked in the gut.

Because salmon in California are managed the way salmon are elsewhere – for acceptably low levels of mortality on threatened and endangered stocks – the lower catch-and-release mortality rates caused by circle hooks enable managers to increase the amount of fishing allowed on stronger stocks in mixed-stock areas.

Circle hooks require a different fishing technique, however, than traditional "J" hooks. Attempting to set a circle hook by rapidly raising the rod tip results in pulling the hook from the fish's mouth without a hook-up. The most effective technique when a bite is detected is simply to reel in line without striking. As the line slowly comes tight, the hook turns and its point sets itself in the fish's mouth near the lip.

The Ocean Salmon Project staff claims its on-the-water research showed that circle hooks, fished properly, are equally as efficient as "J" hooks at catching salmon.

Hub City Information
San Francisco

Population – 808,976 Area Code – 415 County – San Francisco

Hotels & Motels

Parc 55 Hotel, 55 Cyril Magnin St. / 1-800-595-0507 / www.parc55hotel.com
Executive Suites at Archstone South Market, Third and Folsom / 1-888-776-5151 / www.executivesuites-sf.com
Columbus Motor Inn, San Francisco, 1075 Columbus Ave. / 885-1492 / www.columbusmotorinn.com
Hotel Monaco, 501 Geary St. / 292-0100 / www.monaco-sf.com
Sheraton Fisherman's Wharf, 2500 Mason St. / 1-888-393-6809 / www.sheratonatthewharf.com
Chancellor Hotel on Union Square, 433 Powell St. / 1-800-428-4748 / www.chancellorhotel.com

Bed & Breakfasts

The Chateau Tivoli, 1057 Steiner St. / 1-800-228 1647 / www.chateautivoli.com
Hotel Bijou, 111 Mason St. / 1-800-771-1022 / www.hotelbijou.com
Golden Gate Hotel, 775 Bush St. / 1-800-835-1118 / www.goldengatehotel.com

Restaurants

Andalu, 3198 16th St. / Tapas, small plates / 621-2211 / www.andalusf.com
First Crush Restaurant & Bar, 101 Cyril Magnin / French, American / 982-7874 / www.firstcrush.com
South Park Café, 108 South Park / French / 495-7275 / www.southparkcafesf.com
One Market Restaurant, 1 Market St. / American / 777-5577 / www.onemarket.com
Spork, 1058 Valencia St. / American / 643-5005 / www.sporksf.com

Charters

Butchie B. Sportfishing, Fisherman's Wharf / 302-1650 / www.sfsalmon.com
Captain Joe's Cruises & Adventures, Fisherman's Wharf / 752-5886
Bass-Tub Sportfishing Boat, Fisherman's Wharf / 456-9055 / www.basstub.net
Sole Man Sport Fishing, Fisherman's Wharf / 510-703-4148 / www.solemanfishing.com

Launching

Numerous ramps with access to San Francisco Bay in San Francisco and neighboring cities, including those at Alameda Marina, Alameda; Bay View Boat Club, San Francisco; Berkely Marina, Berkeley; Clipper Yacht Harbor, Sausalito; San Leandro Marina, San Leandro.

Fishing Tackle

Hi's Tackle Box, 40 Chestnut Ave., South San Francisco / 650-588-1200
Gus' Discount Fishing Tackle, 3710 Balboa St. / 752-6197

Hospitals

San Francisco General Hospital Emergency Services, 1001 Potrero Ave. / 206-8000
California Pacific Medical Center, Pacific Campus, 2333 Buchanan St. / 600-6000 /
www.cpmc.org

Airport

San Francisco International Airport, about 13 miles south of San Francisco near
junction of Highways 101 and 380.

Sausalito
Population – 7,330 Area Code – 415 County – Marin

Hotels & Motels

Inn Above Tide, 30 El Portal / 1-800-893-8433 / www.innabovetide.com
The Gables Inn, 62 Princess St. / 1-800-966-1554 / www.gablesinnsausalito.com
Hotel Sausalito, 16 El Portal / 1-888-442-0700 / www.hotelsausalito.com

Restaurants

Scoma's Sausalito, 588 Bridgeway / Seafood / 332-9551 /
www.scomassausalito.com
Horizons Restaurant, 558 Bridgeway / Seafood / 331-3232 /
www.horizonssausalito.com
Poggio Trattoria, 777 Bridgeway / Seasonal Italian / 332-7771 /
www.poggiotrattoria.com

Charters

New Rayann, Clipper Yacht Harbor / 924-6851
Outer Limits / 454-3191
Salty Lady / 674-3474
Blue Runner, Harbor Drive and Gate Five Road / 458-8700

Fishing Tackle

Bait Guys, 41 Liberty Ship Way / 331-2676
Salty's Bait & Tackle, 350 Harbor Drive / 332-4200

Berkeley

Population – 102,743 Area Code – 510 County – Alameda

Hotels & Motels

Rodeway Inn, 1461 University Ave. / 848-3840 / www.berkeleyri.com

Doubletree Hotel & Executive Meeting Center Berkeley Marina, 200 Marina Boulevard / 548-7920 / http://doubletree1hilton.com/en_us/dt/hotel/JBKCADT-Doubletree-Hotel-Executive-Meeting-Center-Berkeley-Marina-California/index.do

Bed & Breakfasts

Rose Garden Inn, 2740 Telegraph Ave. / 1-800-992-9005 / www.rosegardeninn.com

Brick Path Bed & Breakfast, 1805 Marin Ave. / 524-4277 / www.thebrickpath.com

Restaurants

Rivoli Restaurant, 1539 Solano Ave. / American / 526-2542 / www.rivolirestaurant.com

Great China Restaurant, 2115 Kittredge St. / 843-7996 / www.greatchinaberkeley.com

Saul's Restaurant & Deli, 1475 Shattuck Ave. / Jewish / 848-3354 / www.saulsdeli.com

Venezia Italian Restaurant, 1799 University Ave. / 849-4681 / www.caffevenezia.com

Charters

Berkeley Marina Sport-Fishing Center, 225 University Ave. / 849-2727 / www.berkeleymarinasport-fishing.com

Berkeley Charter Boats, 225 University Ave. / 849-3333 / www.berkeleycharterboats.com

Happy Hooker Sportfishing / 223-5388

Fishing Tackle

Berkeley Bait & Tackle, 2221 San Pablo Ave. / 849-0432

Berkeley Marina Bait & Tackle Shop, 225 University Ave. / 849-2727

Lucky Bait Shop, 2617 San Pablo Ave. / 704-8990

Hospital

Alta Bates Summit Medical Center, 2450 Ashby Ave. / 204-4444

Airport

Oakland International Airport, 1 Airport Drive / 563-3300

Emeryville
Population – 9,727 Area Code – 510 County – Alameda

Hotels & Motels

Hilton Garden Inn San Francisco / Oakland Bay Bridge, 1800 Powell St. / 658-9300 / www.hiltongardeninn.com

Woodfin Hotel, 5800 Shellmound Way / 1-888-433-9042 / www.woodfinhotelemeryville.com

Restaurants

Rudy's Can't Fail Café, 4081 Hollis St. / Sandwiches, burgers, dinner specials, breakfast served all day / 594-1221 / www.rudyscantfailcafe.com

Hong Kong East Ocean Restaurant, 3199 Powell St. / 655-3388 / www.hkeo.us

Charters

Emeryville Sportfishing, 3310 Powell St. / 1-800-575-9944 / www.Emeryvillesportfishing.com

Fishing Tackle

Emeryville Sportfishing, 3310 Powell St. / 654-6040

Monterey Bay to Morro Bay

From San Francisco it's a couple of hours by car to Monterey Bay, a massively wide indentation in the California coast and the next-closest launching area. There, anglers fish primarily in the bay itself, which tends to be on-again, off-again, because it holds no resident salmon. Sacramento chinook are the target here, and they're just passing through. Expect the fishery to be hot for a while, then slow for a week or so. This tends to be an early fishery, with the best action in April and May.

Many anglers fish hot spots within the bay here, including places such as Soquel Hole, Pajaro fishing hole, Mulligan's Hole, and the Soldier's Club. Ask some of the locals where these are located, and enter the coordinates into your GPS.

Santa Cruz Harbor contains a good launching ramp operated by the Santa Cruz Port District on the northern end of the bay. The next available launch is at Moss Landing, between Santa Cruz and Monterey, and another public ramp is located in Monterey itself.

The coast is virtually empty of launch facilities from Monterey to Morro Bay, near the southern end of the salmon's range, and where sport catches tend to be sparse. The season has opened in recent years in late March or early April here, about the time fish usually begin to show up in significant numbers, mostly three- and four-year-old chinook bound for the Sacramento. Often, the Morro Bay fishery lasts only a week or two, but some years, depending on currents and water temperatures, salmon will remain in the area several weeks.

In good years, party boats from Ventura take salmon in the Santa Barbara Channel. But don't count on finding salmon in catchable numbers south of Morro Bay – it's always a gamble whether they'll migrate close enough for skiff fishermen to go after them.

Among those who contributed information used in this chapter, the author would like to thank:

Allen Grover, senior biologist, California Department of Fish and Game Ocean Salmon Project; Melodie Palmer-Zwahlen, associate marine biologist, California Department of Fish and Game Ocean Salmon Project; Chuck Tracy, staff officer for salmon, Pacific Fishery Management Council; Craig Stone, Emeryville, CA, California sportfishing representative, Pacific Fishery Management Council; Bob Strickland, San Jose, CA, sportfishing representative, Pacific Fishery Management Council; Dave Yarger, Sebastopol, CA, commercial fisherman; Noyo Harbor District, Fort Bragg, CA; Point Arena Harbormaster, Point Arena, CA; Santa Cruz Port District, Santa Cruz, CA; Englund Marine, Crescent City, CA; Tom Sheldrake, Woodley Island Ship Shop, Eureka, CA; Capt. Gerry Brooks, Reel Sportfishing, Santa Cruz, CA.

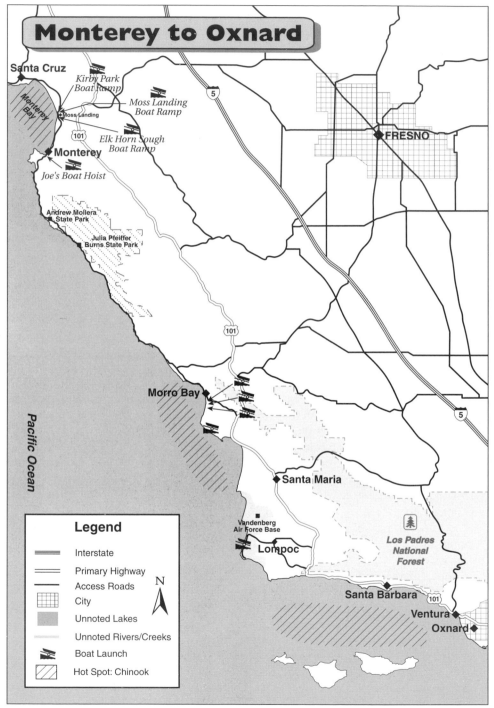

Hub City Information
Santa Cruz
Population – 56,124 Area Code – 831 County – Santa Cruz

Hotels & Motels

Santa Cruz Dream Inn, 175 West Cliff Drive / 1-866-774-7735 /
www.dreaminnsantacruz.com
Bay Front Inn Santa Cruz, 325 Pacific Ave. / 1-800-736-2023 /
www.bayfrontinnsc.com
University Inn & Conference Center, 611 Ocean St. / 1-866-827-2466 /
www.ucscinn.com

Bed & Breakfasts

West Cliff Inn, 174 West Cliff Drive / 1-800-979-0910 / www.westcliffinn.com
Babbling Brook Inn, 1025 Laurel St. / 1-800-866-1131 /
www.innsbythesea.com/babbling-brook

Restaurants

The Crow's Nest, 2218 East Cliff Drive / Seafood, steaks / 476-4560 /
www.crowsnest-santacruz.com
Zachary's Restaurant, 819 Pacific Ave. / American / 427-0646
Gabriella Café, 910 Cedar St. / Eclectic / 457-1677 / www.gabriellacafe.com
El Palomar, 1336 Pacific Ave. / Mexican / 425-7575

Charters

Santa Cruz Sportfishing, departs North Santa Cruz Harbor / 426-4690 /
www.santacruzsportfishing.com
Stagnaro Sport Fishing, Charters & Whale Watching Cruises, departs Santa Cruz
Municipal Wharf / 427-2334 / www.stagnaros.com
Monterey Bay Charters, departs Santa Cruz Harbor / 1-888-662-9800 /
www.montereybaycharters.com
Reel Sport Fishing Santa Cruz, departs Upper Santa Cruz Harbor / 212-1832 /
www.reelsportfishingsc.com
Captain Jimmy Charters, departs Upper Santa Cruz Harbor / 662-3020 /
www.captainjimmycharters.com

Launching

Santa Cruz Port District operates a public ramp in Santa Cruz Harbor. Also, the
Moss Landing Harbor District operates a four-lane public ramp, built in 2007, in
Moss Landing North Harbor, adjacent to Highway 1.

Fishing Tackle

Bayside Marine, 333-B Lake Ave. / 475-2173 / www.baysidemarinesc.com
Andy's Bait & Tackle Shop, 71B Municipal Wharf / 429-1925
The Angler's Choice, 1203 41st Ave., Capitola / 464-1883 /
www.theanglerschoicetackleshop.com

Hospital

Dominican Hospital, 1555 Soquel Drive / 462-7700

Monterey
Population – 30,641 Area Code – 831 County – Monterey

Hotels & Motels

Hotel Pacific, 300 Pacific St. / 800-554-5542 / www.hotelpacific.com
Monterey Bay Inn, 242 Cannery Row / 800-424-6242 / www.montereybayinn.com
Monterey Hotel, 406 Alvarado St. / 1-800-966-6490 / www.montereyhotel.com

Bed & Breakfasts

Old Monterey Inn, 500 Martin St. / 1-800-350-2344 / www.oldmontereyinn.com
Jabberwock Inn, 598 Laine St. / 1-888-428-7253 / www.jabberwockinn.com

Restaurants

Sardine Factory, 701 Wave St. / Seafood, meats / 373-3775 /
www.sardinefactory.com
Rosine's Restaurant, 434 Alvarado St. / Steak, seafood, pasta, salads / 375-1400 /
www.rosinesmonterey.com
Chart House Restaurant, 444 Cannery Row / Seafood, steaks / 372-3362 /
www.chart-house.com
The Crown & Anchor, 150 W. Franklin St. / British pub food / 649-6496 /
www.crownandanchor.net

Charters

Chris' Fishing Trips & Whale Watching, 48 Fisherman's Wharf / 375-5951 /
www.chrissfishing.com/newsite
Randy's Fishing Trips & Whale Watching, 66 Old Fisherman's Wharf #1 /
1-800-251-7440 / www.randysfishingtrips.com/index.html

Launching

City of Monterey operates two free ramps: one two-laner next to Harbormaster's
Office in Monterey Marina, the other, also two lanes, with adjacent fuel dock, at
32 Cannery Row next to Breakwater Cove Marina.

Fishing Tackle

Outdoor World, 2222 N. Fremont St. / 373-3615

Hospital

Community Hospital of the Monterey Peninsula, 23625 Holman Highway / 624-5311

Airport

Monterey Peninsula Airport, 200 Fred Kane Drive / 648-7000 / Non-stop service to Los Angeles, Las Vegas, San Diego, San Francisco, Denver, Phoenix.

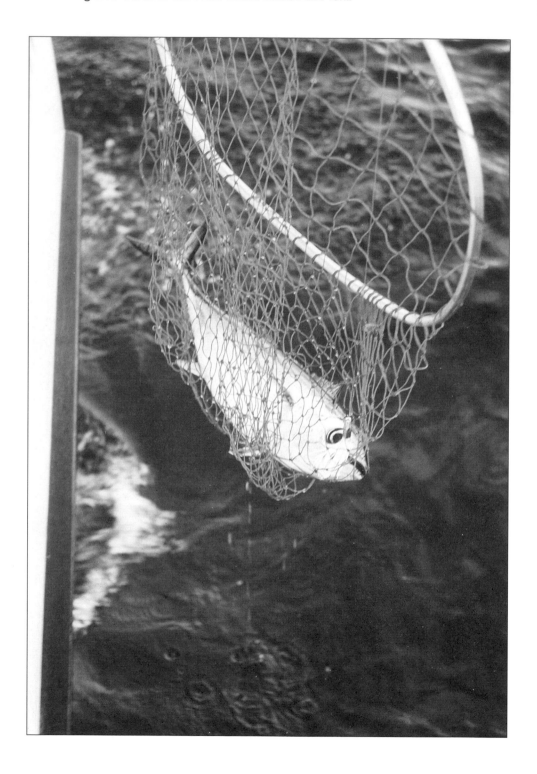

Albacore Tuna

A second major ocean fishery – the albacore tuna fishery – has charged onto the scene to challenge salmon for attention up and down the Northwest coast, and the excitement it generates from California to Washington has attracted burgeoning numbers of enthusiastic anglers.

The fishery calls thousands of anglers each year to venture far over the western horizon with a promise that the inconvenience and expense of the effort, as well as its obvious risks, may be rewarded lavishly.

In California, recreational anglers have targeted albacore for more than 100 years. Their enthusiasm shows no slacking, however, and their albacore-related expenditures now contribute $25 million or more per year to the California economy.

In Oregon and Washington, the presence of albacore has been a recent – if delightful –discovery by sportsmen, who have taken to the fishery with an intensity so often displayed by new converts to anything.

Albacore are pelagic, which means they do not live near the seabed. They spend most of their lives in deep waters seaward of the continental shelf, although they may venture inshore at times.

Like salmon, albacore are migratory. Unlike Pacific salmon, however, albacore live in every temperate and tropical ocean of the world; they breed at sea, unlike salmon, which must reproduce in freshwater; and their migratory proclivities make salmon look almost like stay-at-homes. The North Pacific stock of albacore, which is the one on which West Coast Americans fish, starts its annual migration every spring off the Japanese coast. It arrives off the northern California coast in early summer. Some of the fish turn north to the Pacific Northwest and Canada, and others turn south. With the arrival of autumn storms the fish turn west, and by late in the year end up back in the far-western Pacific.

The California Department of Fish and Game tells of albacore tagged off California being recovered less than a year later some 5,000 miles away. Had they traveled in a straight line from where they were tagged to where they were caught, they would have had to average 17 miles a day of migration for each of the 294 consecutive days they were at large.

In fact, albacore are termed officially by the U.S. National Marine Fisheries Service and by the United Nations Convention on the Law of the Sea a "highly migratory species", and they are managed as such under international agreements. The managers conduct a North Pacific albacore stock assessment every five years, and they say that, while albacore are heavily fished, they appear not to be overfished,

despite an international commercial and sport harvest of hundreds of millions of pounds annually.

Albacore are extremely powerful fish, pound-for-pound much stronger than salmon. They are built for speed, with a body that tapers at both ends, and can reach or surpass 50 miles per hour. Their color fades from metallic blue on the back to a silvery white on the belly, and their most distinguishing physical characteristic is their extremely long pectoral fins which, when held against the body extend well past the anal fin. Biologists believe albacore can live as long as 12 years, maturing at about five years, and can grow to about 4.5 feet in length. They reproduce by broadcast spawning, during which the female releases her eggs and the male fertilizes them outside of her body. Juveniles feed mostly on squid, but their dietary habits change as they mature, consuming fewer squid and more forage fish. Two of their favorite forage fish are sardines and anchovies, and it is these that most anglers use to tempt albacore off the U.S. Pacific coast.

The U.S. coastal fishery, both sport and commercial, usually occurs from about June to October, depending on latitude. Californians typically take about 61 percent of the U.S. sport harvest. Washington anglers are second, with about 27 percent, and Oregonians follow with 12 percent.

Where and When

In California, anglers pursue albacore primarily out of San Francisco Bay and San Diego.

In Oregon, the bulk of the recreational albacore landings usually occur in Newport and Depoe Bay, together. Lesser amounts come ashore in Astoria, Garibaldi, Pacific City, Winchester Bay, Coos Bay, Bandon, Gold Beach, and Brookings.

Most of Washington's recreational catch is landed at Westport. In 2005, for example, Westport accounted for 88 percent of the sport-caught albacore, while Ilwaco ran a distant second with about 10 percent, the balance being landed at Neah Bay or La Push.

Off central California, albacore might show up as early as the end of May. In a good year, they will be present in significant numbers in August, and will continue to show strongly through October. Outside of southern California, albacore are usually available from sometime in June into September or October, depending on the year.

In Oregon, the fishery usually begins during the first two weeks of July, although some years the fish arrive as early as the middle of June. They usually remain until the end of September or middle of October.

In Washington, albacore usually are available mid-July through the end of September, sometimes as late as mid-October.

How to Catch Them

Anglers fish for albacore the same way up and down the coast, and whether you fish aboard a charter out of San Diego, out of Westport, Washington, or out of any location in between, you can expect to utilize similar techniques.

When a charterboat skipper prospects for fish, especially early in the season, he'll do so with jigs that consist of a metal head, a feather or plastic skirt, and a large, two-pronged hook. He will drop a few jigs over the rail and troll them close behind the boat at high speed – 5 to 8 knots.

"Albacore are attracted by the wake," one charter man said. "We'll have probably six lines out, a couple off the stern and a couple off each side. The fish will come up to the wake, see the jig, grab it, and you've got a jig strike."

An albacore hits with great violence, and the stress on equipment is tremendous. Drags are set loose so that the line – or even the rod itself – will not snap on impact. Certain anglers will have been assigned to fish the jigs, and when a hit occurs the angler snatches the rod from its holder on the rail and tries to turn the fish. He tightens the drag so the albacore has something to labor against, and tries to work the fish back toward the boat, drawing the rest of the tuna school with it. Meanwhile, this signals the start of phase two of the fishing effort.

The skipper immediately cuts back on the throttle. If the take was on the left side of the boat he begins a turn to the left. If the take was on the right, he turns to the right, while his crew tosses live anchovies or sardines a few at a time into the water. The chumming with anchovies or sardines, depending on what part of the coast one is fishing, is to concentrate the school of albacore near the boat and, if possible, to induce a feeding frenzy. As soon as the boat stops, anglers down both sides of the boat and across the stern who are not already playing an albacore on a jig grab live-bait rigs, hook a single live baitfish to the terminal end, and toss it into the water at the side of the boat. They fish the anchovy or sardine without weight, stripping out line as the baitfish swims, and keeping plenty of slack in the line. They usually won't have long to wait. When the slack suddenly starts to disappear, it means a tuna has taken the bait.

Albacore rush in and roll onto their sides as they engulf the bait, then streak for deep water. All an angler can do is hang on, try to keep his rod tip up, and ride out that first run until the reel's drag starts to slow the fish. Then the angler tries to turn him. Crewmembers continue to toss baitfish, a few at a time, into the water to keep the albacore school engaged. Multiple hook-ups are the rule.

Experienced anglers use a shorter pull-up and a shorter reel-down with albacore than they do with salmon.

"You want to keep his head pointed toward you," one charter spokesman said, "because once he gets his head pointed away from you, he's really going to take off."

Albacore respond well to jigs early in the season, and often will hit them but not bait. As time passes and their diet preferences shift, they hit both. Eventually, jigs become less effective, and albacore turn their attention almost exclusively to bait.

"August and September are the prime (fishing) months, and for live bait, late August to the middle of September is prime time," the charter man said. "When they really get going on bait, they won't hit jigs anymore. Then you run into the dilemma of, 'How do you find them?'"

At that time, skippers look for feeding birds that denote bait on the surface, and look for albacore jumping.

"So, late in the season you might be traveling around and just looking for jumpers," the charter man said. "Sometimes you can see them jump, and just start throwing bait at them."

You also can see albacore on your fish-finder.

In Oregon, fewer charter boats were equipped to fish with live bait than in Washington and California, because live bait is harder to capture and has not been as readily available there to skippers as it has in the other states. By the end of the first decade of the 21st century, some charterboat companies in Garibaldi, Oregon, were purchasing anchovies in Ilwaco, Washington, on the Columbia River and hauling them down to the Oregon coast. Throughout much of Oregon, however, anglers relied more heavily on artificial baits in their albacore fisheries, sometimes casting plastic swim baits to the albacore.

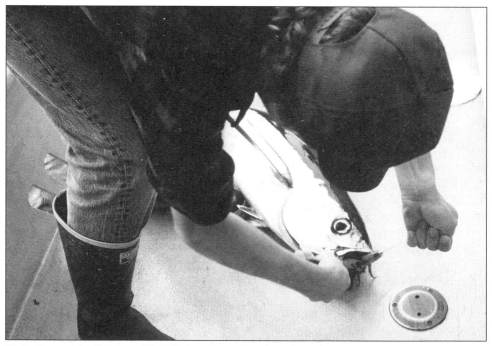

Early in season, albacore will really hammer a jig. Photo by Bob Mottram.

Gear

Live-bait anglers want a fiberglass or graphite-composite rod of 7 or 8 feet that is hefty at the butt, with lots of guides and lots of taper, a baitcasting reel with high-speed retrieve and lots of line capacity, and several hundred feet of 20- to 40-pound-test monofilament line. A short-shanked live-bait hook of 1/0 to 3/0, depending on the size of the bait, is tied directly to the line, and the hook is inserted through the end of the bait's nose or beneath the bone that lies just to the rear of the gills.

Jigs are fished with long, stout rods, heavy-duty baitcasting reels and heavy monofilament lines, 80- or 100-pound-test being common, and leaders as heavy as 120-pound, because of the shock of impact that occurs when trolling at high speed.

Albacore not only are strong pound-for-pound, but often pack a lot of pounds.

"A 10-pounder is a small one," one charter representative said. "They average between 15 and 20. On some trips they'll run into the 25s and 30s, and we've had them in the 40s. You can have a trip where everything is 20 to 25 pounds. We've had lots of trips like that."

Many Northwest charterboat skippers equip their anglers with baitcasting reels that lack a level-wind in the belief that this makes for easier casting of the near-weightless baitfish. A few captains even provide spinning gear, as albacore can be caught on relatively light tackle if an angler is willing to play them carefully.

Some anglers use other kinds of gear.

"My son took a charter group out a few weeks ago with fly rods," one Oregon charterboat skipper said, "and they caught a whole bunch of tuna using both live bait and flies."

In California, anglers usually provide their own gear, although rental rods and reels generally are available. People in that state also provide their own terminal tackle, although some usually is available for sale onboard in case of need.

Where to Find Them

Albacore like a moderate temperature, and you find them in the warm, blue-water current that lies in summer anywhere from 15 to 100 miles or more off the U.S. coast. Albacore anglers go in search of it.

"The threshold temperature for albacore is 58 to 59 degrees," a Washington charterboat skipper said. "But you're looking for blue water, and typically the water out here is green.

"The blue water is very clear. You can see down 100 feet. And you can stand out there and watch yourself cross that line from green water into blue water.

"Albacore like this narrow band between about 58.5 and 62.5 degrees, and they like to stay in it. If the temperature gets lower, they swim right out of it. If it's higher than that, they go down deep to cool off."

Green water off the northern coast in summer might run anywhere from 51 degrees to 57 or 58.

"A good place to find the biggest fish is on the border, where you leave that cooler green water and hit that warmer blue water," the charter skipper said. "There's usually a concentration of feed there, and most of the time you'll run into bigger fish there than you will if you keep heading on out."

In northern California, fish tend to show up first between Morro Bay and Monterey Bay, then move north with the current. Timing varies, depending on water temperature and water color.

The blue-water current swings closer to the beach south of San Francisco, and angles away as it moves north. Deep water exists closer inshore to the south, and at Monterey, Monterey Canyon comes far inshore, so albacore tend to move in closer there.

North of San Francisco, anglers out of Fort Bragg occasionally catch albacore if conditions are just right, and at Eureka and Crescent City, albacore come in quite close at times. Albacore almost never move in very close to the beach off San Francisco Bay, which is a major charter hub, because the continental shelf is so shallow there.

"We don't have deep water off central California until you get out about 20 miles," said a Sausalito skipper, "deep being 600 to 800 feet of water. As you go straight out of San Francisco, you've got a shipping channel that's dredged, and it's only 60 feet deep. At 11 miles you're at about 20 fathoms (120 feet). You drop off the shelf about 28 miles from the beach. You get to 600 feet, and then it just goes down, down, down.

"Some years the albacore come in to right where it drops off. Usually, they're farther out. You often find them at sea mounds that are 45, 50, or 60 miles from the entrance to our bay. Sometimes to the south of us, they're within 20 or 25 miles of shore, but it's long distances from us out of San Francisco Bay."

Virtually no one in the San Francisco charterboat fleet does multiday trips, but some do "extended day trips."

"I do an 18-hour trip," one skipper said. "I leave at 3:30 in the morning and get back in the evening. We primarily troll jigs until we get a hook-up, then use live anchovies or sardines, whatever's available."

At the southern end of the state, San Diego is the major albacore port.

"There are a lot of little coastal towns out of which people operate for albacore," one local skipper said. "From Oceanside to L.A., there's probably 10 different ports that have either private or party boat fleets that run out of them. But most of the time, the albacore are most accessible in Mexican waters, so San Diego is really the hub of albacore fishing in southern California."

In Oregon, the blue-water current often lies farther offshore off the southern part of the coast than it does to the north. Oregon anglers refer to the current as the "blue-water highway", which normally reaches its farthest inshore Oregon position from about Cape Kiwanda to Cape Falcon, an area that spans Tillamook Bay. It is not unusual for the current to be found as close as 25 miles to Tillamook Bay while hovering 60 to 70 miles off Brookings and Gold Beach in the south.

In Washington, skippers typically run in the early season to an area about 60 miles west of the mouth of the Columbia River, which forms the boundary between

Washington and Oregon. That constitutes about an 80-mile run out of Westport, Washington's major albacore-fishing port, and that's about the outer limit of their range. The fish usually work their way north and east over the summer, however, and by the middle of August may be no more than 30 miles west of Westport. Eventually, in a typical year, they'll reach a like distance from La Push and Neah Bay, which lie farther north.

What to Expect

Many Washington charterboat skippers offer day-and-a-half or two-day albacore trips in recognition of the distance that often must be covered in northern waters. Off the Oregon coast, where the albacore tend to gather somewhat closer in, charter trips are almost all of one day's duration. In California, trips range from one day in the north to a week or more in length out of San Diego, from which vessels penetrate far into Mexican waters.

A lot of Washington anglers opt for a day-and-a-half or two-day trip. Typically they leave late in the evening for their run, at about 10 knots, to the fishing grounds. The object is to get to the grounds by first light. If they're early, they'll drift for an hour or two until daybreak, and then drop their gear in the water. On what is called a day-and-a-half trip, they'll stay out a second night, then fish a couple of hours the next morning before heading back. On a two-day trip, they might fish until mid-afternoon of the second day before returning.

A one-day trip in Washington costs the angler about $375 to $400. Day-and-a-half to two-day trips typically run $500 to $600. Cost includes tackle and bait, and every angler gets a bunk. The vessel might provide coffee and rolls, but each angler brings his own sleeping bag, overnight kit, sunscreen, rain gear, motion-sickness pills and a cooler with picnic food and drinks.

In Oregon, charter boats generally offer only one-day trips. Those provided by a charter company in Garibaldi are typical.

"We usually do a 12- to 14-hour trip," the skipper said. "We leave about 4:00am, and we're back at 5:00 or 6:00 that afternoon."

Typically, off Garibaldi, anglers are fishing 25 or 30 miles offshore, and sometimes must travel somewhat north or south to find a school.

"Fifty miles is our limit," the skipper said. It doesn't allow enough time for fishing if you have to spend all that time traveling."

An Oregon trip might cost from $200 to $300, which buys a boat ride, use of gear, and bait if it is available. An angler must provide his own license and must bring his own food and drink in a backpack or cooler, although often the boat will provide coffee.

In northern California, one-day trips are the rule.

"I don't think anybody up here does multiday trips in the party-boat fleet," a San Francisco Bay skipper observed. "Some of us do extended day trips. I do an 18-hour trip that leaves at 3:30 in the morning and gets back in the evening.

In southern California, where the primary albacore port is San Diego, multiday trips are common. An angler can choose among one-day boats and four-, five-, and six-day boats. On longer trips he may be fishing 400 or 500 miles distant.

"Ninety percent of our fishing out of San Diego is in Mexican water," one skipper said. "One-day boats may be operating 40 or 50 miles out of port."

Typically, a San Diego-based boat might fish 40 miles south and 40 miles offshore. The farther south they fish, the closer to the beach they usually are.

Virtually every charter that fishes albacore out of San Diego departs in the evening.

"An overnight trip leaves about 10:00pm and gets back the next night at 7:00pm to 9:00pm," the skipper said. "That's considered a one-day trip."

San Diego boats have bunks, and some have private staterooms. Going rate for an overnight trip is $225. Multiday rates vary significantly, with many in the $200 to $300 per day range. Price of a one-day trip typically does not include food, which often is available for sale on the boat. It usually does include bait, however and, if fishing in Mexico, the cost of a Mexican permit.

Fishing a charter vessel out of San Francisco Bay, an angler can expect to pay $250 to $325 for a 12-hour trip. Some skippers charge for use of trolling gear or live-bait gear. Others furnish the trolling gear for those selected to use it, but might charge a rental fee for the live-bait gear in cases where anglers don't bring their own.

Anglers bring their own food and drink. Some skippers provide use of a microwave oven and an ice chest in which to store drinks.

The Private-Boat Fleet

For many years after the albacore fishery's discovery and initial exploitation in California in the early 1900s, recreational anglers appeared to consider it almost entirely the province of the professional charterboat fleet. Distances were too great, the sea too intimidating and private boats and equipment too inadequate to encourage much participation by private individuals providing their own transportation.

That changed dramatically in the 1990s and the early 2000s, and once the change got underway it mushroomed. Today, half or more of angler trips come aboard private boats, and the increase shows no sign of abating.

During 2007 through 2009, for example, private-boat anglers comprised more than half the total number of anglers in Washington, although they took only 30 to 37 percent of the fish. Average catch per trip for private-boat people during those years ranged from four to five albacore, while charterboat anglers averaged about a dozen.

"Last year, close to 3,000 people fished for albacore off charter boats (in Oregon), including combination trips," an Oregon Department of Fish and Wildlife spokesman said. "And last year, the estimated number of private-boat albacore anglers was 7,700.

"It used not to be that way," he said. "When (albacore fishing) first got popular, charters were the first to start. A lot of them were former commercial fishermen, so they knew how to catch tuna. And they had the range with their larger boats."

What prompted the explosive growth of the private-boat phenomenon?

"It started from a change in awareness," the spokesman said. "A lot of people didn't know we had any tuna species off the (Oregon and Washington) coast, and once the word started to spread, it became popular very fast. I would say that in the last five years the private-boat effort has doubled. And, I would say there are a lot of people who have purchased large boats specifically because they like to fish for tuna."

Astoria, Garibaldi, Depoe Bay, Newport, and Charleston all support a significant private-boat effort, he said

"For the most part it's the larger boats when the fish are farther offshore," the spokesman said. "But when they're 25 miles out, a lot of the smaller boats get out."

A Depoe Bay charterboat skipper confirms the private-boat phenomenon there. He fishes most often for albacore in ocean waters west of Lincoln City, a 25- to 35-mile run from Depoe Day.

"A lot of sport boats go out of Depoe Bay," he said, "a real flotilla. We call them the 'mosquito fleet.'"

The sport boats average about 26 feet in length, he said, and are "really posh" compared to those of a few years ago.

"They're packing some electronics that rival ours," he said.

The great speed of most of the private-boat fleet, relative to the charter fleet, actually gives it a fishing advantage in some instances.

"If they hear something's going on, they'll pick up and run a dozen miles to be where they're supposed to be," the skipper said.

Both California and Washington have matched the Oregon private-boat experience. A big reason for the change no doubt has been the increasing sophistication of marine electronics available at an increasingly economical cost, not to mention the major advances of recent years in the dependability of marine engines and in the designs of boats themselves.

Cost once was a barrier to the purchase of good electronics by the average person. But the price of reliable marine equipment has declined, relative to average income, just as it has for computers. Many, if not most, saltwater anglers now enjoy the benefits of GPS chartplotters, radar, VHF radios, and digital fishfinders, all of which lower the risk of venturing offshore and increase the likelihood of success. Add to these the dependability and power of modern, four-cycle outboard engines, and many boaters see the albacore fishery as being within their grasp.

In California, anglers call fishing in the private-boat fleet "skiff fishing". One charterboat skipper based in San Francisco Bay ties the phenomenon to the robust California economy of the middle to late 1990s.

"People had a lot of money down here," he said. "The economy was booming, and housing values went up. Albacore fishing caught fire – and salmon fishing, too – and people decided they wanted to be their own captains. So they borrowed money on their houses and bought boats.

In the early 2000s, the economy cooled.

"Now it's kind of different," the skipper said. "We find that some of those same people down here don't have those big boats anymore, and they're going fishing with us because it costs them less with us than it did for fuel in their own boats.

"But there still are a lot of recreational boats," he added.

On the northernmost part of the California coast, the skipper said, where albacore sometimes approach the beach quite closely, smaller boats are common in the fishery. The charter fleet out of Eureka and Crescent City consists mostly of what Californians calls "six-pack" boats, he said, each of which carries just a handful of anglers.

"Private boats take advantage of the fish being in closer up there, too," he said, "weather permitting."

At the opposite end of California, private-boat operators are equally active.

"We have a fairly large private-boat fleet," a San Diego charter skipper said. "And if you take southern California as a whole, it's even larger."

From San Diego to Los Angeles, and even beyond, private boats operate out of many coastal communities in search of albacore.

"They vary from good-quality trailerable skiffs up to 60-foot yachts," the skipper said. "The closer the fish come, the smaller the rigs get. But typically, offshore, anything less than 20 feet and 75-horsepower surprises us, although that doesn't mean we don't see it.

A lot of the private-boat operators in southern California embark at night, just like the San Diego charterboat fleet, the skipper said. The object for both is to be on the fishing grounds at first light.

Washington supports a growing private-boat albacore fleet whose success rate is increasing, said a Washington Department of Fish and Wildlife spokesperson. However, Washington's private skippers tend not to take on the ocean at night.

"Typically, private boats leave at daybreak," one Westport charter representative said. "Charter boats typically leave late in the evening. They're running about 10 knots, and the goal is to get out in the area they're going to be fishing before daylight.

"The private-boat guys have 24- to 26-foot boats with a lot of power; boats that can travel 25 or 30 knots," he said. They'll fish for a part of the day and come in that evening."

The same speed advantage works farther to the north, too.

"The fish will come in close off La Push and Neah Bay," he said, "to where it's maybe a 30- or 40-mile run," the charter man said. "A guy in a 26-footer that can travel at 30 knots, he can run out of La Push or Neah Bay and get to the tuna grounds without any trouble at all.

"Charter boats are not nearly that fast," he said, "so we don't take many one-day trips on charters. There's too big a chance of missing the fish in that period of time."

The Bounty

Each albacore produces four lobes of boneless fillet, renowned for its fine flavor and similar in shape to a pork loin or tenderloin of beef. It is the only fish that can be marketed legally in the United States as "white meat tuna".

Skippers carry plenty of ice, and as albacore come aboard, a crewmember immediately bleeds them and ices them down. It is important to lower the temperature of the fish quickly to preserve the quality of the meat.

In Washington, a deck hand will fillet the catch on the way in, and anglers can take the lobes home for canning or freezing. In some ports, they can trade their fillets for fish already canned.

Washington and California had no daily or trip bag limit on albacore, through 2010. In Oregon, the daily limit was 25, but the limit rarely was an issue.

"We usually get three to five fish a person," one skipper said. "They average close to 20 pounds, and some of them have been 30 or better."

Oregon regulations require that fish be brought in whole.

"We unload them at a filleter," the skipper said. "If people want him to fillet them, they pay the filleter $5 a fish."

"Expectation of catch is an important issue," a Washington charter spokesman said. "A lot of private boats come back with three, four, or five fish apiece. That's not bad, and it's not bad for a one-day charter trip. But on a multi-day trip, borderline between a good trip and not so good is eight to ten fish per person. A very successful trip would be 20, maybe even 25. It's very important to think about what you're going to do with these fish when you get home.

"After they're filleted you've got beautiful lobes of albacore," he said. "I like to cut them into chunks for a meal, and then freeze them hard. I barbecue them later. It makes great sushi, too.

"We can the fish, also, using a little salt and a little garlic. It's better than anything you can buy in the store."

Among those who contributed information used in this chapter, the author would like to thank:

Buzz Brizendine, San Diego, California, skipper of the charter boat Prowler; Roger Thomas, Sausalito, California, president of the Golden Gate Fishermen's Association and skipper of the charter boat Salty Lady; Aaron Chappell, Newport Oregon, albacore tuna sampling coordinator for the Oregon Department of Fish and Wildlife; Jeurgen Turner, Depoe Bay, Oregon, skipper of the charter boat Tacklebuster; Mick Buell, Garibaldi, Oregon, skipper of the charter boat Norwestern; Lorna Wargo, marine fisheries biologist for the Washington Department of Fish and Wildlife; and Mark Cedergreen, Westport, Washington, executive director of the Westport Charterboat Association and 2010-11 chairman of the Pacific Fishery Management Council.

Hub City Information
San Diego
Population – 1,359,132 Area Code – 619, 858 County – San Diego

Hotels & Motels

Cabrillo Inn & Suites, 1150 Rosecrans St. / 619-223-5544 / www.cabrilloinnsd.com

Comfort Inn Suites, 632 E St, Chula Vista / 619-426-2500 / http://comfortinncv.com

Days Inn Suites-San Diego, 3350 Rosecrans St. / 1-800-828-8111 /
http://days-in-sea-world.pacificahost.com

Best Western Bayside Inn, 555 W. Ash St. / 1-800-341-1818 / www.baysideinn.com

Bed & Breakfasts

Bed & Breakfast Guild of San Diego / 800-619-7666 / www.bandbguildsandiego.org

Restaurants

Barefoot Bar & Grill, 1404 Vacation Rd. / Sandwiches, salads, pub food /
858-581-5960 / www.paradisepoint.com

Gringo's Cantina, 4474 Mission Blvd. / Mexican favorites / 858-490-2877 /
www.gringoscantina.com

Moondoggies Pacific Beach, 832 Garnet Ave. / Sports restaurant / 858-483-6550 /
www.mondoggies.com

Charters

Fisherman's Landing, 2838 Garrison St. / A 16-vessel fleet / Trips from 1-16 days /
619-221-8500 / www.fishermanslanding.com

H&M Landing, 2803 Emerson St. / A 32-vessel fleet / Local and long-range fishing /
619-222-1144 / www.hmlanding.com

Point Loma Sportfishing, 1403 Scott St. / A 19-vessel fleet / Trips from 6 hours to 17
days / 619-223-1627 / www.pointlomasportfishing.com

Seaforth Sportfishing, 1717 Quivira Rd. / A 16-vessel fleet / Half-day to 1 ½-day trips
/ 619-224-3383 / www.seaforthlanding.com

Launching

Unified Port of San Diego / Operates four free ramps on San Diego Bay, each with
four or more lanes, ample dock space and free parking. Located at Shelter Island,
National City, Chula Vista, and Glorietta Bay in Coronado.

California boat ramp locator website / www.boatrampslocator.com

Fishing Tackle

Anglers Choice Tackle, 1910 Rosecrans St. / 619-223-2324 /
www.anglerschoicetackle.com

Squidco Fishing, 2518 Barnett Ave. / 619-222-8955 / www.squidco.net

Seaforth Sportfishing, 1717 Quivira Rd / 619-224-3383 / www.seaforthlanding.com

Point Loma Sportfishing, 1403 Scott St / 619-223-1627 / www.pointlomasportfishing.com

Dana Landing Market and Fuel Dock, 2580 Ingraham St. / 1-877-685-8537 / www.danalanding.com

Turner's Outdoorsman, Numerous Southern California locations / www.turners.com

Taniguchi, Inc., Commercial & Sport Fishing Supply, 2272 Newton Ave. / 619-234-0431

Sport's Bait & Tackle, 3016 Garrison St. / 619-523-0107

Fisherman's Landing Saltwater Tackle Shop, 2838 Garrison St. / 1-800-566-0273 / www.saltwatertackle.com

Hospital

Sharp Coronado Hospital, 250 Prospect Place, Coronado / 619-522-3600 / www.sharp.com/coronado

Salmon Run Charts

Washington Fisheries

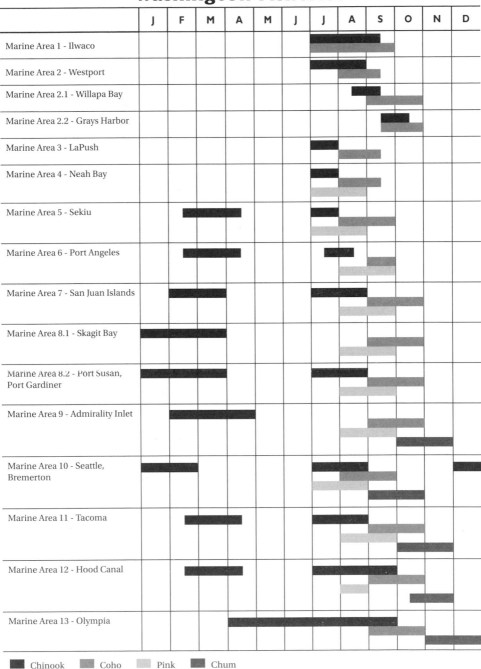

	J	F	M	A	M	J	J	A	S	O	N	D
Marine Area 1 - Ilwaco												
Marine Area 2 - Westport												
Marine Area 2.1 - Willapa Bay												
Marine Area 2.2 - Grays Harbor												
Marine Area 3 - LaPush												
Marine Area 4 - Neah Bay												
Marine Area 5 - Sekiu												
Marine Area 6 - Port Angeles												
Marine Area 7 - San Juan Islands												
Marine Area 8.1 - Skagit Bay												
Marine Area 8.2 - Port Susan, Port Gardiner												
Marine Area 9 - Admirality Inlet												
Marine Area 10 - Seattle, Bremerton												
Marine Area 11 - Tacoma												
Marine Area 12 - Hood Canal												
Marine Area 13 - Olympia												

Chinook   Coho   Pink   Chum

Oregon Fisheries

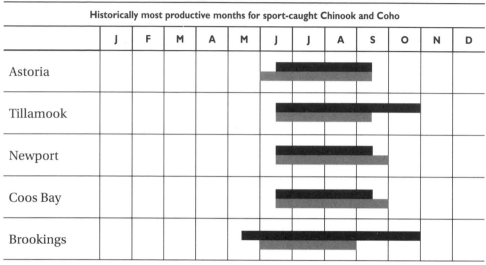

Historically most productive months for sport-caught Chinook and Coho

	J	F	M	A	M	J	J	A	S	O	N	D
Astoria												
Tillamook												
Newport												
Coos Bay												
Brookings												

■ Chinook ■ Coho

California Fisheries

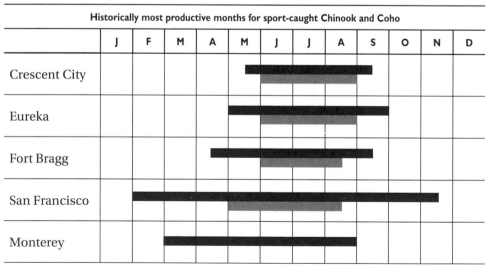

Historically most productive months for sport-caught Chinook and Coho

	J	F	M	A	M	J	J	A	S	O	N	D
Crescent City												
Eureka												
Fort Bragg												
San Francisco												
Monterey												

■ Chinook ■ Coho

Illustrated Knots

An angler needs to know only a handful of good knots in order to fish and boat successfully. The following repertoire should provide a knot for nearly every contingency. (Images and Descriptions © Wilderness Adventures Press, Inc.™)

Fishing

Arbor Knot

Used to attach monofilament line to the spool of a reel.

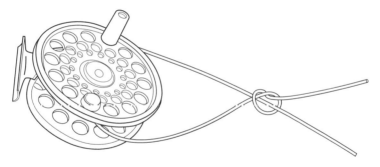

1. Loop the tag end of the line over the spool and tie an overhand knot around the standing line.

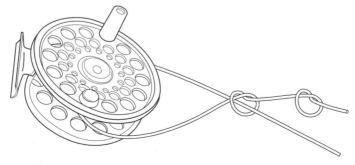

2. Tie a second overhand knot above the first.

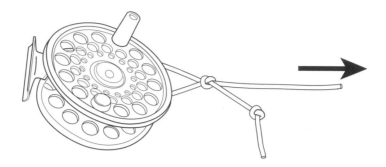

3. Lubricate and tighten by pulling on the standing line until the two overhand knots slip together snugly against the reel arbor. Trim the tag end.

Palomar Knot

One of the simplest yet strongest knots, preferred for attaching monofilament line to a relatively small object.

1. Double the tag end and pass it through the hook eye.

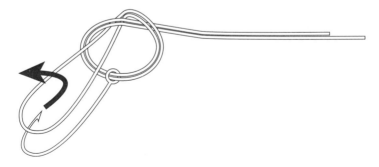

2. Make an overhand knot with the doubled line (around the standing line), leaving a loop in the end.

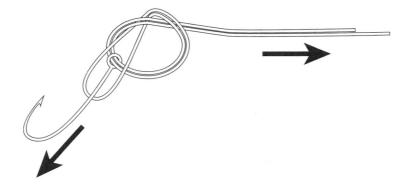

3. Bring the hook through the loop and pull on the standing and tag ends to begin tightening.

4. Lubricate and finish tightening by pulling on the standing end. Trim tag. Palomar knot, one of the simplest yet strongest knots, preferred for attaching monofilament line to a relatively small object.

Improved Clinch Knot

Improved clinch knot, best knot for attaching monofilament line to an object too large to conveniently accept a Palomar knot.

3-6x

1. Thread the tag end through the hook eye.

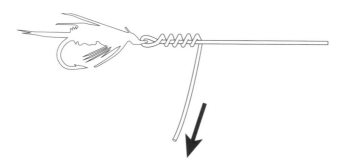

2. Twist it 3 to 6 times around the standing line.

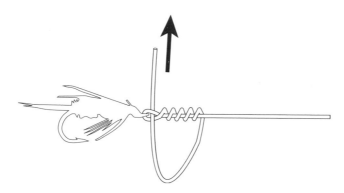

3. Push the tag end through the loop formed at the hook eye.

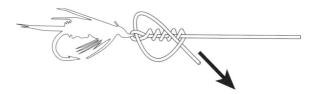

4. Bring the tag end through the loop formed between the hook eye and the top of the knot.

5. Lubricate and tighten by pulling on the standing line and hook. (Keep your fingertips behind the point of the hook.) The coils should sit down smoothly and evenly against the hook eye.

Snell Knot

Snell knot, best knot for attaching leader to a mooching or trolling hook.

1. Bring the end of your line through the hook eye, and form a big loop, with one side of the loop along the hook shank. Bring the tag end of the line through the eye a second time and align it along the shank as shown.

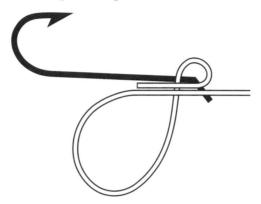

2. Take the big loop and wrap it around both lines and the shank five or six times.

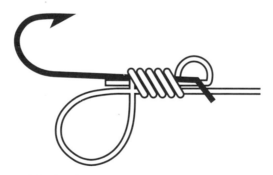

3. Pull the slack out of the big loop and pull the line tight.

Boating

Cleat Hitch

Cleat hitch, for mooring a boat to a cleat.

1. Pull the mooring line taut and wrap it once around the base of the cleat and back around the cleat's near horn.

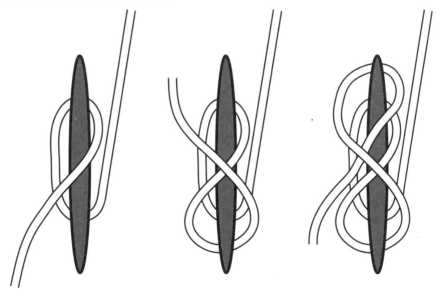

2. Wrap it around each horn in a figure eight pattern one time.

3. To tie it off, wrap it around once more, pulling the tag end of the line under the last wrap as shown, and pull tight.

Anchor Bend

Anchor bend, for tying a line to an anchor.

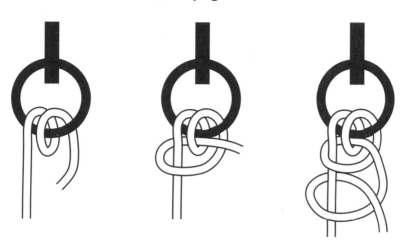

1. Loop your anchor line around the anchor ring twice, leaving enough room in the loops to bring the line back through them.

2. Bring the tag end of the line in front of the line over the standing line, and then back through the two loops from step 1. Tighten.

3. Bring the tag end over the standing line again, then through the loop that is formed. Pull it tight.

Bowline

Bowline, a very versatile boater's knot, creates an unslippable loop. Easily untied, even after it has been under stress.

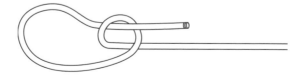

1. Form a small loop in the standing line—the farther back from the end you make this loop, the bigger the finished loop—and bring the tag end of the rope up through it.

2. Bring the tag end around the standing line and back through the small loop.

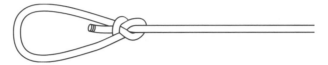

3. Tighten. (To undo this knot, press on the "bight," which is located next to the standing line.)

Clove Hitch

Clove hitch, for mooring a boat to a piling or tying a fender to a rail.

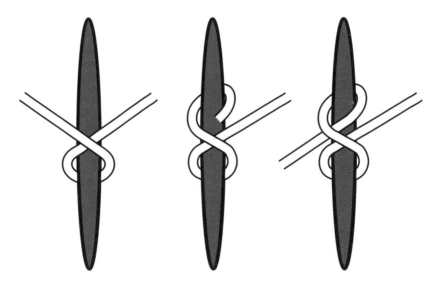

Wrap the mooring line once around the stationary object, bringing the tag end over the standing line. Pass it around the object once more, and then through the gap just created. Pull Tight.

How to Rig Herring

Photos by Karen Mottram

1. To rig plug-cut herring, start with bright, unmarked bait and a sharp knife. Slice off the head, cutting on an angle from front to back as shown, and also on an angle from top to bottom by tilting back of blade toward herring's head. This puts a beveled edge on the bait to make it spin. Practice will teach at how sharp an angle the bevel should be.

2. Remove entrails with the head. They must be removed to obtain proper action from the bait.

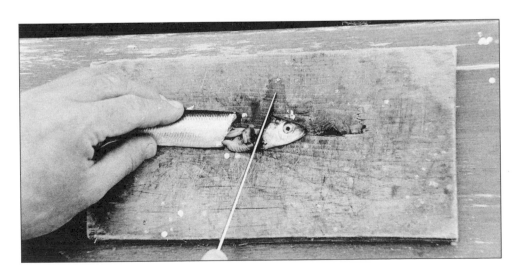

3. Insert the trailing hook of a two-hook mooching rig into the body cavity and out through the short side of beveled bait. Pull entire hook out through the hole.

4. Insert the leading hook of a two-hook mooching rig into the body cavity and out near the spine.

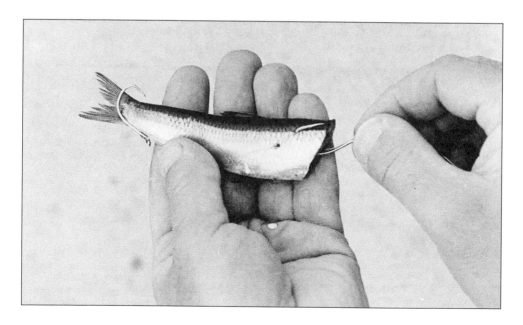

5. Plug-cut herring is ready to fish. You may let the trailing hook dangle, or you may anchor it in the bait near the tail with the point exposed. Always test the bait for proper action by pulling it alongside the boat before fishing. The bait should spin erratically, imitating an injured herring.

Alternative method

1. Insert the trailing hook through the fleshy portion of the herring above the body cavity, exiting on the side of the herring.

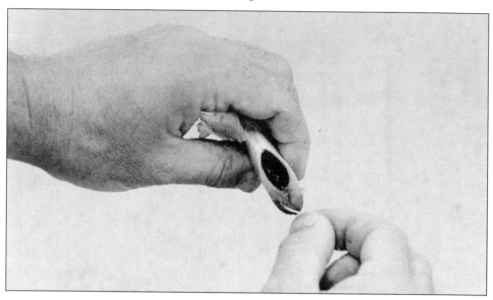

2. Pull the trailing hook all the way through the hole, and insert the leading hook into the same hole.

3. Pull the leading hook all the way through the hole, then insert it just behind the hole and anchor it high in the side of the herring near the spine, with the tip exposed.

4. Tighten the leading hook by pulling on the leader above it, drawing the eye of the hook back into the original hole through which both the trailing hook and the leading hook were inserted.

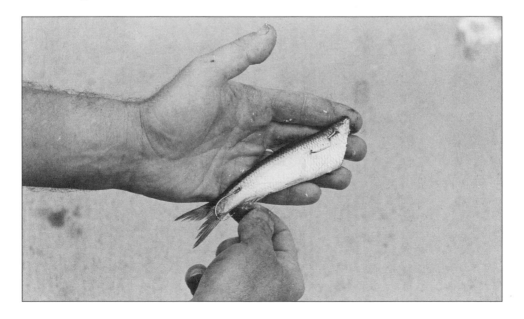

5. The bait is ready to fish. Always test it in the water before fishing.

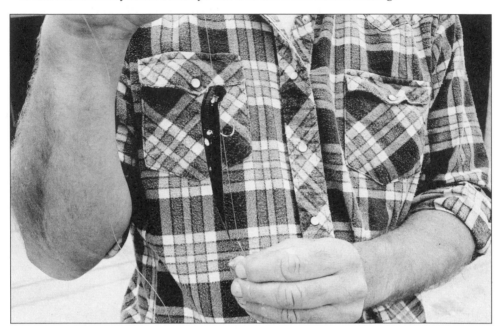

6. Simplest of many ways to rig a whole herring, and a very effective one, is to insert the leading hook through the head between the herring's eye and its mouth, from left to right.

7. Without pulling the hook all the way through the hole, turn the shank and re-insert the point into the head behind the herring's eye. Push the point all the way through the head so it emerges on the same side of the head as the hook's eye. Simply let the trailing hook dangle.

8. Ready to fish. Always test by pulling alongside the boat before fishing.

Salmon Filleting

Photos by Karen Mottram

1. To fillet a salmon properly, you need a hard cutting surface and a good-quality, flexible fillet knife. Give the knife a few strokes on the stone or the steel before you use it. The knife must be ultra-sharp to do the job well. Start with a fish whose internal organs, including gills, have been removed, and whose bloodline along the spine has been scraped and rinsed away.

2. Remove scales from your salmon by directing a hard stream of water from a garden hose along the fish from tail to head, opposite the direction in which the scales lie. The sooner this is done after the fish is killed, the easier the scale removal. Now slice off the head just behind the gill cover and discard. (Some people retain heads and backbones for stock or for crab bait. They may be frozen until needed.)

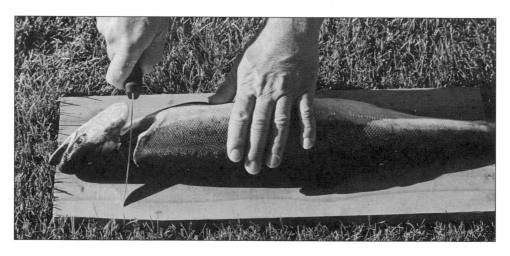

3. Lay knife against the top side of the spine, blade parallel with the ground, and slice toward the tail, keeping blade flat and cutting through ribs as you proceed.

4. Cut all the way to the tail, keeping blade flat atop the spine the entire time.

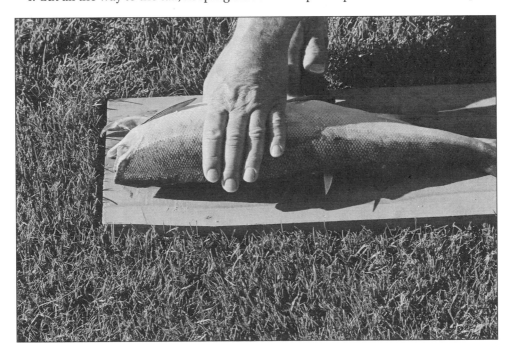

5. Top side of fish will come away from the rest of the carcass at the tail.

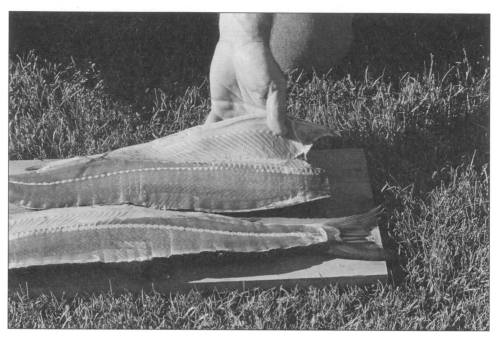

6. Trim off the curved cleithrum bone and the pectoral fin that is attached.

7. Lay piece skin-side down and, starting near center line, trim away ribs in one piece, holding the knife blade flat and slicing carefully through the meat just below the ribs. Discard ribs.

8. You may wish to remove and discard the fatty belly strip. Some people like to retain it.

9. Turn the other side of the fish flesh side down and repeat the process, slicing carefully along the top of the spine with a flat blade to remove the meaty portion from the spine. Repeat steps 6, 7, and 8.

10. Slice each side into serving-size portions.

11. The finished product. Tail sections are bone-free. One line of rib-size bones remains in each of the other pieces. You may remove them with pliers, but if left in, bones are large and easy to avoid when eating.

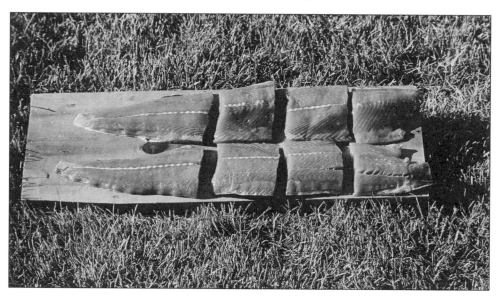

Coastal Tackle Shops
California
(alphabetical by town)

Bakersfield

Custom Fishing Rods
16 P St.
661-324-2523

Second Amendment Sports
2523 Mohawk St.
661-323-4512
www.2ndamendmentsports.com

Benicia

Benicia Bait & Tackle
509 Claverie Way
707-745-4921
www.beneciabait.com

Berkeley

Berkeley Bait & Tackle
2221 San Pablo Ave.
510-849-0432

Berkeley Marina Bait & Tackle Shop
225 University Ave.
510-849-2727

Lucky Bait Shop
2617 San Pablo Ave.
510-704-8990

Bodega Bay

Diekmann's Bay Store
1275 California 1
707-875-3517
www.diekmannbaystore.com

Capitola

The Angler's Choice
1203 41st Ave.
831-464-1883
www.theanglerschoicetackleshop.com

Chino Hills

Turner's Outdoorsman
4200 Chino Hills Parkway, Suite 600
909-590-7225
www.turners.com

Corona

Turner's Outdoorsman
2246 Griffin Way
951-736-8007
www.turners.com

Costa Mesa

Glenn's Tackle Shop
1145 Baker St. #A
714-957-1408
www.gottackle.com

Crescent City

Englund Marine & Industrial Supply
201 Citizens Dock Road
707-464-1650
www.englundmarine.com

Lunker Fish Trips Bait & Tackle
2095 Highway 199
707-458-4704

Rick's Haircuts Outdoor Store & Tackle
646 A St.
707-464-2186

Sandie's Marine & Sport
110 Anchor Way
707-465-6499

Emeryville

Emeryville Sportfishing
3310 Powell St.
510-654-6040

Eureka

Bucksport Sporting Goods
3650 Broadway
707-442-1832

Englund Marine & Industrial Supply
2 Commercial St.
707-444-9266
www.englundmarine.com

Redwood Marine
8 W. Sixth St.
707-443-7029
www.redwoodmarine.com

Fort Bragg

Mendocino Coast Tackle & Sport
32450 North Harbor Dr.
707-964-3710

Fountain Valley

Turner's Outdoorsman
18808 Brookhurst
714-965-5151
www.turners.com

Fresno

California Bait & Tackle
4516 E. Belmont Ave.
559-454-1155

Fisherman's Warehouse
4320 W. Shaw Ave.
559-225-1838
www.fishermanswarehouse.com

Huntington Beach

CharkBait
16561 Bolsa Chica St.
714-846-6452
www.charkbait.com

Mako Matt's Marine
6411 Edinger Ave.
714-893-7743
www.makomattsmarine.com

Pacific Edge
5042 Edinger Ave.
714-840-4262
www.pacificedgetackle.com

Kearny Mesa

Turner's Outdoorsman
8199 Clairemont Mesa
858-278-8005
www.turners.com

Long Beach

Fisherman's Hardware
2801 E. Anaheim St.
562-434-8311

Seeker Rod Co.
1340 W. Cowles St.
562-491-0076
www.seekerrods.com

Los Angeles

Bob's Sporting Goods Center
2003 Sawtelle Blvd.
310-478-2638

Fishing Time
317 N. Western Ave.
323-466-7181
www.fishingtimeusa.com

Joy Fishing Tackle & Camping
4918 Santa Monica Blvd.
323-664-0808
www.abupro.com

Lindell's Tackle Box
11203 S. Western Ave.
323-418-0094

Martin's Fishing Tackle
2821 ½ S. Western Ave.
323-731-5549

Purfield's Pro Tackle
12512 W. Washington Blvd.
310-397-6171
www.purfieldsprotackle.com

Manteca

Fisherman's Warehouse
2201 E. Yosemite Ave.
209-239-2248
www.fishermanswarehouse.com

Marina Del Rey

Marina Del Rey Sportfishing
13759 Fiji Way
310-822-3625
www.marinadelreysportfishing.com

Modesto

Auto Life Outdoors
901 N. Carpenter Rd.
209-574-1400
www.autolifeoutdoors.com

Bill's Sport & Bait Shop
2001 Crows Landing Road
209-537-4294

Grandsons Bait and Tackle
1400 10th St.
209-566-9516

Stop N Shop Bait & Tackle
1914 Crows Landing Rd.
209-537-8221

Monterey

Outdoor World
2222 N. Fremont St.
831-373-3615

Morro Bay

Jerry's Marine & Tackle
1158 Scott St.
805-225-1005

Virg's Sportfishin'
1215 Embarcadero
805-772-1222

West Coast Light Tackle
1124 Front St.
805-772-4576

Newport Beach

Anglers Center
419 Old Newport Blvd.
949-642-6662
www.anglerscenter.com

J D's Big Game Tackle
406 South Bay Front
949-723-0883
www.jdsbiggame.com

Norwalk

Turner's Outdoorsman
11336 Firestone Blvd.
562-929-4056
www.turners.com

Oceanside

Anglers Tackle Store
1413 North Coast Highway
760-967-1897

Ken's Custom Reel
1351 Harbor Drive N
760-967-7335

Pacific Coast Bait and Tackle
2110 South Coast Highway, Suite E
760-439-3474
www.pacificcoast-baitandtackle.com

Orange

Turner's Outdoorsman
1932 N. Tustin
714-974-0600
www.turners.com

Pacifica

New Coastside Bait & Tackle
1604 Francisco Blvd.
650-359-9790

Pasadena

Turner's Outdoorsman
835 S. Arroyo Pkwy.
626-578-0155
www.turners.com

Point Arena

Cove Coffee & Tackle
790 Port Road
707-882-2665

Rancho Cucamonga

Turner's Outdoorsman
11738 San Marino St., Suite B
909-923-4422
www.turners.com

Redding

Strictly Fishin' Guide & Tackle
2451 Athens Ave.
530-241-4665
www.strictlyfishin.net

Redondo Beach

Redondo Sport Fishing Co.
233 North Harbor Dr.
310-372-2111
www.redondosportfishing.com

Turner's Outdoorsman
2323 Hawthorne Blvd.
310-214-8724
www.turners.com

Reseda

Turner's Outdoorsman
19329 Vanowen St.
818-996-5033
www.turners.com

Sacramento

Broadway Bait Rod & Gun
1701 Broadway
916-448-6338

Delta Bait & Tackle
8140 Freeport Blvd.
916-665-6588

Fisherman's Warehouse
9035 Folsom Blvd.
916-362-1200
www.fishermanswarehouse.com

Romeo's Bait & Tackle Shop
8120 Freeport Blvd.
916-665-1788

Sacramento Pro Tackle
2390 Northgate Blvd.
916-925-0529

Salinas

Bokanovich Custom Rods & Repairs
38 La Mirada Crt.
831-424-9699

The Tackle Box
1012 N. Davis Rd.
831-757-9797

San Bernardino

Turner's Outdoorsman
491 W. Orange Show Rd.
909-388-1090
www.turners.com

San Diego

Anglers Choice Tackle
1910 Rosecrans St.
619-223-2324
www.anglerschoicetackle.com

Dana Landing Market and Fuel Dock
2580 Ingraham St.
877-685-8537
www.danalanding.com

Fisherman's Landing Saltwater Tackle Shop
2838 Garrison St.
800-566-0273
www.saltwatertackle.com

Point Loma Sportfishing
1403 Scott St.
619-223-1627
www.pointlomasportfishing.com

Seaforth Sportfishing
1717 Quivira Rd.
619-224-3383
www.seaforthlanding.com

Sport's Bait & Tackle
3016 Garrison St.
619-523-0107

Squidco Fishing
2518 Barnett Ave.
619-222-8955
www.squidco.net

Taniguchi, Inc., Commercial & Sport Fishing Supply
2272 Newton Ave.
619-234-0431

San Francisco

88 Fishing Tackle
2360 San Bruno Ave.
415-467-1268
www.88fishingtackle.com

Gus' Discount Fishing Tackle
3710 Balboa St.
415-752-6197

San Jose

Fisherman's Warehouse
1140 S. De Anza Blvd.
408-873-0113
www.fishermanswarehouse.com

San Jose

Ly's Sporting & Fishing Goods
1051 E. Capitol Expressway
408-629-9644

Mel Cotton's Sporting Goods
1266 W. San Carlos St.
408-287-5994
www.melcottons.com

San Marcos

Turner's Outdoorsman
2085 Montiel
760-741-1570
www.turners.com

San Rafael

Western Sport Shop
902 Third St.
415-456-5454
www.westernsportshop.com

Santa Barbara

Frank's Bait & Tackle
230 Stearns Wharf #B
805-965-1333

Hook Line & Sinker
4010 Calle Real #5
805-687-5689

Santa Cruz

Andy's Bait & Tackle Shop
71B Municipal Wharf
831-429-1925

Bayside Marine
333-B Lake Ave.
831-475-2173
www.baysidemarinesc.com

Santa Monica

Lincoln-Pico Sporting Goods
2017 Lincoln Blvd.
310-452-3831

Santa Rosa

Western Sport Shop
2790 Santa Rosa Ave.
707-542-4432

Sausalito

Bait Guys
41 Liberty Ship Way
415-331-2676

Salty's Bait & Tackle
350 Harbor Drive
415-332-4200

Signal Hill

Turner's Outdoorsman
2201 E. Willow St.
562-424-8628
www.turners.com

Solana Beach

Blue Water Tackle and San Diego Fly Shop
124 Lomas Santa Fe Dr, #207
858-350-8505
www.sandiegoflyshop.com

South San Francisco

Hi's Tackle Box
40 Chestnut Ave.
650-588-1200

Stockton

Jolly Bait & Tackle
101 W. Charter Way
209-948-6344

Outdoor Sportsman
4969 West Lane
209-957-4867
www.outdoorsportsman.biz

Thornton Road Bait & Tackle
9242 Thornton Road
209-473-2239

Vacaville

Guns Fishing & Other Stuff
197 Butcher Rd.
707-451-1199
www.gunsfishing.com

West Covina

Turner's Outdoorsman
357 N. Azusa Ave.
626-858-8948
www.turners.com

Oregon
(alphabetical by town)

Astoria

Astor Court Grocery
690 Alameda Ave.
503-325-4650

Englund Marine & Industrial Supply
95 Hamburg Ave.
503-325-4341
www.englundmarine.com

Bandon

Bandon Baits
110 First St. S.E.
541-347-3905

Port-O-Call
155 First St. S.E.
541-347-2875

Brookings

Chetco Riverside Market
98877 N. Bank Chetco River Road
541-469-4496
www.chetcoriversidemarket.com

Four M Tackle
16060 Lower Harbor Rd.
541-469-6951

Harborview Enterprises
222 Cove Road
541-469-8890

Riverside Market
98877 North Bank Chetco River Rd.
541-469-4496

Sporthaven Marina
16374 Lower Harbor Road
541-469-3301

Charleston

Basin Tackle Shop
63510 Kingfisher Road
541-888-3811

Clackamas

D & G Bait Inc.
15981 S.E. 122nd Ave.
503-557-2248

Great American Tackle Shop
16122 S.E. 82nd Dr.
503-650-2662

Poulsen Cascade Tackle
15875 S.E. 114th Ave #N
503-655-2828
www.poulsencascadetackle.com

Coos Bay

Bite's On Bait & Tackle
750 Newmark Ave.
541-888-4015

Englund Marine & Industrial Supply
91146 Cape Arago Highway
541-888-6623
www.englundmarine.com

Tackle Shack
1165 Newmark Ave. #A
541-808-2180

Gearhart

Bud's Campground & Grocery
4412 Highway 101 N.
503-738-6855

Gold Beach

Four Seasons RV Resort
96526 North Bank Rogue River Rd.
541-247-4503

Gold Beach

Gold Coast Products
94180 Seventh St.
541-247-5706

Jot's Resort Tackle Shop
94360 Wedderburn Loop Road
1-800-367-5687
www.jotsresort.com

Rogue Outdoor Store
29865 Ellensburg Ave.
541-247-5706

Gresham

Buley's
6630 S.E. 182nd Ave.
503-665-1747

Hammond

Charlton Deep Sea Charters
71 Tyee St.
503-861-2429
www.charltoncharters.com

Happy Valley

Throbbin'rod Tackle Co.
8711 S.E. Owen Dr.
503-794-9188

Hillsboro

Catcher Co.
5285 N.E. Elam Young Parkway, #B700
503-648-2643

Lake Oswego

Angling Spoken Here
5765 Windfield Loop
503-624-8603

Milwaukie

Crowe's Bait
7499 S.E. Overland St.
503-771-2341

Newport

Englund Marine & Industrial Supply
880 S.E. Bay Boulevard
541-265-9275
www.englundmarine.com

Harry's Bait & Tackle
404 S.W. Bay Boulevard
541-265-2407

Oak Grove

GI Joe's Sports & Auto Stores
15600 S.E McLoughlin Blvd
503-653-5611

Oregon City

Fisherman's Marine & Outdoor
1900 Mcloughlin Blvd. #60
503-557-3313

Portland

Fisherman's Marine & Outdoor
1120 N. Hayden Meadows Drive
503- 283-0044
www.fishermans-marine.com

Martin's Tackle Co.
7608 S.E. 70th Ave.
503-775-6221

Ollie Damon's
236 S.E. Grand Ave.
503-232-3193

Sports Authority
10245 N.E. Cascades Parkway
503-493-7374
www.sportsauthority.com

Swan Island Marine Supply Co.
4855 N Lagoon Ave.
503-285-6694

Reedsport

Reedsport Outdoor Store
2049 Winchester Ave.
541-271-2311

Stockade Market & Tackle
2850 Country Club Court
541-271-3800

Turman Tackle
139 N. Third St.
541-271-0586
www.turman-tackle.com

Sandy

The Reel Tackle Shop
39261 Proctor Blvd.
503-668-7490

Seaside

Trucke's 1-Stop
1921 S. Roosevelt Dr.
503-738-8863

Tillamook

Tillamook Sporting Goods
2207 Main Ave. N., Suite B
503-842-4334
www.tillamooksportinggoods.com

Troutdale

Jack's Snacks & Tackle
1208 E. Historic Columbia River
503-665-2257
www.jackssnackandtackle.com

Warrenton

Tackle Time Bait Shop
530 E. Harbor St.
503-861-3693
www.tackletime.net/baitshop

West Linn

Promotion Fishing Products
22768 Johnson Road
503-722-1576
www.promotionfishingproducts.com

Winchester Bay

Salmon Harbor Charters Tackle Shop
495 Beach Blvd.
541-271-2010

Stockade Market & Tackle Shop
350 Beach Boulevard
541-271-3800

Washington
(alphabetical by town)

Anacortes

Ace Hardware
1720 Q Ave.
360-293-3535

West Marine
918 Commercial Ave.
360-293-4262
www.westmarine.com

Auburn

Auburn Sports & Marine
810 Auburn Way N.
253-833-1440
www.auburnsportsmarineinc.com

Bellingham

Norm's Bait & Tackle
1801 Roeder Ave., Ste. 168
360-671-3373

West Marine
3560 Meridian St.
360-650-1100
www.westmarine.com

Yeager's Sporting Goods
3101 Northwest Ave.
360-733-1080
www.yeagerssportinggoods.com

Burlington

Holiday Market Sports Center
895 Nevitt Rd.
360-757-4361

Everett

Hepman's Big Fish Bait
307 W. Mukilteo Boulevard
425-252-7920

Herman's Big Fish Bait-Tackle
307 W. Mukilteo Blvd.
425-252-7920

Jerry's Surplus
2031 Broadway
425-252-1176

John's Sporting Goods
1913 Broadway
425-259-3056
www.johnssportinggoods.com

West Marine
1716 W. Marine View Dr. #A
425-303-1880
www.westmarine.com

Fife

Sportco Warehouse Sporting Goods
4602 20th St. E.
253-922-2222
www.sportco.com

West Marine
3212 20th St. E
253-926-2533
www.westmarine.com

Forks

Forks Outfitters
950 S. Forks Ave.
360-374-6161
www.forksthriftway.com

Olympic Sporting Goods
190 S. Forks Ave.
360-374-6330

Friday Harbor

Lfs Marine Supplies
50 Second St.
800-426-8860

Nash Brothers Sporting Goods
280 Spring St.
360-378-4612

West Marine
313 Spring St., #306
360-378-1086
www.westmarine.com

Ilwaco

Englund Marine & Industrial Supply
123 Howerton Way
360-642-2308
www.englundmarine.com

Kelso

Metro Tackle & More
412 S. Pacific Ave.
360-673-4690
www.metrotackleandmore.com

Lacey

Cabela's
1600 Gateway Boulevard N.E.
360-252-3500
www.cabelas.com

Lakewood

Zak Tackle Manufacturing Co.
10910 26th Ave.
253-584-8559
www.zaktacklemfg.com

Longview

Bob's Sporting Goods
1111 Hudson St.
360-425-3870
www.bobsmerch.com

Lynnwood

Ted's Sports Center
15526 Highway 99
425-743-9505

Neah Bay

Big Salmon Resort
Bayview Ave.
1-866-787-1900
www.bigsalmonresort.net

Olympia

Larry's Tackle Closet
2036 Arab Drive S.E.
360-943-8057

Tom's Outboard
221 East Bay Drive N.E.
360-754-3882
www.tomsoutboard.com

Visionhooks & Tackle
2302 4th Ave. W.
360-866-7775
www.visionhooksandtackle.com

Port Angeles

R & R Marine Supply
1222 E. Front St.
360-452-7062

Swain's General Store
602 E. First St.
360-452-2357
www.swainsinc.com

Port Townsend

Henery Do It Best Hardware
218 Sims Way
360-385-5900
www.henery.doitbest.com

Swain's Outdoor
1121 Water St.
360-385-1313

West Marine
2428 Washington St.
360-379-1612
www.westmarine.com

Puyallup

Go-Fish-N-Tackle Shop
1033 E. Main
253-251-0034

Zak Tackle Manufacturing Co.
2301 E. Pioneer #B
253-584-8559

Seattle

Happy Hooker Bait & Tackle
955 Alaskan Way W.
206-281-5289

Linc's Fishing Tackle & Honda
501 Rainier Ave. S.
206-324-7600

Outdoor Emporium
1701 Fourth Ave. S.
206-624-6550
www.sportco.com

Seattle Marine & Fishing Supply Co.
2121 W. Commodore Way
206- 285-7925
www.seamar.com

West Marine
1275 Westlake Ave. N
206-926-0356
www.westmarine.com

West Marine
6317 Seaview Ave. N.W.
206-789-4640
www.westmarine.com

Sekiu

Olson's Resort
444 Front St.
360- 963-2311
www.olsonsresort.com

Van Riper's Resort
280 Front St.
888-462-0803
www.vanripersresort.com

Shoreline

Anglers Choice
20222 Ballinger Way N.E.
206-364-9827
www.anglerschoiceinc.com

Tacoma

J.T. Tackle
3110 N. 26th St.

Narrows Marina
9001 S. 19th St.
253-564-3473
www.narrowsmarina.com

Point Defiance Marina
5912 N. Waterfront Drive
253-591-5325
www.metroparkstacoma.org

Tumwater

Tumwater Sports Center
6200 Capitol Way S.E.
360-352-5161
www.tumwatersports.com

Westport

Englund Marine & Industrial Supply
280 E. Wilson Ave.
360-268-9311
www.englundmarine.com

Hungry Whale Enterprises
1680 S. Montesano St.
360-268-0136

Woodinville

Doug's Boats and Outdoor
13410 N.E. 175th St.
425-483-2001
www.dougsboatsandoutdoor.com

Woodland

Fishermen's Depot
1230 Lewis River Rd. #A
360-225-9900

G. Loomis, Inc.
1359 Down River Dr.
360-225-6516
www.gloomis.com

Harper's Tackle & Outdoor
660 Goerig St.
360-841-8292

Lamiglas, Inc.
1400 Atlantic Ave.
360-225-9436
www.lamiglas.com

Talon
1552 Down River Dr.
360-225-8247
www.talon-graphite.com

Charter Services
California
(alphabetical by town)

Berkeley

Berkeley Charter Boats
225 University Ave.
510-849-3333
www.berkeleycharterboats.com

Berkeley Marina Sport-Fishing Center
225 University Ave.
510-849-2727
www.berkeleymarinasport-fishing.com

Drifter
Berkeley Marina
510-849-2727

El Dorado
Berkeley Marina
510-849-3333

Flying Fish
Berkeley Marina
415-898-6610
www.flyingfishsportfishing.com

Hali
Berkeley Marina
510-755-6989

Happy Hooker Sportfishing
510-223-5388

New Easy Rider
Berkeley Marina
510-849-3333

Crescent City

Chartle Charters
Sometimes serves Crescent City. Based in Brookings, Oregon.
541-251-4562
www.chartlecharters.com

Golden Bear Fishing Charters
Departs Crescent City's Inner Harbor
707-951-0119
www.goldenbearfishingcharters.com

Emeryville

C-Gull 2
Emeryville Marina
510-654-6040

Captain Hook
Emeryville Marina
510-654-6040

Emeryville Sportfishing
(for the Emeryville fleet)
3310 Powell St.
800-575-9944
www.Emeryvillesportfishing.com

New Huck Finn
Emeryville Marina
510-654-6040

New Salmon Queen
Emeryville Marina
510-654-6040
www.salmonqueen.com

New Seeker
Emeryville Marina
510-654-6040

New Superfish
Emeryville Marina
510-654-6040

Rapid Transit
Emeryville Marina
510-654-6040

Eureka

Full Throttle Sportfishing
601 Startare Drive
707-498-7473
www.fullthrottlesportfishing.com

King Salmon Charters & Yacht Club
1137 King Salmon Ave.
707-442-3474

Fort Bragg

A Fishy Business
707-964-7609

All Aboard Adventures
Noyo Harbor
707-964-1881
www.allaboardadventures.com

Anchor Charter Boats
Noyo Harbor
707-964-4550
www.anchorcharterboats.com

Fort Bragg Sport Fishing
Noyo Harbor
707-961-9692
www.fortbraggsportfishing.com

Lady Irma II
230 Azalea
707-964-3854

Noyo Fishing Center
32440 N. Harbor Dr.
707-964-3000
www.fortbraggfishing.com

Noyo Harbor at Fort Bragg

Telstar Charters
32390 N. Harbor Drive
707-964-8770
www.gooceanfishing.com

Half Moon Bay

Huli Cat
H Dock, Pillar Point Harbor
650-726-2926
www.hulicat.com

Pillar Point Harbor

New Captain Pete
800-572-2934
www.sfsportfishing.com/newcaptainpete

Queen of Hearts
Dock H-3
510-581-2628
www.fishingboat.com

Riptide
H Dock
888-747-8433
www.riptide.net

Monterey

Chris' Fishing Trips & Whale Watching
48 Fisherman's Wharf
831-375-5951
www.chrissfishing.com/newsite

Randy's Fishing Trips & Whale Watching
66 Old Fisherman's Wharf #1
800-251-7440
www.randysfishingtrips.com

Newport Beach

Newport Landing Sportfishing
309 Palm St. #A
949-675-0550
www.fishnewportlanding.com

Richmond

Fishing Fool IV
Marina Bay Yacht Harbor
510-654-6040

Fury
Point San Pablo Yacht Harbor
800-499-6465
www.furysportfishing.com

Hook'd Up Sportfishing
707-655-6736

San Diego

Alexes Sportfishing
1717 Quivira Rd.
619-990-0926

Baja Sport Fishing, Inc.
2408 Congress St.
800-770-2341
www.bajasportfishinginc.com

Dana Landing
2590 Ingraham St.
619-224-2513

Fisherman's Landing
2838 Garrison St.
619-221-8500
www.fishermanslanding.com

H&M Landing
2803 Emerson St.
619-222-1144
www.hmlanding.com

Islander Charters
2838 Garrison St.
619-224-4388
www.islander-charters.com

Mission Bay Sportfishing
1551 Mission Bay Dr.
619-555-1212
www.missionbaysportfishing.com

Point Loma Sportfishing
1403 Scott St.
619-223-1627
www.pointlomasportfishing.com

Qualifier 105
619-223-2786
www.qualifier105.com

Red Rooster III
2801 Emerson St.
619-224-3857
www.redrooster3.com

Rock-N-Roll Sport Fishing
619-342-6137

San Diego Fishing Adventures
Shelter Island Drive
760-402-9917
www.sandiegofishingadventures.com

Seaforth Sportfishing
1717 Quivira Rd.
619-224-3383
www.seaforthlanding.com

Sportsman's Dock
1617 Quivira Rd.
619-224-3551

The Long Run
  1880 Harbor Dr.
  858-336-6594
  www.thelongrunsportfishing.com

Voodoo Sportfishing
  1880 Harbor Dr., Suite F
  858-735-7078
  www.voodoosportfishing.com

San Francisco

Bass-Tub Sportfishing Boat
  Berth 4, Fisherman's Wharf
  415-456-9055
  www.basstub.net

Butchie B. Sportfishing
  Foot of Jones, Fisherman's Wharf
  415-302-1650
  www.sfsalmon.com

Captain Joe's Cruises & Adventures
  Fisherman's Wharf
  415-752-5886

Captain Joey
  Fisherman's Wharf
  415-892-2353

Chucky's Pride
  Fisherman's Wharf
  415-564-5515

Happy Days
  Fisherman's Wharf
  415-752-5886
  www.captainjoes.com

Kitty Kat
  Fisherman's Wharf
  415-752-5886
  www.captainjoes.com

Lovely Martha
  Berth 3, Fisherman's Wharf
  650-871-1691
  www.lovelymartha.com

Miss Farallones
  Fisherman's Wharf
  925-689-0900

Primetime
  Fisherman's Wharf
  888-405-9333
  www.primetimesportfishing.com

Sole Man Sport Fishing
  Fisherman's Wharf
  510-703-4148
  www.solemanfishing.com

Wacky Jacky
  Fisherman's Wharf
  415-586-9800

San Rafael

Jim Cox Sport Fishing Charters
  925-261-9820

Santa Cruz

Captain Jimmy Charters
  Departs Upper Santa Cruz Harbor
  831-662-3020
  www.captainjimmycharters.com

Fish'n Dan's Guide Services
  209-352-0224

Monterey Bay Charters
  Departs Santa Cruz Harbor
  888-662-9800
  www.montereybaycharters.com

Reel Sport Fishing Santa Cruz
Departs Upper Santa Cruz Harbor
831-212-1832
www.reelsportfishingsc.com

Santa Cruz Sportfishing
Departs North Santa Cruz Harbor
831-426-4690
www.santacruzsportfishing.com

**Stagnaro Sport Fishing, Charters &
Whale Watching Cruises**
Departs Santa Cruz Municipal Wharf
831-427-2334
www.stagnaros.com

Sausalito

Blue Runner
Harbor Drive and Gate Five Road
415-458-8700

Captain Jack's Sport Fishing
800-475-8643
www.captainjacks.net

Hog Heaven
415-382-7891

New Rayann
Clipper Yacht Harbor
415-924-6851

Outer Limits
415-454-3191

Salty Lady
415-674-3474

Oregon

(alphabetical by town)

Astoria

Dielman's Northwest River
665 15th St.
503-338-7467

Martin's Big Fish Adventures
503-351-0650
www.martinsbigfish.com

Sea Star Fishing Charters
92163 Aspmo Rd.
866-373-3474
www.seastarfishingcharters.com

Tiki Charters
350 Industry St.
503-325-7818
www.tikicharter.com

Todd Dielman Fishing
91120 Youngs River Road
503-338-7467
www.dielmansguides.com

Bandon

Prowler Charters
325 First St. S.E.
888-347-1901
www.prowlercharters.com

Brookings

Chartle Charters
541-251-4562
www.chartlecharters.com

Strictly Salmon
866-682-6394

Tidewind Sport Fishing & Whale Watching
16368 Lower Harbor Road
541-469-0337
www.tidewindsportfishing.com

Wild Rivers Fishing
98203 County Hwy. 808
541-813-1082

Charleston

Betty Kay Charters
541-888-9021
www.bettykaycharters.com

Depoe Bay

Custom Fishing Charters
253-228-0883
www.customfishingcharter.com

Dockside Charters
270 Coast Guard Place
800-733-8915
www.docksidedepoebay.com

The Mariner at Depoe Bay
Dock 1, Depoe Bay Harbor
541-270-6163
www.depoebaymariner.com

Tradewinds Charters
Highway 101 downtown
800-445-8730
www.tradewindscharters.com

Garibaldi

Garibaldi Charters
Seventh and Highway 101
800-900-4665
www.garibaldicharters.com

Kerri Lyn Charters
611 Commercial
503-355-2439

Linda Sue III Charters
304 Mooring Basin Rd.
503-355-3419

Secret Island Fishing
500 Biak St.
907-738-4500
www.secretislandfishing.com

Sidewinder Charters
Departs Garibaldi Marina
360-740-7888
www.sidewindercharters.com

SIGGI – G Ocean Charters
611 S. Commercial
503-322-3285
www.siggig.com

Troller Deep Sea Charter
304 Mooring Basin
503-322-3666

Gold Beach

Fish Oregon Fishing Guide Service
94575 Chandler Rd.
541-247-4138
www.fishoregon.com

Fishboss Guide Service
28379 Mateer Road
800-263-4351
www.fishchinook.com

Five Star Charters
Port of Gold Beach
888-301-6480
www.goldbeachadventures.com

Mark Vanhook Guide Service
541-247-6702
www.markvanhookguideservice.com

Hammond

Defiance Charters
Departs from Hammond Marina
503-440-2413
www.defiancecharters.com

Newport

Captain's Charters
343 S.W. Bay Boulevard
800-865-7441
www.captainsreel.com

Newport Marina Store and Charters
2128 S.E. Marine Science Drive
541-867-4470
www.nmscharters.com

Newport Tradewinds Deep Sea Fishing
653 S.W. Bay Boulevard
800-676-7819
www.newporttradewinds.com

Yaquina Bay Charters
1000 S.E. Bay Boulevard
866-465-6801
www.yaquinabaycharters.com

Reedsport

Rivers End Guide Service
3421 Ridgeway Drive
888-388-3125
www.umpquafishing.com

Seaside

Perry's Fishing Adventures
84647Junction Road
866-738-6991
www.fishingwithval.com

Tillamook

Fishing Oregon
7350 Vaughn Rd.
503-842-5171
www.fish-oregon.com

T & S Guide Services
4025 Brickyard Rd.
503-842-2071

Warrenton

B J's Guide Services
91994 Spirit Place Rd.
503-440-1249

Charlton Charters
470 N.E. Skipanon Drive
503-861-2429
www.charltoncharters.com

Gale Force Guides
90425 Par Rd.
503-861-1494
www.galeforceguides.com

Len Self Professional Fishing
90803 Hwy. 101
503-861-0554

Merrin Fisheries Thunderbird
45 N.E. Harbor Place
503861-1270

Tackle Time Charters
530 E. Harbor St.
503-861-3693
www.tackletime.net

Winchester Bay

Krista Jay Charters
182 Bay Loop
541-271-5698

Salmon Harbor Charters
495 Beach Boulevard
541-271-2010
www.salmonharborcharters.com

Strike Zone Charters
465 Beach Boulevard
800-230-5350

Washington
(alphabetical by town)

Anacortes

Anacortes Highliner Charters
Skyline Marina, 2011 Skyline Way
360-770-0341
www.highlinercharters.com

Catchmore Charters
Skyline Marina
360-293-7093
www.catchmorecharters.com

Dash One Charters
Skyline Marina
360-293-6450
www.dashonecharters.com

R&R Charters
Skyline Marina
360-293-2992
www.rrcharters.com

Sea Hawk Salmon Charters
Skyline Marina
360-424-1350
www.seahawksalmoncharters.com

Des Moines

Tight Lines Sport Fishing
19602 Second Ave. S.
866-363-1559
www.tightlinessportfishing.com

Edmonds

All Season Charters
300 Admiral Way, Suite 102
877-943-9590
http://biznw.com/fishing

Puget Sound Sport Fishing
T Dock on Admiral Way
206-546-5710
www.pugetsoundsportsfishing.com

Everett

AAA Fishing Charters
Port of Everett
800-783-6581
www.aaafishingcharters.com

All Star Fishing Charters
1726 W. Marine View Dr.
800-214-1595
www.allstarfishing.com

Big King Salmon Charters
Port of Everett
425-776-7688
www.bigkingsalmoncharters.com

Brett's Guide Service
Based near Everett, launches various
locations
425-359-3284
www.brettsguideservice.com

Excel Fishing Charters
Port of Everett
877-805-1729
www.excelfishingcharters.com

Northwest Fishing Charters
O Dock, Port of Everett
206-949-0221
www.nwfishingcharters.com

Possession Point Fishing Charters
Port of Everett
866-652-3797
www.possessionpointfishing.com

Ridge to River Outdoors
Based near Everett, launches various
locations
425-478-9133
http://ridgetoriveroutdoors.com

Ilwaco

Beacon Charters
332 Elizabeth St.
360- 642-2138
www.fishbeacon.com

Coho Charters & Motel
800-339-2646
www.cohocharters.com

Pacific Salmon Charters
191 Howerton Way
800-831-2695
www.pacificsalmoncharters.com

Sea Breeze Charters
800-204-9125
www.seabreezecharters.net

Sea Sport Fishing Charters
221 Howerton Way
866-211-6611
www.seasportfishingcharters.com

La Push

All-Ways Fishing
La Push Marina
360-374-2052
www.allwaysfishing.com

Fun Fleet Charter Co.
La Push Marina
888-819-4603
www.ijustwannagofishin.com

Top Notch Ocean Charters
La Push Marina
888-501-5887
www.forks-web.com/jim/salt

Neah Bay

Big Salmon Resort
Bayview Ave.
866-787-1900
www.bigsalmonresort.net

Jambo's Sportfishing
425-788-5955
www.jambossportfishing.com

Port Orchard

Venture Charters
1777 Bay St.
360-895-5424
www.venturecharterboats.com

Seattle

A Spot Tail Salmon Guide
Shilshole Bay Marina
7001 Seaview Ave. N.W.
206-295-7031
www.salmonguide.com

Adventure Charters
Shilshole Bay Marina
206-789-8245
www.seattlesalmoncharters.com

All Star Fishing Charters
Shilshole Bay Marina
800-214-1595
www.allstarfishing.com

Fish Finders Private Charters
Shilshole Bay Marina
206-632-2611
www.fishingseattle.com

Tyee Charters
Shilshole Bay Marina
206-799-2530
www.tyeecharters.net

Shelton

Puget Charters
51 S.E. Arabian Rd.
360-490-8482
www.pugetcharters.com

Tacoma

Captain Jerry's Charters
1101 Dock St.
253-752-1100
www.tacomasportfishing.com

Fox Island Salmon Charters
Departs from Point Defiance
253-549-0745
http://foxislandsalmoncharters.com

Vashon

Onco Sportfishing & Guide Services
877-483-0047
www.oncosportfishing.com

Westport

Advantage Charters
Float 12
800-689-5595
www.advantagecharters.com

Angler Charters
2401 Westhaven Dr.
800-422-0425
http://anglercharters.net

Buccaneer Tours & Charters
2101 Westhaven Dr.
800-851-8687

Cachalot Charters

2511 N. Westhaven Drive
800-356-0323
www.cachalotcharters.com

Deep Sea Charters
Opposite Float 6
800-562-0151
www.deepseacharters.biz

El Matador Charters
320 Dock St.
360-580-0093

Ms Magoo Sportfishing
Float 6
360-648-3017
www.msmagoosportfishing.com

Ocean Charters
Across from Float 14
800-562-0105
www.oceanchartersinc.com

Salmon Charters
Float 8
888-266-5168
www.salmoncharterswestport.com

Westport Charterboat Association
www.charterwestport.com

Westport Charters
Across from Floats 8/10
800-562-0157
www.westportcharters.com

Westport Sportfishing
271 E. Dock St.
866-964-8862
www.westportsportfishing.com

Glossary

Aft - Nautical term meaning at or near the stern of a boat or in the direction of the stern.

Attractor – Any device used in conjunction with a bait or lure to attract fish either visually or sonically to bait or lure.

Blackmouth – An immature chinook salmon, so-called because of the black gum line characteristic of chinook.

Bycatch – Any non-targeted fish, individually or in the aggregate, captured unintentionally while fishing for another.

Dodger – A metal attractor that swings from side to side as it precedes a bait or lure, creating vibrations and imparting action to bait or lure. Used in trolling for salmon.

Fathom – A nautical measure of water depth, equaling six feet.

Flasher – A rotating plastic or metal attractor that precedes a bait or lure, imparting action to bait or lure and vibrations to the water. Used in trolling for salmon.

Gunwale – The top edge of the side of a boat. Pronounced gun'-nel.

Hoochie – A plastic lure resembling a squid that is trolled behind a flasher in fishing for salmon.

Jig – A metal lure, usually of lead, shaped somewhat like a herring or a candlefish and containing a single- or multiple-pointed hook. It usually is fished by raising and lowering the rod tip from a few inches to a few feet to produce a fluttering action as the lure descends.

Knucklebuster (reel) – A direct-drive reel with relatively large spool, similar in design to a fly-fishing reel, with which one turn of the reel handle produces one turn of the spool.

Level-wind (reel) – A reel with a device that moves from side to side across the spool as the spool turns in order to distribute line evenly across the spool during a retrieve.

Mooching – A technique for fishing with live or dead bait fish by dangling the bait in the water beneath a weight and imparting action to the bait by moving the rod tip or by putting a boat's motor in and out of gear.

Plug-cut – A method of removing the head of a bait fish, particularly a herring, with a tapered cut that imparts an enticing action to the body of the bait when it is mooched or trolled.

Port – Nautical term for left side.

Race – A genetically related group within a species, such as spring-, summer- and fall-returning races of chinook salmon.

Spreader – A device with two rigid, wire arms that stretch in opposite directions. A spreader is attached to the terminal end of a fishing line and is used most often when fishing for halibut or other bottom fish. A weight is attached to the end of the shorter arm, and a leader and hook to the end of the longer arm. A spreader enables an angler to lower gear in the water without wrapping hook and leader back around the main line.

Starboard – Nautical term for right side.

Stern – The back of a boat.

Transom – The rearmost surface of a boat's hull, to which an outboard motor often is attached.

Tule – A term describing early-spawning fall chinook salmon common to the lower Columbia River, to distinguish them from later-spawning chinook that reproduce farther upriver. Tules reach the river as adults typically already in their spawning phase, and reproduce in lower Columbia River tributaries. Widely used for many years in Columbia River hatchery programs, they contribute significantly to fisheries in the lower river and in the ocean off the Washington coast. Pronounced too'-lee.

Index

A

Albacore Tuna 217–227
Anacortes 128–129
Anchor Bend 234
Arbor Knot 230
Astoria - Warrenton 174–175

B

Background on Fish Management Issues
     87–89
Bait 39–40
Bandon 185
Berkeley 209
Boats 65–69
Boats and Motors 63–72
Bowline 234
Brining Herring 49
Brookings 191

C

California Coast 193–215, 228–229
  California Fishing Licenses 195
  California Information Sources 195
  Crescent City and Eureka 196–201
    Map 198
  Fisheries Management 193–195
  Fort Bragg to Tomales Bay 201–202
  Hub Cities
    Berkeley 209
    Crescent City 199–200
    Emeryville 210
    Eureka 200–201
    Fort Bragg 202
    Monterey 214–215

    San Diego 228–229
    San Francisco 207
    Santa Cruz 213–214
    Sausalito 208
  Monterey to Morro Bay 211–215
    Map 212
  San Francisco 203–210
    Map 204
California Fishing Licenses 195
California Information Sources 195
Chartplotters 77
Chinook 90
Chum 92
Cleat Hitch 234
Clove Hitch 235
Coho 91
Columbia River 169–176
  Map 170
Coos Bay 185–186
Crescent City 199–200
Crescent City and Eureka 196–201
  Map 198
Crossing the Bar 154–155

D

Dedication 7
Depoe Bay 180
Downriggers 17

E

Electronics 73–86
Emeryville 210
Eureka 200–201
Everett 137–138

F

Fish Finders 76
Florence and Reedsport 182–183
  Map 184
Fort Bragg 202
Fort Bragg to Tomales Bay 201–202

G

Gold Beach 190
Gold Beach and Brookings 187–191
  Map 188

H

Hood Canal 116–121
  Map 118–119
How to Jig 58–61
How to Rig Herring 236–242
Hub Cities
  Anacortes 128–129
  Astoria - Warrenton 174–175
  Berkeley 209
  Brookings 191
  Coos Bay 186
  Crescent City 199–200
  Depoe Bay 180
  Emeryville 210
  Eureka 200–201
  Everett 137–138
  Fort Bragg 202
  Gold Beach 190
  Ilwaco 164–165
  La Push 163
  Monterey 214–215
  Neah Bay 102
  Newport 180–181
  Olympia 152
  Port Angeles 114
  Portland 173
  Port Townsend 115
  Reedsport 183
  San Diego 228–229
  San Francisco 207–208

  Santa Cruz 213–214
  Sausalito 208
  Seattle 144–145
  Sekiu / Clallam Bay 107
  Tacoma 151–152
  Tillamook 175–176
  Westport 163–165

I

Illustrated Knots 230–235
Improved Clinch Knot 232

J

Jigging 50–62

L

Laptop Computers 84–85
Lines 34
Lower Columbia River and Washington
    Coast
  Map 157, 160, 166

M

Meatlines 19
Monterey 214–215
Monterey to Morro Bay 211–215
  Map 212
Mooching 32–49
Mooching Rods 32–33
Mooching Techniques 44–46
Motors 69–72
Multifunction Units 75–76

N

Neah Bay 98–102, 102
  Map 100
Newport 180–181
Newport and Depoe Bay 177–181
  Map 178
North Puget Sound 130–138
  Map 134–135

O

Oregon Coast 167–191
  Columbia River 169–176
    Map 170
  Coos Bay 185–186
  Fisheries Management 167–168
  Florence and Reedsport 182–183
    Map 184
  Gold Beach and Brookings 187–191
    Map 188
  Hub Cities
    Astoria - Warrenton 174–175
    Brookings 191
    Coos Bay 186
    Depoe Bay 180
    Gold Beach 190
    Newport 180–181
    Portland 173
    Reedsport 183
    Tillamook 175–176
  Newport and Depoe Bay 177–181
    Map 178
  Oregon Fishing Licenses 168
  Oregon Information Sources 168
  Tillamook Bay 171–176
Oregon Fishing Licenses 168
Oregon Information Sources 168

P

Palomar Knot 231
Pink 91–92
Planers 16–17
Plug Cutting Herring 41
Port Angeles 114
Port Angeles to Port Townsend 108–115
  Map 111
Port Orford 185
Port Townsend 115
Preface 9–14

R

Radar 79–80
Radios 81–84
Reedsport 183
Reels 21, 35–37
Rigging Plug-cut Herring 42
Rigging Whole Herring 40
Rods 20

S

Salmon Filleting 243–248
Salmon Identification and Reproductive Behavior 90–93
  Chinook 90
  Chum 92
  Coho 91
  Pink 91–92
  Sockeye 93
Salmon Season-Setting 88–89
San Diego 228–229
San Francisco 203–210, 207–208
  Map 204
Santa Cruz 213–214
Sausalito 208
Seattle and Central Puget Sound 139–145
  Map 142
Sekiu to Pillar Point 103–107
  Map 104
Sekiu / Clallam Bay 107
Snell Knot 233
Sockeye 93

T

Tacoma and South Puget Sound 146–153
  Map 148–149
Terminal Gear 21–22
The San Juans 122–129
Tillamook 175–176
Tillamook Bay 171–176
Trolling 15–31

W

Washington Coast 94–166
  Hood Canal 116–121
    Map 118–119

Hub City Information
  Anacortes 128–129
  Everett 137–138
  Ilwaco 164–165
  La Push 163
  Neah Bay 102
  Olympia 152
  Port Angeles 114
  Port Townsend 115
  Seattle 144–145
  Sekiu / Clallam Bay 107
  Tacoma 151–152
Lower Columbia River and Washington
  Coast
  Map 157, 160, 166
  Westport 163–165
Neah Bay 98–102
  Map 100
North Puget Sound 130–138
  Map 134–135

Port Angeles to Port Townsend 108–115
  Map 111
Seattle and Central Puget Sound 139–
  145
  Map 142
Sekiu to Pillar Point 103–107
  Map 104
Tacoma and South Puget Sound 146–
  153
  Map 148–149
The San Juans 122–129
  Map 124–125
Washington Fishing Licenses 97
Washington Information Sources 97
Washington Coast Fisheries Management
  95–97
Washington Fishing Licenses 97
Washington Information Sources 97